Think again.
The best essays from *Prospect*
1995-2020

Think again.
The best essays from *Prospect*
1995-2020

Think again. Think *Prospect*

Published April 2020 in the UK by
Prospect Publishing Ltd,
Prospect, 2 Queen Anne's Gate
London SW1H 9AA

A CIP catalogue record for this book is available from the British Library.

ISBN (Paperback) 978 1 5272 5974 4

Designed by Mike Turner and Chris Tilbury
Printed and bound by CPI Group (UK) Ltd, Croydon, CR0 4YY

www.prospectmagazine.co.uk

For Clive, who has kept the show on the road

Contents

Economics

Culture and ideas

Science

Stranger than fiction

Families

Contributors

Neal Ascherson has been a journalist for 60 years. He is the author of *Black Sea* and *Stone Voices: The Search for Scotland*

Philip Ball is the author of many books of popular science. In 2019 he won the William Thompson, Lord Kelvin medal for his writing

Marcus Chown is a science writer, journalist and broadcaster. He is the author of *The Magicians: Great Minds and the Central Miracle of Science*

Tom Clark is editor of *Prospect* and the co-author of *Hard Times: Inequality, Recession, Aftermath*

Ed Docx is a writer and novelist. *Let Go My Hand* came out in 2017

David Edmonds is a radio feature maker at the BBC World Service

Francis Fukuyama is Olivier Nomellini Senior Fellow at Stanford University. His most recent book is *Identity: Contemporary Identity Politics and the Struggle for Recognition*

David Goodhart is the founding editor of *Prospect*

John Gray is a philosopher and writer. His latest book is *Seven Types of Atheism*

Isabel Hilton is a writer and visiting professor at King's College London

Christopher Hitchens was a columnist, essayist and journalist. He died in 2011

Peter Hitchens is a journalist and author. He now writes for the *Mail on Sunday*

Clive James was a critic, journalist, broadcaster and author of more than 50 books. A regular columnist for *Prospect*, he died in 2019

Sam Knight is a writer and journalist. He was associate editor of *Prospect* between 2011 and 2016 and is now a staff writer at the *New Yorker*

Ivan Krastev is chairman of the Centre for Liberal Strategies in Sofia. His book *The Light that Failed*, co-authored with Stephen Holmes, came out in 2019

Sam Leith is an author and literary editor. Until 2018 he wrote a regular column for *Prospect*

Joris Luyendijk is a Dutch non-fiction author and news correspondent

Bronwen Maddox edited *Prospect* between 2010 and 2016

Bryan Magee was a British philosopher, broadcaster and author. He died in 2019

Andrew Marr is a journalist, author and broadcaster

Pankaj Mishra is an Indian author and essayist. *Age of Anger: A History of the Present* came out in 2017

Ray Monk is a philosopher and writer. He has written biographies of Ludwig Wittgenstein and Bertrand Russell

Evgeny Morozov is a contributing editor at the *New Republic*

Ferdinand Mount was head of Margaret Thatcher's Policy Unit in the 1980s. He edited the *Times Literary Supplement* from 1991 to 2002

Peter Pomerantsev is a journalist, author and television producer

Sameer Rahim is managing editor of *Prospect*. His novel *Asghar and Zahra* came out in 2019

Angela Saini is an award-winning science journalist and author of *Superior: The Return of Race Science*

Will Self is a novelist and journalist. His new memoir is *Will*

Robert Skidelsky is an economic historian and biographer of John Maynard Keynes

Wendell Steavenson is an author and journalist who has written for *Prospect* for two decades

Adam Tooze is a historian and a professor at Columbia University. *Crashed*, his history of the financial crisis, won the 2019 Lionel Gelber Prize

Alison Wolf is Sir Roy Griffiths Professor of Public Sector Management. She sits as a cross-bench peer in the House of Lords

Introduction

Tom Clark

"A new publication," began *Prospect*'s opening editorial in October 1995, "requires an explanation, even a justification." For David Goodhart, who had walked away from a good job at the *Financial Times* to set the magazine up, those words must have been heartfelt. Like the founding chair, Derek Coombs, he was risking a lot in the notoriously unprofitable field of highbrow publishing, in order to embark on something new—but what?

In page one of issue one, the founding editor went on to explain how curious British minds were missing out on the sort of extended high-class polemics and canonical overviews that Americans had long lapped up from top US writers and thinkers in publications such as the *Atlantic* and the *New Yorker*. In the quarter-century since, *Prospect* has been true to the mission of filling that gap.

I'll leave it to readers of this anniversary compendium of our best essays to judge for themselves whether or not the magazine has also succeeded in Goodhart's other founding ambition to be "a home for those writers who can see further into the future than the rest of us." Twenty-five years is a very long time in the prognostication business: few would have guessed the extent to which *Prospect* would go digital, with millions of readers online each year, plus a weekly podcast. It was just over a year into the magazine's life that a rudimentary website was announced by a small notice in our pages which read "*Prospect* joins the nerds." Prediction is an inherently hit and miss affair.

That is a point powerfully made by our opening selection of pieces on "Britain." We start with Neal Ascherson's state of the nation address "When was Britain?" published in May 1996. His sharp ear for the "estuary" accent coming out of public schools and his feel for the vague power of English nationalism still resonate, but other lines betray how mid-1990s Britain was another country. Structurally, we were still in a unitary state: he writes about a Scottish parliament only in a conditional future tense. Politically, we were yet to see the rise (never mind the fall) of New Labour, at a time when it was still that bit easier to imagine vigour and imagination—"fresh air, intellectual exercise and new parliamentary majorities," as Ascherson puts it—could solve the big problems without provoking big divisions.

Above all else, however, as we look back from 2020, it is Ascherson's confident conclusion that "in the end, the union of Europe can replace the unions... around which the UK was built," which exposes just how far our island story has, for better or worse, moved on. The following two essays, by Dutchman Joris Luyendijk—with the self-explanatory title "How I learnt to loathe England"—and the insider-outsider, Russian-born, English-raised Peter Pomerantsev, both eloquently attest to how national identity has hardened since the Brexit referendum. Still, *Prospect* has always sought to take the long view, and as a brilliant student of history as well as a journalist, Ascherson would have been less caught off guard than many from the years of "things can only get better" complacency. Even in 1996, he saw at least the potential for "a deadly confluence ahead. The river of Eurosceptic xenophobia is beginning to converge with the river of intolerant English nationalism."

I hope I'm not striking the tone of a preachy pro-European at this point, because one other distinctive quality of *Prospect* has been to avoid lapsing into shrill tribalism. We have always, as Goodhart wrote in his opening editorial, been willing to "offer space to contrary temperaments," picking pieces not on the basis of where they are coming from politically, but rather whether the author could write, and whether they had something to say.

It is as a result of this pluralism, I am sure, that the core identity of the magazine has survived pretty well intact, even as Goodhart himself evolved from a contrarian progressive into a contrarian post-liberal, then handed the reins to Bronwen Maddox, who hailed from the *Times* and mostly shared its "muscular" pro-western worldview, and then again as she in turn handed over to me, with my own background on the *Guardian* left. A strikingly high proportion of our subscribers have been with us throughout this whole journey, and so too have quite a few of the writers. Isabel Hilton, Ray Monk, Wendell Steavenson, Philip Ball and Francis Fukuyama are just some of the writers included here who wrote for *Prospect* back in the Goodhart years, and have also written for me.

And it's not just the same thinkers and writers who keep popping up in our pages, it's very often also the same themes. Take social mobility (or the lack of it) and "meritocracy," contested ideals which both appear in different ways in this collection in pieces from Ivan Krastev, in the context of post-Communist eastern Europe, and Alison Wolf's writing on the "rise of the super-family."

Identity, likewise, has kept bubbling back in different forms, with some *Prospect* pieces sounding early alarms about the rising discomfort with immigration, years before the issue came to dominate British politics. More recently, however, we've also found plenty of room for pieces from writers who see things from the other side of, as it were, the diversity divide—including our own Sameer Rahim, whose essay on the "The good Muslim delusion" details how western powers have been trying, and failing, to dictate what Islam should be for centuries.

The last 25 years have dramatically sharpened awareness about which voices are deemed to have the authority to write the kind of canonical piece to which *Prospect* aspires, especially in terms of gender. We've made some (if imperfect) progress on that front of late. But this collection from the vaults represents the world of ideas and letters as it has historically been reflected in the pages of *Prospect* over the course of its life, and we've made no attempt to tamper with that.

What has been in the DNA of the magazine from the off is *argument*: the testing not of who happens to be saying something, but of what is being said. And the thread that runs through an archetypal *Prospect* piece is very much an argumentative one, even when we are tackling subjects normally covered in a more informative or discursive tone—witness, in this collection, Angela Saini on medicine, or Will Self on love. The magazine relishes starting arguments in fact, as can be seen here in the 1998 family row over the legacy of the 1960s engineered between the Hitchens brothers. And, as loyal subscribers will know, the Duel—in which two intellectual combatants swap letters for and against a proposition—remains one of our most recognisable and popular features.

The insistence on picking holes and subjecting every passing fashion to scrutiny is not to everyone's taste, but—especially in foreign policy and economics—the past 25 years have proven the worth of writers who challenge conventional wisdom. The west's post-war hopes of a new liberal order have been exposed as naive, and its talk of nation building has been the cover for an approach that has left the Middle East in flames. (Maddox is firmly committed to the Atlantic alliance—she wrote a book called *In Defence of America*—and yet her essay on the Afghan war in this collection powerfully illustrates just how much has gone wrong.)

And then, of course, there was the 2008 crash, an event so seismic that we've not included any of *Prospect*'s earlier economic coverage in this book. Instead we have picked out Robert Skidelsky's magisterial meditation, within months of Lehman Brothers toppling, on exactly what kind of failure it was. Then there is Adam Tooze's eloquent explanation—a decade on from the first bite of the crunch—about exactly how things had gone wrong in the banks, and the scarcely-understood mechanism by which they were eventually pulled back from the brink. Remarkably, such was the grip of the pre-crash conventional wisdom, much of this was new to most of us. Tooze went on to elaborate his thesis in an award-winning history of the crisis.

One familiar phrase in that first editorial—a phrase coined, indeed, by *Prospect* contributor Francis Fukuyama—was "the end of history." It is a phrase that instantly illuminates just how different the 1990s were from our own time: in the intervening quarter of a century history has had its revenge. Some of the consequences of that might have been ugly, but they make it plainer that there is indeed an "explanation, even a justification" for a magazine of remorseless argument. Because in our world there should be few illusions about anyone having the final word. Which suits *Prospect* just fine.

Britain

When was Britain?

The assertion of national identities within the United Kingdom has left Britain in an identity muddle. Englishness, stripped of Britishness, has acquired illiberal connotations. Can a benign English identity now "come out" within a European embrace?

Neal Ascherson

May 1996

"Jim Bloggs, 101 Inkerman Terrace, Scratfield, Staffordshire, England, Great Britain, Europe, the World, the Galaxy, the Universe..." When schoolchildren used to write things like that in the front of their books, they were producing a classic old model of identities. It was a concentric model. It was seen from the central dot of all those concentric rings: the individual. Your house was the nearest ring; the universe the most remote. It was also a list of overlapping memberships. You "came from" the Potteries, but were also English. You were British, but also European, Terran, Galactic, Universal.

The question which the model does not answer is this: which of these identities, if any, has priority? By which ring does the central dot wish to be identified by others? Pope John Paul II, who derives some of his theology from 19th-century Polish patriotic mysticism, also leaves this question open. In his view, God created humanity in three concentric categories: individual, family and nation. But which is the defining identity, and which might you be entitled to betray in order to save one or both of the others? There the faithful receive no clear guidance.

The schoolchild's site of identity could be the house. It could be the continent. It could, when the child becomes a self-obsessed first year student, be the dot itself: "I am myself, and nothing else." It could be several different rings at once. In the past, we used to ask a stranger: "Where do you come from?" But these days people are more often asked *who* they are—a different, more loaded matter. The answer is usually the name of a state or a nation. This is a learned response; ordinary people did not always think like that. In parts of Belorussia, language, religion and custom vary from village to village, and the only common cultural experience is of brutality at the hands of invaders. There, peasants who are confronted with "who are you?" will often reply: "We are *tutejszy*—we are 'from here' people." But the world will not allow them that answer for much longer.

Identity is now a problem in Britain, too. To talk about an "identity crisis" would be exaggerated. But there is an enormous identity muddle. Many people have difficulty finding a satisfactory answer to the question of who they are. And this muddle has developed with astonishing speed. Fifteen years ago, the suggestion that the British were not sure who they were would have seemed absurd. No people in the world were more placidly certain about their identity and suffered less angst about it.

This new muddle is healthy. It pains some, and gives others vertigo. But it is part of Britain's adaptation to the new world and its disorder, of which the European Union (EU) is the leading edge. This adaptation does not just mean institutional change or a less "sceptred isle" approach to national sovereignty. All that is necessary. But with it comes a change in the way in which the British understand themselves as a political community, an ethnicity, a nation, a people—however you name it. We have to transform not only ourselves, but also the names we give ourselves.

Like almost all British problems of modernisation, the identity muddle relates to the archaic nature of Britain's constitutional system, now a unique survival in Europe. This system was set up by a limited and primitive reform: the principle of absolutism was not abolished, but simply transferred from the English crown to parliament. This was a process which had begun with the democratic hopes of the English revolution but ended in the compromise settlement of 1688-89. This settlement enabled the future British state to escape the political influence of the Enlightenment almost entirely—to say nothing of the French revolution. This has not only deprived Britain of institutional reforms such as a written constitution, a code of administrative law, or a citizenship based on a "culture of rights." It has kept out of British usage the very language used by all European states to describe their political societies.

Take the distinction between "state" and "nation." Although in the past these definitions were more pliable, they are now reasonably standardised, on the continent and beyond. "Nation" describes an extensive community which feels united by a common culture. A state is the set of institutions which a nation (or group of nations) may set up as the structure of government and administration. Not all nations decide that they must have an independent nation state of their own. Some (like the Catalans) are for the moment satisfied with self-government within a larger multinational state. But in the last two or three centuries, most communities which have defined themselves as "nations" have tried to establish their own states. The difference between nation and state was quite clear to them. It was expressed with brutal clarity in the old Soviet passports: "Nationality: Ukrainian (or Kazakh or Jewish). Statehood: Soviet."

In Britain that difference has never been fully understood. England and Britain are sometimes referred to as nations, sometimes as states. Most seriously—because this is a misunderstanding which gets in the way of comparing like with like in Europe—the phrase "multinational state" is almost never applied to the UK. And yet that is what the UK is. It is not tidy or symmetrical in its diversity. The UK consists of two ancient kingdoms united by treaty, one conquered Celtic nation, the rump of another and a scatter of islands. One component—England—is 10 times as populous as all the others put together. In spite of that diversity, the state governing these nations is tightly centralised. This centralism, which grew far more painful and constricting with the huge growth of state bureaucracy after 1945, arises from the absolutist doctrine of parliamentary sovereignty whose roots stretch back to 1688. Under this doctrine, sovereignty cannot be shared or distributed.

The confusion in the UK over identity and terminology is mostly English confusion. For the past few decades, at least, Welsh and Scottish subjects of the UK have found it fairly easy to define themselves as Welsh or Scottish by nation, but British by citizenship (or statehood). The word "English" has been through many vicissitudes, especially in England. Until recently, English people used the word "England" to describe the main island of the archipelago; in my youth London politicians visiting Scotland referred to "England's victory over Hitler" or "England's special relationship with America." The Scots silently resented this, although there had been a time in the late-18th and early-19th centuries when middle-class Scots travelling on the continent were proud to name their culture "English."

Then, some 25 years ago, a change set in. I believe it was the huge expansion of higher education in the 1960s, rather than the nationalist surges in Scotland and Wales during the 1970s, which encouraged it. The English began to use the term "British" to describe not only the other inhabitants of the multinational state—but themselves. It was not just that the political and media classes grew aware (led by the BBC) of how irritated Scottish and Welsh audiences became when they were called English. The change went further; the term "English" began to acquire a vaguely improper, even negative flavour to English ears. It implied not only obtuseness to the sensibilities of others, but a right-wing nationalist self-assertion ("There'll always be an England!") which was best left to football hooligans or Prom audiences. Before political correctness was even heard of, Englishness became politically incorrect.

Some, like Enoch Powell on the right and AJP Taylor on the left, continued to say England when they meant England. Others ducked out. Absurdities appeared, such as travel guide references to "Britain, land of hedgerows, cream teas and thatched cottages." It looked as if a new nation called Britain was being invented. Closer inspection showed that the word "British" was merely substituting for the word "English." Was there, then, never a *nation* called Britain? Can we ask, as Professor Gwyn Williams memorably asked about Wales: "When was Britain?"

The answer is that a common culture did come to exist in certain areas of life, after the Anglo-Scottish union of 1707. "Britishness" existed during wartime and on the frontiers or in the trading houses of the empire, both as a set of standards and as a commitment to defend the particularly British way of doing things. "Britishness" also described a battery of political conventions, involving aspirations to fair, non-corrupt government. As time passed, a *homo britannicus* was actually bred, although never in sufficient numbers to compose a nation rather than to lead it. This was the British upper class as it existed by the mid-19th century, which wore the same tweeds, remembered the same public schools, spoke with the same accent and owned almost all the land between Land's End and John O'Groats. The social and political eclipse of this class is an important factor in the decline of this shortlived "British" identity. To take a small example, boys and girls emerging from public schools now mostly speak with versions of the "estuary" accent of southeast England. The voice of the ruling class is no longer "above locality" but has become the voice of one geographical region. More importantly, Margaret Thatcher was the first Conservative prime minister to be instantly identifiable as English rather than "British."

Recently I attended a meeting of broadcasters and historians to debate a project for a millennium television series on British history. When was Britain? Many thought that the series should start with the Roman conquest—as if the Roman province of Britannia, which did not extend to Ireland or beyond southern Scotland, had developed in some linear way into the UK. Others acknowledged that in effect Britain as a single "experience" could not have existed before 1603 (union of crowns) or 1707 (union of parliaments), but they proposed to bolt on extra programmes which would rush through the separate histories of Scotland, Wales or Ireland before their respective incorporations by England.

This seemed to beg the question. But my own suggestion—that the series should be called "From England to Great Britain: the Story of English Imperial Expansion"—was greeted coldly. A generation ago, it would have probably seemed acceptable to a similar gathering. In 1995 it reeked of incorrectness. The broadcasters professed to fear that such an approach might give offence at the Celtic peripheries. In reality they were not prepared to accept that there is no such animal as a British history which goes back 2,000 years. To put it another way, they were reluctant to come out as English.

Coming out, all the same, has always been an English option. Since the confusion between England and Britain descended, there have been many in Scotland and Wales who have wanted the English national identity to reassert itself. At least, runs the argument, we would know where and who we were. Great Britain would be revealed as the multi-ethnic state it is. And then a rational future for that state could be worked out. The fearsome "West Lothian question" rests on this confusion of British-English identity. It complains that if there were a Scottish parliament with power over internal affairs, then Scottish Westminster MPs would be able to vote on bills concerning English education, while English Westminster MPs would not be able to vote on Scottish education. Conversely, if the Scots MPs were deprived of the right to vote on purely English legislation, then Westminster might find itself with two conflicting majorities: a Labour majority on British matters, but a Tory one on English matters. Government would become impossible.

The logical remedy would be to establish an English parliament as well as a British one. The UK should be reformed into a quasi-federal structure with three (or four, counting Northern Ireland) national parliaments and a central legislature dealing with foreign affairs, defence, shared services and macro-economic policy. Logical—but given the present state of political awareness south of the border, unthinkable. The House of Commons in the palace of Westminster is perceived by the English as England's ancient parliament, the ark of the covenant honoured and fought over between crown and people through the centuries, the chalice of national liberty and sovereignty. The notion that this sacred place should be diminished to a sort of under-used federal chamber, with hot, living debate on the laws of England evicted to the Queen Elizabeth Conference Centre across Parliament Square, would seem to most English people like a monstrous, senseless act of vandalism.

But what if the English did come out of the closet to embrace their own national identity? This is beginning to happen. Here and there, Englishness is being displayed without the fig leaf of Britishness. In the 1992 election campaign, John Major told his Scottish audience candidly that he was English, and therefore not entirely qualified to understand their feelings. This was significant. Thatcher, similarly, had made no pretence to the old upper class "British" culture and was widely identified in Scotland (pejoratively) as "English." But she still felt entitled to instruct the Scots about their true national character—and did so, in her notorious "sermon on the mound" before the general assembly of the Church of Scotland. Major's humility was not only a contrast. It marked a slight but perceptible change in the relationship of ethnicity to authority in Britain. To govern, it is no longer necessary to deny one's Englishness.

If we learn to read them, there are other signs of a reviving English identity. Newspapers such as the *Independent*, founded only 10 years ago, are content to be perceived as essentially "English" papers for the English reader—even the southeast English reader. The *Guardian* and the *Observer*, in contrast, still strain dutifully to be "British" in their emphasis—although their proportion of readers outside the M25 ring or north of Watford is not much greater than that of their *Independent* rivals. In scholarship, English nationalism is clearly on the move. We have studies claiming that the Anglo-Saxon peasantry—Thatcherites *avant la lettre*—developed an individualistic entrepreneurial culture long before the rest of Europe escaped from primitive collectivism. Or that the post-Roman Saxon "invaders" were in fact a tiny elite minority who so dazzled the Romano-British population that they persuaded it to change its language, religion and material culture to that of the newcomers. This theory tries to demonstrate that England really "is" Britain in an ethnic, genetic sense. England therefore would have a continuity which did not start merely at the Dark Ages but reached back for many more millennia: perhaps into the early Iron Age, perhaps even further. It was in this spirit that the archaeologist Lord Renfrew has spoken of ancestral territories which "we" have possessed for many thousands of years.

But if it is true that the English are beginning once again to claim English national identity, is that an entirely healthy development? Clearly, there is a gain in lucidity when British identity is under discussion. But beyond that is a larger, murkier question. What is modern English nationalism going to be like? Could it turn out to be a great deal less "civic" than peripheral Celtic nationalisms? Could it adopt a vengeful and irrational form which would set itself against any reform seeming to diminish this English-dominated Britain? This is a question which nobody asks. We should. So far, English opinion has been strikingly tolerant of Scottish and Welsh aspirations to self-government. John Major apparently believes that his appeals in 1992 to "defend the union" against Labour's devolution plans went down well with English voters. There is little hard evidence to support him, but the point is that he has begun to "play the English card." At a certain moment, English nationalism may begin to rise and come to meet him or his successor.

English nationalism has been mobilised by a variety of (mostly tiny) political groups for brief periods in the first half of this century. Putting their experience together, a disconcerting picture emerges. In his book *Blood and Belonging*, Michael Ignatieff makes the rough contrast between "ethnic" and "civic" nationalism, between the atavistic wish to plunge back into the imaginary past and the modernising impulse to construct a new, responsible society which joins the world on its own terms. Surprisingly, English nationalism registers at a point towards the ethnic end of this scale. It has been xenophobic (anti-French, anti-Irish and anti-semitic), ruralist rather than urban, deeply suspicious of industrial society and the "uprooting" influence of modern life. As Patrick Wright suggests in his book *The Village that Died for England*, this blood-and-soil emphasis left English nationalism open to fascist infection in the 1920s and 1930s. Compared to the respectable, small town reformism of mainstream Welsh or Scottish nationalism, the English version is not a pretty sight.

And here the idea of "Britishness" acquires an unexpected function. It may be that feeling British has protected the English nation against its own worst instincts. We all know what happened when post-Habsburg Austrians decided to feel German in the 1930s. The fiction of a British "nation" has kept English nationalism in check. It has channelled its passions into empire building, into defensive wars against continental powers, into pride in British social achievements—whether as the old "workshop of the world" or as the site of a national health service envied by most of the world. Britain survived the loss of colonial empire surprisingly well. Colonies and dominions became independent, but Britain itself did not change dramatically. It did not lose its identity by losing its empire. The question is whether the next transition can be so successful.

Britain is multinational, but it no longer consists of the English, the Scots, the Welsh and the Irish—plus "a few refugees and foreigners." There are now some five million British subjects whose ethnic origins are outside Europe: principally in the Indian subcontinent or the Caribbean. Very few of them want to remain in foreign enclaves, living exclusively within the culture of their roots. Almost all of them are happy to venture out and inhabit overlapping rings of identity. There is the ring which has to do with their daily life and schooling in these islands. There is the ring which contains the cultural traditions of their family and milieu which relate to lands far from Britain. And, in most cases, there is the "political" ring with the designation of British citizenship in passport and other official documents.

These inhabitants of Britain raise several questions about identity. First of all, who do they think they are? A few years back, there was a hopeful anticipation that these immigrant communities would emerge as the last true Britons—that they would define themselves as proudly "British" above any petty local ethnicities. They would, in short, replace the gentry as the authentic British class. This would have been a piquant outcome. The "true Brit" would turn out to be a child of the empire—not only son or daughter of those who had created it, but also of the black and brown millions whom it ruled. The reality is more complex. Yes, they do see themselves as British, but usually with the qualification—"black British" or "British Muslim." To add to the complexity, in Glasgow or Cardiff, locally born children may even say that they feel "Scottish" or "Welsh." Maybe they are becoming like the Jewish community in Scotland, which, with its roots mostly in Poland or Lithuania, has regarded itself for 100 years as Scottish as well as Jewish, with "British" honoured as citizenship rather than culture.

There is, then, no living heir to British cultural identity. This fact makes the rise of English nationalism, freed of its "British" restraint, all the more dangerous. At one level, it leaves the non-European communities ideologically defenceless; the Britain which "built the empire" and brought them to London, Bradford, Liverpool and Cardiff no longer exists to justify their presence. And at the wider political level, we can begin to see a deadly confluence ahead. The river of Eurosceptic xenophobia is beginning to converge with the river of intolerant English nationalism. If they become one torrent, England may cease to be a country where men and women with ideals would care to live—and not only men and women whose skin is black or brown.

Europhobia, as a party political disease, can be rooted out by fresh air, intellectual exercise and new parliamentary majorities. But intolerant English nationalism cannot. Instead, it must be confronted, educated and slowly tamed. Sooner or later, England will have to come to terms with being English. I leave aside intricate questions such as whether Scottish independence—if it ever came to pass—would produce two successor states, one called Scotland and the other, presumably consisting of England, Wales and Northern Ireland, no longer entitled to call itself Britain or the United Kingdom. The immediate problem is whether English national identity can be managed in a much looser version of the British state, without allowing the unregenerate aspects of English nationalism to break through.

Here I am optimistic. It would be a cruel irony if the long prophesied, long delayed "post-imperial hangover" arrived because of the decentralisation of Britain itself. This does not have to happen. The path to safety lies through the EU. If the Union can both "widen" and "deepen," then a new notion of identity will emerge. In Northern Ireland there has already been profound and hopeful discussion of how different cultural traditions can co-exist by separating cultural identity from traditional political allegiances to London or to Dublin. This can be the future for Britain.

It is a long road. But in the end, the union of Europe can replace the unions—forcible or contractual—around which the UK was built. The pressure will be taken out of identity. To be Welsh and British, or simply Welsh and European, will no longer imply an unresolved tension with England. To be English in Europe will no longer imply an unresolved nostalgia for "Great Britain." But children will continue to imagine their concentric rings of identity reaching out to all humanity and beyond, and in this archipelago of ours, one of them will be called "Britain." The difference will be that no single ring will have sovereignty over the others. Those children, our grandchildren, will be Lords of all the Rings, the heirs to an infinity of identity.

How I learned to loathe England

Six years in your company has convinced me: you lot need time alone

Joris Luyendijk

November 2017

When I came to live in London with my family in 2011 I did not have to think of a work or residency permit. My children quickly found an excellent state primary school, and after a handful of calls we enjoyed free healthcare, and the right to vote in local elections. The only real bureaucratic hassle we encountered that warm summer concerned a permit to park. It all seemed so smooth compared to earlier moves to the United States, Egypt, Lebanon and Israel/Palestine. Then again, this time we were moving in with our cousins—weren't we?

We had arrived as fellow Europeans, but when we left this summer to return to the Netherlands we felt more like foreigners: people tolerated as long as they behave. At best we were "European Union nationals" whose rights would be subject to negotiations—bargaining chips in the eyes of politicians. As we sailed from Harwich, it occurred to me that our departure would be counted by Theresa May as five more strikes towards her goal of "bringing down net immigration to the tens of thousands."

The Dutch and the British have a lot in common, at first sight. Sea-faring nations with a long and guilty history of colonial occupation and slavery, they are pro free-trade and have large financial service industries—RBS may even move its headquarters to Amsterdam. Both tend to view American power as benign; the Netherlands joined the occupations of Afghanistan and Iraq. Shell, Unilever and Elsevier are just three examples of remarkably successful Anglo-Dutch joint ventures. I say "remarkably" because I've learnt that in important respects, there is no culture more alien to the Dutch than the English. (I focus on England as I've no experience with Wales, Scotland or Northern Ireland). Echoing the Calvinist insistence on "being true to oneself," the Dutch are almost compulsively truthful. Most consider politeness a cowardly form of hypocrisy. Bluntness is a virtue; insincerity and backhandedness are cardinal sins.

So let me try to be as Dutch as I can, and say that I left the UK feeling disappointed, hurt and immensely worried. We did not leave because of Brexit. My wife and I are both Dutch and we want our children to grow roots in the country where we came of age. We loved our time in London and have all met people who we hope will become our friends for life. But by the time the referendum came, I had become very much in favour of the UK leaving the EU. The worrying conditions that gave rise to the result—the class divide and the class fixation, as well as an unhinged press, combine to produce a national psychology that makes Britain a country you simply don't want in your club.

I am terribly sorry for my pro-EU middle-class friends in England, and even more sorry for the poor who had no idea that by supporting Brexit they were voting to become poorer. But this is England's problem, not the EU's: the nation urgently needs some time alone to sort itself out. So when those first "Leave" votes came in, I found myself making fist pumps at the television.

On the morning of 24th June 2016 the middle-class parents at my children's school were huddling together in shock over the result. One or two were crying quietly when a working-class mother I knew walked up to a well-to-do mother who had been canvassing for Remain. "OUT! OUT! OUT!", she shouted as she wagged her index finger. Then she walked off in triumph, back to her working-class friends at the other end of the playground.

Over the years, I had learned she was a warm person, yet on that day something stronger burst out. She had used the referendum to try to smash that expensive middle-class toy called the EU and it had worked. At last, for the first time in decades, those who felt like life's losers openly defied the winners, and carried an election. Now her country would have £350m a week to spend on the number one worry for people like her: the NHS.

I've seen a good deal in England which suggested that, just maybe, not all was well with the collective psyche—the in-your-face binge drinking, the bookies stoking gambling addiction on every high street, the abject but routine neglect of public housing which went undiscussed until the Grenfell Tower fire.

But that scene on the morning after the referendum encapsulates my disappointment with the country. Not only the division, but also the way it had been inflamed. Why would you allow a handful of billionaires to poison your national conversation with disinformation—either directly through the tabloids they own, or indirectly, by using those newspapers to intimidate the public broadcaster? Why would you allow them to use their papers to build up and co-opt politicians peddling those lies? Why would you let them get away with this stuff about "foreign judges" and the need to "take back control" when Britain's own public opinion is routinely manipulated by five or six unaccountable rich white men, themselves either foreigners or foreign-domiciled?

Before coming to Britain I had always thought that the tabloids were like a misanthropic counterpoint to Monty Python. Like many Europeans, I saw these newspapers as a kind of English folklore, laying it on thick in the way that theatrical British politicians conduct their debates in the House of Commons. Newspapers in the Netherlands would carry on their opinion pages articles by commentators such as Oxford scholar Timothy Garton Ash—giving the impression that such voices represented the mainstream in Britain. Watching *QI* before coming to the UK, I remember seeing Stephen Fry banter with Jeremy Clarkson and imagining the former was the rule, and the latter the exception. Living in London taught me that it is the other way around. George Orwell is still correct: England is a family with the wrong members in charge.

This has been a bitter pill to swallow for this Smiths fan who grew up in the 1980s on a cultural diet of Tolkien, Le Carré, *The Young Ones*, *Spitting Image* and *The Singing Detective*—these books being available in every library, and the programmes carried by our national broadcaster. I never knew much about French culture and politics, so if I had discovered that they are vile it would have meant travelling a far smaller mental distance. But the English? They were our liberators, a term still used more than 70 years after my mother saw the "Tommies" enter her home town of Eindhoven.

Until the tabloids are reformed and freed from editorial interference by their plutocratic owners, the rageful misunderstanding that I saw in the school playground will not go away. Tabloid readers will sometimes see through the bias on particular issues and against particular people, as many did when they voted for the demonised Labour leader Jeremy Corbyn in June. But when it comes to Europe and the world beyond, the campaign of chauvinism has been so unremitting, over so many decades, that it is much harder to resist. And, as things stand, the journalists at those publications could never come out and admit that they have misjudged Brexit—that would mean not only losing face, but very likely losing their job. Indeed, where is the investigative reporting about the exact quid pro quo when Rupert Murdoch or *Daily Mail* editor Paul Dacre come out in support of, say, Theresa May? Most British journalists, with a few noble exceptions, are too terrified of the press barons to pursue such questions.

That scene at my children's school last year showed up another side of English society: entrenched inequality. In the Netherlands, schools are not ranked, and nor are universities. Sought-after secondary schools and universities use a lottery to decide who is admitted—the opposite of the generally hyper-competitive and market-based English model. (There have been experiments with school lotteries in England, but these have run into outrage because of the perception that giving every child an equal chance is—in some unspecified way—profoundly unfair.)

You could, if you've been as frustrated by the Dutch educational system as I was, characterise it as institutionalised mediocrity. But the good thing about it is that it really doesn't matter for your identity or your prospects exactly which school or university you went to—not in the way it does in England. Dutch people are unfamiliar with that English ritual where two highly educated people try to work out which one has the edge: state school or private? Oxford, Cambridge, or some other place? If Oxbridge, what college?

I have seen plenty of English middle-class parents jump through crazy hoops to get their children into the "right" school. I have seen friendships ripped apart when one couple sends their daughter to a private school and the others do not. I was not surprised to read that Corbyn's second marriage collapsed over the question of whether to send his son to a selective school.

It is quite ironic that a nation that gave the world the term "fair play" sees the fact that rich children receive a better education than poor ones as a perfectly natural thing. I remember asking around at the *Guardian*, where I had been hired to investigate the City of London, why this progressive newspaper did not put the school system centre stage. This is how the elites clone themselves, is it not? The answer: most of our management and prominent writers went to private school themselves and most are sending their children there, too, so that would invite the charge of hypocrisy. I struggle to blame those former *Guardian* colleagues knowing that two thirds of all top jobs in England today go to the 7 per cent of children who have attended private schools. Are you really going to sacrifice your child's prospects to make an individual stand which will change nothing?

Nor do I blame working-class people for seething at a system where by the time you are 11 the die is cast, and where—to add insult to injury—you are constantly told that this is a meritocracy where all that counts is hard work and being "aspirational" (a word that does not even exist in Dutch). And one in which you hear everyone talk about "public schools." That is like calling a taxi a form of "public transport" or, indeed, naming dilapidated zones of social housing "estates." (Seriously, middle-class Englanders, how will you ever straighten yourselves out if you can't even say what you mean, and mean what you say?)

If I were English and working class, the loaded dice and the accompanying cant would make me very bitter—a bitterness that was cleverly harvested by the "Leave" camp. Yes, there were factors beside class that bore on the vote: voters in London and Scotland broke for "Remain," and pensioners broke for "Leave." But class was central: the connection between voting "Leave" and having finished education early was just as strong as the endlessly-discussed age dimension. And the same bitterness will, surely, be harnessed again until the root cause is addressed.

There is another, final, side to this class system *à l'Anglaise*. It seems to breed a perspective on the world that is zero-sum. Your class system is a form of ranking. For one to go up, another must go down. Perhaps this is why sports are such an obsession. There, too, only one can win. It was striking for this Dutchman to see an innocuous school dance be concluded with the designation of a winner. The result: all the other eight-year-olds went home slightly or clearly annoyed for not having won. Why not just let them dance? There seems to be in English culture—with its adversarial courtrooms, and its parliamentary front benches two swords' length apart—an almost reflexive need to compete, to conclude a process by declaring a winner. The expectation that English children will learn to put a brave face on the hurt of losing doubtless deepens the scars.

The English consequently struggle to understand the "one plus one is three" concept of co-operation so fundamental to the EU. The word "compromise" has an almost negative ring in English popular culture; the idea gets dismissed as "fudge," rather than a worthwhile outcome that can help everyone save face.

Could there be a causal relationship between English hostility to the EU and this wider adversarial culture? Does it make English soil especially fertile for those press barons to plant their seeds of slander? I began to wonder about when this hostility began to hurt. I was surprised by this feeling since, until then, I had never given the European side of my identity much thought. I have often heard Muslim friends say that it was only the attacks of 9/11 that had made them Muslim. Suddenly everybody regarded them as Muslims and so, over time, they began to feel as such. Something similar happened to me when the EU referendum campaign started.

I began to realise that there are powerful people in England who actively want the EU destroyed. They are full of aggressive contempt for everything the Union stands for. Even David Cameron could not bring himself to go to Oslo with other EU leaders to receive the 2012 Nobel Peace Prize. Given the deep competitiveness of the English, it may be that they need the EU to feel superior; we may have lost the empire and be less than 1 per cent of the world's population but at least we're not "Yurup."

This attitude then justifies the enduring ignorance about the EU, its member states and European culture generally. "We don't even know who they are," shrieked Brexiteer Andrea Leadsom during a televised debate about the EU's so-called five presidents. You could tell she thought this was a really good argument to use: we don't know who they are, so that must be their fault.

The superiority complex feeds a sense of entitlement, which Cameron played to by demanding "concessions." The word says it all. Apparently membership is a favour of the English people to the EU and in exchange there must be rebates, opt-outs and special status. Every "Remain" as well as "Leave" supporter that I have spoken to automatically assumed I would be against Brexit.

Consider that Brexiteer line—the EU "needs us more than vice versa." It's abject nonsense, as was the presumption that after the Brits voted to leave, other EU countries would follow.

In October last year Peter Foster, who is the Europe Editor and an increasingly rare measured voice on the *Daily Telegraph*, wrote an article calling on Theresa May to "accept publicly that the European side has as much right to guard their interests as the UK does." He then continued that, "it might also be worth acknowledging that, on balance, the EU27 also has more power to protect its interests in these negotiations than Britain does."

Just imagine the French centre-right newspaper *Le Figaro* or its German equivalent *Die Welt* publishing an opinion piece pleading with its readers to understand that "the British people have national interests, too." The thought would never occur. That is the difference between England on the one hand and serious European countries on the other.

This, then, was how, for the first time in my life, I began to feel European. Though no pro-EU federalist, I was suddenly being defensive over something I had never actively supported. In fact, I think there are good reasons for the Netherlands to leave the EU, just as there are good reasons to stay. The EU is a dilemma full of trade-offs. But what I do think is that if the EU is to become truly democratic it needs to conduct an honest and open debate about what it wants to be, and then build the structures to go with it. An existential debate of that kind followed by either dismantling or reinvention requires good faith. This is almost entirely missing from the English side where "Remain," too, campaigned on the promise that the UK could veto any further integration. Hence my support for Brexit.

Ever since the referendum, friends from across the world have been enquiring whether it is true that the British have gone mad. Without those six years in London, I would have unhesitatingly said "yes." "A temporary bout of insanity" still seems the preferred explanation in much of Europe and among many British Remainers. But years of immersion in English culture and society have convinced me that actually, the Brexit vote should instead be seen as the logical and overdue outcome of a set of English pathologies.

Which brings me to my real anxiety. It is extremely difficult to see a scenario in which this whole Brexit saga could end well.

The Tories are seared by Europe, as they have been for a generation, only now with more intensity; Labour looks incapable of overcoming its own divisions on the question. Neither party dares to speak the truth to millions of people who have voted for a "have your cake and eat it" option that was never on the menu. How to carry out the will of the majority when the majority voted for something that does not exist?

Legally, politically and logically the EU cannot give the UK the kind of deal that would draw this chapter to a happy close. Britain will pay a horrible price for a hard Brexit. The alternative should be a sweet soft deal, except that this will then encourage every EU member state to demand their own special arrangement, and that would be the end of the EU. The fact that even Remainers keep exhorting the EU "not to punish us" demonstrates just how incapable the English are of reckoning with anyone else's point of view.

The one real alternative is that Britain reverses course, gets on its knees, and begs to be let back in. This could be the most dangerous outcome of all. While the imagination of many "Leave" voters remain in the grip of the tabloids, any concession to the reality of national interests risks inflaming rage and cries of betrayal. As for the EU, it is first and foremost a rule-based organisation. If the rules around Article 50 were bent to allow Britain back in on special terms, then the whole edifice is undermined. Scotland should be let in if it wants, and Northern Ireland too. But England is out and must be kept out—at least until it has resolved its deep internal problems. Call it nation building.

Excuse me, are you English?

I never thought I could be English.
Now I'm not sure I want to be

Peter Pomerantsev

January/February 2020

I have only met Dominic Cummings once, but the meeting had a profound impact on my identity. It took place in a pub near the Islington home of the "Leave" campaign mastermind, some months after the Brexit referendum and many before he arrived in Downing Street with Boris Johnson.

It was a casual meeting, not an interview, and I wasn't taking notes. But I hope I'm not betraying anyone's trust when I relate being stunned that—when looking back at the referendum campaign—Cummings used the phrase "the problem for people like you is..." From the context, it was clear that by "people like you" he meant a new category of the English electorate called "Remainers," a type of Englishness that he was identifying me with. And this was stunning because it was the first time I had ever been identified as any part of the English people.

I'm a first-generation immigrant with a blatantly non-Anglo surname; I have no relatives in England aside from my utterly un-English mother; I've lived at least half of my life in what you people call "abroad." I've sometimes exercised my right to vote, but it wouldn't have occurred to me to associate suffrage with identity. I voted for practical concerns in places where I pay my taxes, the same as I would have voted in any country where I might reside.

At first, I thought Cummings's identification of me an accident. But when I travelled across the country to cover the 2017 election I heard the same sentiment: "It must be hard for people like you," I was told; "Brexit is all the fault of people like you." And while Brexiteers saw me as the other part of the English people, so Remainers embraced me. As a Cornish friend who works at a multinational organisation told me: "There are many English people who are like you, and you can join us."

Something fundamental has shifted in the possibility of becoming English. For the first time I have the option to join this once-exclusive club. On the one hand this seems convenient, as my British passport is the only one that I have. But what does it say about the English that they suddenly want to invite me in? And why, when I stand at the edge of this half-open door, do I find myself pausing?

A nation in gradation

As far back as I can remember, I never thought I could be English. Or to be more precise, the only way I thought I could be accepted by the English was to insist I wasn't one of them. Let me explain. I grew up in the 1980s. As a child I worked out that the English were obsessed with difference, with the micro-gradations of class and postcode, accent, county and school. This deification of differentiation was even expressed in small details of urban design, in those park benches with little dividers between every seat. It was expressed more dramatically in relationships. When I transitioned between state and private schools at the age of seven, a friend's parents told my mother that we could no longer play together as we were now "in different classes." My Soviet-raised mother was horrified: what were these arbitrary distinctions?

Through my early childhood what felt like utterly unnatural class definers, distinctions that had nothing to do with me, were shaping everything around me. It felt as if some alien set of selves, with centuries of brooding hatreds, was being imposed onto mine. If this was what being English meant, I wanted none of it. Thankfully that wasn't the deal on offer anyway.

"Do you feel Russian or English?" my classmates' parents would constantly ask me. I quickly worked out it was something of a trick question. It wouldn't do to become English too fast, a sure sign you hadn't grasped the differentiation game. The most English thing I could possibly do, I realised, was to insist on *not* being English. So, even though I'd only spent the first nine months of my life in the USSR, I identified myself as "Russian." In many ways this was absurd. Though I spoke Russian at home my family was from Ukraine. But saying I was Ukrainian, when I didn't even know anyone who spoke the language, seemed dishonest too. What was I meant to say: that I was Soviet? That was ridiculous: my family had run away from that regime. In any case Russia, Ukraine, the USSR—all these were abstractions to me. There was no sizeable Russian émigré community in London that I could be part of. "Russia" was shorthand for our family of three, a secret language we could speak in the street and no one understood, a texture of sound so much more boisterous than the breeziness of English. Russia and Ukraine were vast splodges upon the map that hung in our kitchen, part of the bigger splodge of the USSR, splattered with coffee, wine and cooking oil, a territory I could only populate with books that I had read. Is that where I came from—books?

I was only "Russian" in the sense that it was a way of being non-English in a very English way. This half-in, half-out identity had advantages. On the one hand I could enjoy the many pleasures of being in England, learn only the way someone living here can the stubborn sense of self-worth that even the poorest here possess, which is so striking if you know cultures where even the super-rich are mental serfs. But it also meant that I could avoid being pulled into the disheartening English class distinctions. As a "Russian" I didn't have a class, I was just foreign. I didn't have to carry around all the class guilt and loathing.

The only trouble I had with my very English Russianness was that my spoken English was a little too good. "Your English is so perfect, one would never suspect you are a Russian," I would be told, and would feel my speech was somehow deceptive (what should I do—fake a Russian accent to be more genuine?).

The language proficiency became a bigger problem when, as a student, I found myself in Scotland. In Edinburgh I would be constantly mistaken for an English person, with all the national resentments that comes with. It could take a while to explain, sometimes not in the most friendly situation, that, despite my speech, I wasn't English.

Edinburgh may not have been English either, but it was a concentration of all the identity disasters that I had always done my damnedest to avoid. Class differences were represented geographically: the upper and upper-middle classes on the higher hills of New Town; the middle classes on the flat plains of Bruntsfield; the working classes on the lower slopes of Leith. And then there were the tensions between the English and the Scots. If it had ever occurred to me to think of myself as "British," Scotland made me realise how fraught that identity is too. Becoming "English" meant having to take on the ghastly games of class identity; becoming "British" meant having to take on the mutual loathing of two nations stuck in an ancient and often abusive marriage.

I left the UK straight after university, and returned a decade later with three small children and an actually Russian wife in tow. Much had changed in the intervening decade. Russian was no longer a secret language on London's streets. While I had been one of the few non-English kids in school, my children were in classes where over half, sometimes more like 90 per cent, could be some sort of immigrant. My children still weren't English and would describe themselves as Russian, but it was much less of a big deal for them to be non-English.

And then came the referendum and that chat with Cummings—and my fragile constructions of being non-English English seemed suddenly irrelevant. Here seemed a project for a new English identity, loosely referred to as "Remainers," where my foreign origins helped qualify me to join.

New worlds, old hatreds

Here, however, is my first problem with becoming an "English Remainer"—I'm European. Not "European" in some abstract, cultural sense, but in the much narrower meaning of the political European project, the EU. As a teenager, in between my London childhood and Scottish student years, I lived in Munich, where I attended a special "European School," one of a dozen or so such educational institutions created by the founders of the EEC and EU to create young people "in mind European." (Boris Johnson briefly attended one as well.) The "European" idea nurtured in the school was not about imposing a supra-identity. We didn't hail the European flag or sing "Ode to Joy" in the mornings. The educational innovation was to have you study history and geography in another language and from another point of view. So I was in the English section of the school, and studied history and geography in French. Someone in the Dutch sections could have studied them in German. The Germans, from a French point of view, and so on.

While your distinct connection to your nation of origin was maintained (you still followed the broader curriculum of your own country), you were being simultaneously taught to be able to understand the point of view of others. In many ways this reflected the EU's own logic, a project whose aim is not some woolly cosmopolitanism, but a way of squaring the circle of nationalism and the need for co-operation on a crowded continent. "European" is a way of doing things, a constant effort to understand others and compromise, to smooth polarisation.

The "Remainer" versus "Brexiteer" divide which now cleaves right through English identity operates with the polar opposite of such a logic. It's all about constructing in-out groups. It's a crass divide engineered by propagandists. Moreover, I'm not convinced the "Remain" versus "Leave" identities are all that stable or whole. Below the surface, I see the old class and national divisions I've always veered away from. Leave-Remain has quickly become a new way of talking about old Anglo-Scottish tensions. Meanwhile, among English political elites, what is purportedly a row about "Europe" is also an older dance of class ambition.

It is the story of up-and-coming middle-class men like Cummings, Michael Gove or Dominic Raab, men from relatively humble families, strivers who went to slightly the wrong schools and wouldn't have made the right societies at Oxford, challenging the smug, upper-middle-class and lower-upper-class aristos who ruled the country and the Conservative Party. These up-and-coming men formed an alliance with reactionary grandees such as Lord Salisbury—a former power-broker in parliament's upper house and the great-great grandson of the gloomy, bewhiskered Victorian premier. The power of such men goes back centuries, but their influence had seemed on the wane. Together these two groups ganged up against the urbane Osbornes and Camerons of this world.

"Europe" is just a proxy for this game. In another dynamic a Cummings or Gove might have been pro-Europe, if that was the anti-status quo pose that would have allowed them to stab the arrogant class above them. In this Edwardian play Johnson is the rakish opportunist, ready to transform himself to suit the zeitgeist, a humorous symbol of a society that has lost its sense of order and propriety. There would also be walk-on parts for ardent Catholic Leavers like Jacob Rees-Mogg and Iain Duncan Smith, so desperate to prove they belong with the high Anglican elite they became the most furious advocates of English anti-Europeanism.

"The irony is that for generations," the Catholic journalist Kate Maltby told me, "it has been a core tenet of conservative thought in this country—especially amongst conservative Catholics and Anglo-Catholics—to stress our cultural debt to Rome, in both the classical and religious senses. TS Eliot, when he said that 'there is no such thing as an English classic,' asserted the cultural supremacy of pan-Europeanism. This used to be the orthodox position. So when you see senior Catholic Conservatives like Duncan Smith or Rees-Mogg laud Brexit as some kind of new English Reformation, it represents a huge disconnect from that English Roman Catholic tradition. Or perhaps, a rejection of it."

Rather than fostering stable new selves, the Brexit debate has surfaced and sharpened old complexes and hatreds. If anything, the debate has become more class obsessed. Posh boys have long dominated English politics, but Brexit has been contemporaneous with a heightened public loathing for Etonians and accusations of how the boarding school system has created an elite that has led the country into ruin—feelings that must have been stirring underneath for quite a while.

And then there's the anti-semitism debate. While focused on a justified critique of a Labour Party leadership that appears to have missed how some of its domestic fans and international "friends" are text-book anti-semites, what's interesting is that this question has surfaced now, in the spasms of identity unrest around Brexit. Just as the country is questioning the assumptions about who it is, so English Jews are wondering whether they have been truly accepted.

The Brexit referendum asked the country "who are you?", a question so explosive it is rarely asked directly, and in the shock of scrambling for an answer every latent hatred, insecurity, hidden resentment and unresolved discomfort has been dredged up. And so, three decades after being constantly asked "what nationality is it you feel?" I find the roles reversed. It's now the English who need to answer the question of who they are. But is there a way to do this that is less self-destructive, that gets us talking productively to each other, and about ourselves?

Cracking mirrors

"Psychoanalysts are a bit suspicious of the word 'identity,'" Josh Cohen told me, when I called to ask him whether there were any insights his profession could grant us into how to talk about who we are. "Identity in the strict sense is what never differs from itself, whereas psychoanalysis tends to think of selfhood as a fragile patchwork of different identifications—parents in the first instance, but then teachers, group leaders, rock stars, the list could and does go on. The French psychoanalyst Lacan speaks of the 'mirror stage,' the moment in early childhood when we see ourselves in the mirror and mistake ourselves for a cohesive, integral being, rather than the diffuse and contradictory creatures we actually are. In our effort to shore up this artificially complete version of ourselves, which we call our 'identity,' we are liable to become aggressive."

And so amid a disturbing discussion about identity, Cohen suggested, psychoanalysts might suggest "getting people to think about identification as a process" and talking "through the different patterns and paths that lead us to adopt an identity." Because, Cohen explained, "it's amazing, once you start to think about it, the sheer number of identifications—personal relationships and cultural influences and value systems and so on—that go into the transmission and making of a self."

National identities don't necessarily operate in the same way as an individual's psyche, but there is a useful parallel to make here with Brexit. In response to the impossible question of "who are you?" implicit in the referendum—a sort of enforced glance into a national mirror—we have both retreated and been pushed into a series of binary identities which, when you prod them, fall apart, and by the very dint of their fragility become ever more aggressively defended. "Many psychoanalysts have noted how it's impossible to have a nuanced, ambivalent discussion about Brexit," Cohen told me. "You have to be for or against." Recent social research echoes this. At King's College Bobby Duffy has showed how British people tend to agree about many salient issues—minority rights, say, or how to govern the economy—but this long-established ability to find common ground in many fields of policy runs counter to strong emotional polarisation: something, or someone, is pushing us apart.

To think how we can move beyond the nasty in-out groupings that have come to dominate our discourse, it's worth gaining perspective from other countries. Ever since the collapse of the USSR, my birth country of Ukraine has been going through one long period of turbulence around its national identity. Propagandists, foreign and domestic, have worked to split the country into a supposedly solid pro-European, anti-Soviet, Ukrainian-speaking West Ukraine, and a supposedly pro-Russian, pro-Soviet, Russian-speaking East Ukraine. However, when my small research initiative at the LSE conducted polling and focus groups across the country, we found such binaries were far too crude to do justice to diverse values and aspirations, and even attitudes to history in Ukraine, on both sides of the supposed divide. Parts of society which had been defined in different categories due to geography and language had much in common with one another. Others that had been clumped together had more in common with groups that had been defined as their adversaries. We now work with local Ukrainian media to explore stories that move beyond the east-west divide, that widen the aperture of possible experiences Ukrainians define themselves through.

Here in England, there is a panoply of unarticulated experiences that need to be explored. As the journalist Ben Judah once told me, the Jewish English experience has barely been covered in our culture. We lack the most basic family-saga novels that track the generational journey from Brick Lane to Hampstead Garden Suburb, and all the games around acceptance along the way. Judah has advocated for a British museum of immigration, that could compare and cross-relate the experiences of different immigrant groups over the centuries.

Perhaps one of the newer experiences covered could be of people like me, the more recent non-English English. Why do we come to England? Why do we stay? Once he'd fled the Soviet Union my father could have chosen to be a refugee in any number of western countries. He chose England because he wanted to work at the BBC World Service, and there is much to make sense of how the World Service has made possible identifications with this country.

And why did I bring my kids back to be brought up here? It wasn't simply because of the language—any international school would have been fine for that. Nor was it because overpriced London is such a world city—there are others. No, it was because I wanted them to go through the same self-reflections about not being English that I did. Partly so we would have that in common, but more importantly because I think the way the English don't accept you is a powerful way of thinking about who you really are. I was always faintly horrified by how my émigré Soviet relatives would become American in moments after they moved to the US, like seeing someone disappearing under quicksand. How can you, as an immigrant, start working out who you are if you are co-opted so quickly? The difference now is that the English, too, are sliding away from subtle differentiations and towards simplistic identities which are easy to join and all the more awful for it. In my insistence to avoid them, am I the last English person left?

The world beyond

The greengrocer's revenge

The fall of communism in 1989 was a great relief to citizens of the eastern bloc. So why have millions of them come to be angry at the ruling elites who made them freer, wealthier and citizens of the EU?

Ivan Krastev

October 2009

The revolutions of 1989, which saw communist governments toppled across eastern Europe, used to be considered among the continent's most agreeable. The left praised them as an expression of people power and the victory of civil society against the state. The right celebrated them as a triumph of the free market and the free world. But the combination of the global economic crisis and the rise of political populism in eastern Europe is challenging long-held assumptions. The financial crisis has put neoliberal capitalism on trial and the claim that democracy is best at delivering growth has been shaken by the success of China.

The geopolitical gains from the end of the Cold War now also look uncertain. Writing in the *Observer* in September 2008, the philosopher John Gray prophesied that "the upheaval we are experiencing is more than a financial crisis." He argued that "the era of American global leadership, reaching back to the Second World War, is over… a change as far-reaching in its implications as the fall of the Soviet Union." And the EU's declining global relevance is acknowledged even by Brussels. The revisionists' hour has arrived.

The revolutions have always been celebrated for setting people free. But an alternative interpretation of the events of 20 years ago is gaining ground: that in 1989, the elites broke free. It is easy to dismiss this as a conspiracy theory. It is not, however, easy to ignore its political followers. In eastern Europe, populism—a political doctrine that pits the interests of "ordinary people" against the "elites"—is on the rise. Populists have held power in Poland, Slovakia and Bulgaria. But why should people be angry at their ruling elite, when these rulers have made them freer, wealthier and citizens of the EU?

Václav Havel wrote about the ordinary eastern bloc citizen in a 1978 essay, "The Power of the Powerless." Havel imagined a greengrocer who places a sign in the window of the shop where he works. The sign reads "Workers of the world, unite!" Yet the greengrocer doesn't care about the proletariat and its unity. The slogan was a declaration of loyalty to those in power, and a plea to be left alone by them. Since 1989, of course, the greengrocer has been free to take down the sign. But how else did he fare during the past 20 years?

Perhaps the greengrocer succeeded in privatising the shop. He may have replaced the sign with one reading "The best fruit in town" (with his customers complaining that one lie had been supplanted by another). But his situation may not have improved. In the 1990s, the communist welfare state was replaced by a post-communist farewell state. He could have avoided paying taxes—but would have been forced to pay off the local criminals who wielded the real authority instead. More probably he failed to take control of the shop. If it was in a desirable location it was probably privatised by his boss. Subsequently, the greengrocer may have lost his job, and therefore his social status and his financial security.

It is quite likely that the greengrocer's son left the country to work in western Europe, and that his daughter's children received a poor education in the local school. One of his neighbours probably got rich and constantly complained about the ineffectiveness of the state. Perhaps a newly arrived supermarket took away his customers. And the greengrocer was haunted by the spectre of comparisons: comparing his lot with how he lived before, or how his peers live in western Europe. He may now live a life of anxiety and disappointment.

This picture is not exaggerated. A 2003 Bulgarian study found that only 15-20 per cent of people had benefited from the transition from communism, measured in terms of income, social mobility and consumption. Only 5 per cent of people identified themselves as winners from the transition.

And there have been even darker outcomes. According to a study published in the *Lancet* earlier this year, rapid privatisation increased the death rate in the former Soviet Union and eastern bloc by 13 per cent in the early 1990s. Russian life expectancy fell by almost five years between 1991 and 1994.

So it is not hard to understand why the greengrocer may hate his post-communist rulers and blame them for his problems. (He is, however, unlikely to be nostalgic for Communism.) But paradoxically, political populism in eastern Europe rose after the situation had improved—when the decade or so of lawlessness and oligarchic capitalism was, for most countries, over. What then is driving the discontent?

In 2004, two prominent left-wing sociologists, Andrei Raichev and Kancho Stoychev, published a book, *What Happened? A Story About the Transition in Bulgaria—1989-2004*. The book had a clear and unabashed message. The transition is over. Political polarisation is over: there is no right and left any more. Communism was our common past (stop being hysterical about it), capitalism is our common future (stop being frightened by it). It is pointless to talk about citizens or subjects. The new society is populated only by consumers and failed consumers. The transition was messy, painful and unjust, but it fulfilled its function of transforming communism into a market democracy and in selecting the new elites to run it. This new elite are a strange breed: they have the brains of bankers, the manners of waiters and the dreams of teenagers. They are not in the business of governing, but of managing and entertaining—part of the service industry. And they look powerless, so they are less likely to be threatened by social movements from below.

What Happened? caused a sensation in Bulgaria's sleepy intellectual landscape. Raichev and Stoychev were also successful businessmen—shareholders in the country's first golf course—and so numbered among the new elite. The book was taken as a manifesto: the emancipated elites proclaiming victory over the rest of society and declaring their independence, not caring if the public hated them, it seemed. Most of the book's critics did agree with its argument that the meritocratic groups in the old elite were the main beneficiaries of the revolution. But they did not share the authors' benevolent view of the transition. The left was infuriated by their anti-egalitarianism and the right by their assertion that the revolution led to the re-legitimisation of communist elites.

Whether Raichev and Stoychev are correct or not, the fall of the Berlin Wall divorced eastern bloc elites from the rest of their societies. Under communism, elites had everything but could not enjoy it openly. They hid in special shops and Mercedes with dark windows. The price they paid for privilege in an ideologically egalitarian society was permanent insecurity. Stalin's purges and Mao's Cultural Revolution were reminders of what can go wrong for those at the top. The transition to communism, unlike to capitalism, was never over.

While communist elites were brutal, they were also accessible—they were obliged to mix with the ordinary people. It was an ideological imperative and a precondition of the party's control over society, but it was also an unavoidable reality imposed by shortages. The key to understanding late communist society is the mysterious (and at the same time prosaic) practices that the Russians called *blat*, the Poles *zalatwic sprawy* and the Bulgarians *vruzki*: the informal arrangements, exchanges of services, black market deals, party contacts and connections that people used to get along or ahead.

Today, the greengrocer may well earn more money than in communist times, but he has lost his well-connected friends. Twenty years ago, even a member of the elite had to befriend his greengrocer if he wanted fresh fruit. He had to return a favour if the greengrocer asked him. In the perverse world of the shortage economy, the greengrocer decided who would get what. He was powerless and powerful at the same time. He "owned" the shop without taking the risks of real ownership. Corruption both eroded and sustained communism, by redistributing not only goods but also power. The exchange of favours unintentionally empowered the weak.

But, while the greengrocer benefited from the corruption of the communist system, he became the victim of the post-communist corruption. The revolution liberated him from having to decorate the shop with ideological nonsense. He gained the freedom to talk, to travel, to vote, to consume. But he lost his limited leverage over the elites. The power of the ballot is more abstract than the tangible influence he derived from his connections. Now there is no need for anybody to befriend the greengrocer to get fresh fruit. He cannot ask for favours from powerful customers. The modern politician talks to the voters through television and listens via opinion polls. And the rise of social inequality has been accompanied by a process of social segregation. A recent study in Bulgaria found that low-income people have virtually no contact with those with high incomes.

Many Bulgarians disliked *What Happened?* for being a self-serving, if half-true, justification of the status quo. But what shocked them was the realisation that the authors were spokesmen for the new meritocracy: the rule of those with competence and training. After being ruled for half a century by mediocre party loyalists, the protagonists of the 1989 revolutions desired meritocracy. That belief, much more than democracy, was the common ground on which communist reformers and anti-communist dissidents met. As an illustration, in the early sessions of the March 1990 roundtable talks that paved the way for free elections in Bulgaria, the communist leaders started off by addressing their opponents as "comrades." When the opposition objected, the only compromise that could be agreed on was to use academic titles.

The late 1990s saw the opening of the post-communist economies and the end of large-scale privatisation. At that point, meritocrats began to replace the oligarchs as the backbone of the establishment in eastern Europe. Thuggish insiders were slowly replaced by well-educated outsiders. Today, throughout the region, income is more closely related to educational status than any other factor. Mastery of the English language and education at a western university is the best predictor of a person's success. The meritocratic elites—those with education and talent—are the real winners of the transition.

Meritocracy is the natural utopia of post-political societies. It promises competent leadership, the opportunity to enjoy a private life (with no need for civic participation), and social mobility through education. But the eastern European experience sheds light on a broader global backlash against meritocracy fuelled by the economic crisis. Meritocracy is preconditioned on good education systems, on a sense of community and responsibility among the elites, and on rational voters who reward performance. These conditions do not exist.

Plus, as Michael Young foresaw in *The Rise of the Meritocracy* (1958), meritocracy creates a world with clear, justifiable winners and losers. As a consequence elites, convinced of the legitimacy of their success, tend to have little compassion for the poor, at least less than their predecessors. Liberal philosophers such as John Rawls have argued that just inequality is more acceptable to people than unjust inequality. But the opposite may be true in the former eastern bloc. Under communism, being a loser could be an expression of moral principle. Being a loser in a meritocratic society is much more psychologically devastating: it simply means that you have failed.

The elites have never had it so good. Traditional aristocratic elites were saddled with duties and were brought up to perform them. Generations of their forebears, who looked down on them from portraits on the walls of their castles, had done these duties before, which meant they were taken seriously. In Britain, for example, the proportion of the upper class who died in the First World War was greater than the proportion of the lower classes. But the new elites do not know sacrifice.

Their children don't die in wars. The mobility of the meritocratic elites make them practically independent from the pressure of the state. In his book *The Revolt of the Elites* (1995), American social critic Christopher Lasch distinguishes meritocratic elites from their predecessors by their lack of interest in leadership and their wish to escape from the common lot. They are not dependent on their country's education system (their children go to private schools) or national health service (they can afford better hospitals). And they have lost what anthropologist Ivaylo Ditchev calls "emotional citizenship"—the tendency to share the passions of their community.

The end of communism set in motion the process that has liberated the meritocratic elites from fear, guilt, ideology, the chains of community, national loyalty and even from the necessity to govern. This is the true legacy of 1989 and the key to understanding the rise of populism in eastern Europe. The populists do not offer a real alternative, nor are they egalitarian. Their attraction lies in their promise to renationalise the elites, to re-establish the constraints that were removed in 1989. The covert aim of populists is to inject fear and insecurity into the life of elites, or even imprison them (the one thing elites cannot escape is the justice system). It is not a struggle for justice or equality, but for intimacy. Populists are like an abandoned wife who cannot accept her husband's new freedom and indifference and will do everything to remind their partner that they are still married.

Armed with the ammunition of the global financial crisis, the populists' campaign to renationalise the elites will continue. It remains to be seen how successful their counter revolution will be in undoing the legacy of 1989.

How dictators watch us on the web

The internet is meant to help activists, enable democratic protest and weaken the grip of authoritarian regimes. But it doesn't. In fact, the web is a boon for bullies

Evgeny Morozov

December 2009

My homeland of Belarus is an unlikely place for an internet revolution. The country, controlled by authoritarian president Alexander Lukashenko since 1994, was once described by Condoleezza Rice as "the last outpost of tyranny in Europe."

Its last presidential election in March 2006 was followed by a short-lived and unsuccessful revolution. The initial protests were brutally suppressed. But where public rallies couldn't succeed, protesters turned to more creative forms of insurgency: flash mobs. In a flash mob, social media or email is used to assemble a group of people in a public place, who then perform together a brief, often surreal action. Some young Belarusians used the blogging service LiveJournal to organise a series of events in Minsk with subtle anti-government messages. In a typical flash mob, the youngsters smiled, read newspapers or ate ice-cream. There was nothing openly political but the subtext was: "It's better to lick ice-cream than the president's ass!" The security services made many arrests, but their actions were captured in photos that were posted on LiveJournal and on photo-sharing websites like Flickr. Western bloggers and then traditional media picked up the news, drawing attention to the harsh crackdown.

Details of this rebellion have since been celebrated by a cadre of mostly western thinkers who believe that digital activism can help to topple authoritarian regimes. Belarusian flash mobs are invoked to illustrate how a new generation of decentralised protesters, armed only with technology, can oppose the state in ways unthought of in 1968 or 1989. But these digital enthusiasts rarely tell you what happened next.

Enthusiasm for the idea of digital revolution abounds. In October, I was invited to testify to the Commission on Security and Co-operation in Europe in Washington DC—a hotchpotch of US congressmen, diplomats and military officials. The group was holding a hearing titled: "Twitter Against Tyrants: New Media in Authoritarian

Regimes." I would once have happily accepted the premise, but recently my thinking has changed. From 2006-08 I worked on western-funded internet projects in the former Soviet Union—most with a "let's-promote-democracy-through-blogs" angle. But last year I quit. Our mission to use the internet to nudge citizens of authoritarian regimes to challenge the status quo had so many unexpected consequences that, at times, it seemed to be hurting the very causes we were trying to promote.

At the hearing, I was the lonely voice of dissent in a sea of optimism. In one speech, Senator Sam Brownback, a Republican known for his conservative Christian views, implored us to "tear down the new walls of the 21st century, the cyber-walls and electronic censorship technology used by tyrants."

Jon Stewart, host of the satirical programme *The Daily Show*, recently poked fun at a similar suggestion from a congressman that the web was freeing the peoples of Iraq, Afghanistan and Iran: "What, we could have liberated them over the internet? Why did we send an army when we could do it the same way we buy shoes?" Unfortunately, critical voices like his are rare. The majority of the media, so cranky when reporting the internet's impact on their industry, keep producing tear-jerking examples of the marriage of political protest and social media. And what a list it is: Burmese monks defying an evil junta with digital cameras; Filipino teenagers using SMS to create a "textual revolution;" Egyptian activists using encryption to hide from the all-seeing-eye of the *mukhabarat*; even Brazilian ecologists using Google maps to show deforestation in the Amazon delta. And did I mention Moldova, China and Iran? These cyber-dissidents, we are told, now take their struggles online, swapping leaflets for Twitter updates and ditching fax machines for iPhones.

But that isn't what happened in Belarus. After the first flash mob, the authorities began monitoring By_mob, the LiveJournal community where the activities were announced. The police started to show up at the events, often before the flashmobbers did. Not only did they detain participants, but they too took photos. These—along with the protesters' own online images—were used to identify troublemakers, many of whom were then interrogated by the KGB, threatened with suspension from university, or worse. This intimidation didn't go unnoticed. Soon, only hardcore activists would show up. Social media created a digital panopticon that thwarted the revolution: its networks, transmitting public fear, were infiltrated and hopelessly outgunned by the power of the state.

The Belarusian government shows no sign of being embarrassed by the fact it arrested people for eating ice-cream. Despite what digital enthusiasts tell you, the emergence of new digital spaces for dissent also lead to new ways of tracking it. Analogue activism was pretty safe: if one node in a protest network got busted, the rest of the group was probably okay. But getting access to an activist's inbox puts all their interlocutors in the frame, too. The result is a cat-and-mouse game in which protesters try to hide from the authorities by carving out unconventional niches. In Iran, dissidents used to be active on Goodreads, an international social networking website for book-lovers. Here they quietly engaged in conversations about politics and culture, unseen by the censors—that is, until the *Los Angeles Times* helpfully published an article about what was going on, tipping the authorities off.

Social networking, then, has inadvertently made it easier to gather intelligence about activist networks. Even a tiny security flaw in the settings of one Facebook profile can compromise the security of many others. A study by two MIT students, reported in September, showed it is possible to predict a person's sexual orientation by analysing their Facebook friends; bad news for those in regions where homosexuality carries the threat of beatings and prison. And many authoritarian regimes are turning to data-mining companies to help them identify troublemakers. TRS Technologies in China is one such company. It boasts that "thanks to our technology, the work of 10 internet cops can now be done by just one."

This does not mean that cyber-dissent is an illusion. There are three main strands to the "democracy by tweets" theory. First, despite my caveats, the internet can, if used properly, give dissidents secure and cheap tools of communication. Russian activists can use hard-to-tap Skype in place of insecure phone lines, for example. Dissidents can encrypt emails, distribute anti-government materials without leaving a paper trail, and use clever tools to bypass internet filters. It's now easier to be a "one-man NGO": with Google Docs, you can do your own printing, lowering the risk of leaks. Second, new technology makes bloody crackdowns riskier, as police are surrounded by digital cameras and pictures can quickly be sent to western news agencies. Some governments, like Burma and North Korea, don't care about looking brutal, but many others do. Third, technology reduces the marginal cost of protest, helping to turn "fence-sitters" into protesters at critical moments. An apolitical Iranian student, for instance, might find that all her Facebook friends are protesting and decide to take part.

This third point, however, needs careful examination. The argument goes like this. Thanks to the internet, governments have lost their monopoly on controlling information, while citizens have acquired access to other sources of knowledge and the ability to organise more safely. Many people will use this access to learn more about democracy, which will unshackle them from government propaganda. They will use this new power to push the government on accountability (as has happened to a limited extent in China, where online campaigners have had corrupt local officials sacked). When the next crisis strikes—such as the flawed Iranian election in 2009, or high fuel prices in Burma in 2007—citizens will turn to the internet to see how unpopular the regime has become. Discovering others of like mind, they will see the protests and, if the regime hasn't responded with violence, join to create a "snowball" capable of crushing the most rigid authoritarian structure.

Social scientists have named these snowballs "information cascades." They explain why, when most citizens may believe that a revolution will not succeed, they will still pour into the streets if everyone else is protesting; so many people can't be wrong. Perhaps the most famous example is described in a 1994 paper by UCLA political scientist Susanne Lohmann. She sought to explain the sudden appeal of the "Monday demonstrations" in the East German town of Leipzig, which began in September 1989. Lohmann argues that the East German fence-sitters watched the protests unfold and, noting the lack of government retaliation, decided to join in. In the circumstances, it was the most rational thing for them to do.

It's not hard to see how the internet might amplify information cascades and so strengthen the position of activists. The point is made most famously by the American web guru Clay Shirky. He is a darling of the social media world, a consultant for government, corporate and philanthropic bodies, and a source for reporters seeking quotes on how the internet is changing protest. He is also the man most responsible for the intellectual confusion over the political role of the internet. Shirky adapted Lohmann's theories for the age of MySpace in his bestseller *Here Comes Everybody* (2008). The major lesson he drew from Leipzig is that people should "protest in ways that the state was unlikely to interfere with, and distribute evidence of their actions widely." Why? Protesters are in a win-win situation: "If the state didn't react, the documentation would serve as evidence that the protesting was safe. If the state did react, then the documentation of the crackdown could be used to spur an international outcry."

But the truth is often different. In Belarus, most fence-sitters watched the state's response and, acting rationally, went searching for higher fences. In Iran this year, the famous video of Neda Agha-Soltan, murdered in the streets, went viral and she became a symbol of the "green revolution." Whether it encouraged any fence-sitters is much less obvious.

Information cascades often fail to translate into crowds, even without state fear-mongering. Last year's anti-Farc protests in Colombia—aided by Facebook—attracted huge crowds. But this year's anti-Chávez protests did not, although they were organised by the same group using the same methods. The aim was for 50m people to rally worldwide but only a few thousand turned up. The same has been true when people have tried to organise protests in Azerbaijan and Russia.

Yet even if the internet doesn't always bring people out onto the streets, its adherents have another, subtler, argument. For democracy to succeed, they say, you need civil movements to help make protests more intense, frequent and well attended. A vibrant civil society can challenge those in power by documenting corruption or uncovering activities like the murder of political enemies. In democracies, this function is mostly performed by the media, NGOs or opposition parties. In authoritarian states—or so the story goes—it is largely up to lone individuals, who often get locked up as a result. Yet if citizens can form ad-hoc groups, gain access to unbiased information and connect with each other, challenges to the state become more likely. And social theorists like Robert Putnam argue that the emergence of such groups increases social capital and trust among citizens.

It is true that the internet is building what I call "digital civic infrastructure"—new ways to access data and networks to distribute it. This logic underlies many western efforts to reshape cyberspace in authoritarian states. The British Foreign Secretary David Miliband has enthused about the potential of the communications revolution to "fuel the drive for social justice." "If it's true that there are more bloggers per head of population in Iran than in any other country, this makes me optimistic," he has also said. In early November, US Secretary of State Hillary Clinton announced Civil Society 2.0, a project to help grassroots organisations around the world use digital technology, which will include tuition in online campaigning and how to leverage social networks.

But the emergence of this seemingly benign infrastructure can backfire on western governments. The first snag is that turning the internet into a new platform for civic participation requires certainty that only pro-western and pro-democracy forces will participate. Most authoritarian societies, however, defy easy classification into the "good guys vs bad guys" paradigms of the Bush era. In Egypt, for example, the extremist Muslim Brotherhood is a political force—albeit mostly missing from the Egyptian parliament—that can teach Hosni Mubarak a lesson about civic participation. It has an enviable digital presence and a sophisticated internet strategy: for example, campaigning online to get activists released from prison. Western governments shouldn't be surprised when groups like this become the loudest voices in new digital spaces: they are hugely popular and are commonly denied a place in the heavily policed traditional public sphere.

Similarly, the smartest and most active user of new media in Lebanon is not the western-backed government of Saad Hariri, but the fundamentalist troublemakers of Hezbollah, whose suave manipulation of cyberspace was on display during the 2006 war with Israel. In Russia, the internet has given a boost to extreme right-wing groups like the Movement Against Illegal Immigration, which has been using Google Maps to visualise the location of ethnic minorities in Russian cities and encouraging its members to hound them out. Criminal gangs in Mexico are fond of YouTube, where they flaunt their power by uploading videos of their graphic killings. Generally, in the absence of strong democratic norms and institutions, the internet has fuelled a drive for vigilante justice rather than the social variety Miliband was expecting.

And it gets worse. Ultra-loyalist groups supporting Thailand's monarchy were active during both the September 2006 coup and more recent street protests, finding anti-monarchy material that needed to be censored via a website called Protecttheking.net. In this, they are essentially doing the job usually reserved for the secret police. In much the same way, the Iranian revolutionary guards posted online photos of the most ardent protesters at the June 2009 rallies, asking pro-Ahmadinejad Iranians to identify them. And in August 2009 religious fundamentalists in Saudi Arabia launched a campaign to identify YouTube videos they found offensive and pressure the company to delete them—a form of digital "hacktivism" which must be delighting the official censors.

And it doesn't help that anyone with a computer and an internet connection can launch a cyber-attack on a sovereign nation. Last year I took part in one—purely for the sake of experiment—on the websites of the Georgian government. As the Russian tanks were marching into South Ossetia, I was sitting in a cafe in Berlin with a laptop and instructions culled from Russian nationalist blogs. All I had to do was to input the targets provided—the URLs of hostile Georgian institutions (curiously, the British embassy in Tbilisi was on that list)—click "Start" and sit back. I did it out of curiosity; thousands of Russians did it out of patriotism. And the Russian government turned a blind eye. The results of the attack were unclear. For a brief period some government emails and a few dozen websites were either slow or unavailable; some Georgian banks couldn't offer online services for a short period.

Yet while the internet may take the power away from an authoritarian (or any other) state or institution, that power is not necessarily transferred to pro-democracy groups. Instead it often flows to groups who, if anything, are nastier than the regime. Social media's greatest assets—anonymity, "virality," interconnectedness—are also its main weaknesses.

So how do repressive governments use the internet? As we have seen, the security services can turn technology against the logistics of protest. But the advent of blogging and social networking has also made it easier for the state to plant and promote its own messages, spinning and neutralising online discussions before they translate into offline action. The "great firewall of China," which supposedly keeps the Chinese in the dark, is legendary. In truth, such methods of internet censorship no longer work. They might stop the man on the street, but a half-determined activist can find a way round. And more often than not, official attempts to delete a post by an anti-government blogger will backfire, as the blogger's allies take on the task of distributing it through their own networks. Governments have long lost absolute control over how the information spreads online, and extirpating it from blogs is no longer a viable option. Instead, they fight back. It is no trouble to dispatch commentators to accuse a dissident of being an infidel, a sexual deviant, a criminal, or, worst of all, a CIA stooge.

Moreover, the distracting noise of the internet—the gossip, pornography, and conspiracy theories—can act as a de-politicising factor. Providing unfettered access to information is not by itself going to push citizens of authoritarian states to learn about their government's crimes. Political scientists talk about the preference for non-political information as "rational ignorance." It's a fancy way of saying that most people, whether in democracies or not, prefer to read about trivia and what's useful in daily life—restaurant and film reviews and so on—than about the tedious business of governance.

One study from early 2007, by a Saudi academic, showed that 70 per cent of all content swapped by Saudi teenagers via Bluetooth was pornographic. Authoritarian governments know that the internet could be a new opium for the masses. They are tolerant of rampant internet piracy, as in China. In many cases, they push the cyber-hedonistic pursuits of their youth. Government-controlled internet providers in Belarus, for example, run dedicated servers full of pirated digital goodies for their clients to download for free. Under this new social contract, internet users are allowed plenty of autonomy online—just so long as they don't venture into politics.

We shouldn't kid ourselves. Nobody knows how to create sustainable digital public spheres capable of promoting democracy. Western interventions can even thwart the natural development of such spaces. Governments usually give cash to a favoured NGO—often based outside the authoritarian state in question—which has the job of creating new social media infrastructure: group blogs, social networks, search engines and other services that we take for granted in the west. The NGOs then hire local talent to work on a Belarusian Twitter or an Egyptian version of the blog-search platform Technorati.

Yet these services work because they are born in entrepreneurial cultures where they can be speedily built and adapted to local needs. The stodgy form-filling process of angling for the next juicy grant, which in truth drives nearly all NGOs, is a world away from a free-wheeling Palo Alto start-up. The result is a clumsy arrangement in which NGOs toil away on lengthy, expensive and unnecessary projects instead of ditching them when it becomes apparent they won't work and moving on to the next idea. Despite millions of dollars poured into the former Soviet Union, NGO-funded new media projects that are alive and kicking a year after the original grant has ended can be counted on the fingers of one hand.

So should we stop funding projects that use the internet to promote democracy? Of course not. Even a sceptic like me can see the upside. Western governments and NGOs shouldn't abandon their digital democracy push, they should just improve it. One way would be to invest in tools that help make digital civic spaces less susceptible to government spin. There are some interesting prototypes—particularly based around Wikipedia edits—that supply readers with visual hints that some contributors may not be trustworthy. As Twitter and Facebook emerge as platforms for cyber-activism in authoritarian states, it is essential they are aware of their new global obligations, including the need to protect the data entrusted to them by activists. Elsewhere, cyber-attacks on NGOs are poised to intensify. We in the west should be prepared to step in and help the dissenting voices, providing free and prompt assistance to get back online as soon as possible.

Some consistency in dealing with cyber-attacks is also needed. If we treat cyber-attacks that Russian nationalists launch on Estonian or Georgian targets as crimes, we cannot approve when our own "hacktivists" launch similar attacks on Iranian government websites. And western governments should refrain from confirming paranoid autocrats' theories about a Twitter revolution, thus necessitating a crackdown. During the Iran protests this year, the US state department called Twitter executives and asked them to delay maintenance of the site so Iranians could continue using it to protest. There was no better way to confirm Iranian suspicions that the US government was somehow behind the protest.

One final idea. Let us in future be a bit more sceptical about the need to recreate the protest wheel. In almost all countries run by authoritarian regimes there is an untapped mass of activists, dissidents, and anti-government intellectuals who have barely heard of Facebook. Reaching out to these offline but effective networks will yield more value than trying to badger bloggers to take up political activities. Western embassies working on the ground in authoritarian states often excel at identifying and empowering such networks and new media literacy should become part of diplomatic training. After all, these old-school types are the people who brought democracy to central and eastern Europe. And it will probably be them who win freedom for China and Iran too.

The case for an Afghanistan inquiry

Britain needs answers to five questions about its longest war

Bronwen Maddox

September 2013

At the height of the summer, David Cameron flew unannounced into Kabul and Helmand province to explain why, after Britain had spent 12 years battling to defeat the Taliban, he was pressing for talks with them. In open-necked dark shirt and trousers, standing out starkly against the ranks of soldiers in desert fatigues, he shrugged off the recent remarks of Lieutenant-General Nick Carter, Britain's top general in Afghanistan and Nato's deputy commander in the conflict—that for a decade Britain and the United States had missed crucial chances to talk to the Taliban.

"You can argue about whether the settlement we put in place after 2001 could have been better arranged. Of course you can make that argument," the prime minister said, gesturing with his sunglasses, before adroitly announcing that, to mark Armed Forces Day, the fines collected from banks for improperly fixing interest rates would go towards creating a permanent memorial for the 444 British personnel killed in Afghanistan. He concluded: "We want peace and stability in Afghanistan, we want the return of the Taliban back to their country."

Twelve years ago, that would have been an astounding statement—an apparent bald contradiction. Now, it is a measure of how completely the Afghan conflict has confounded early goals, as well as a victory, at last, for the notion that military effort is futile without a political deal for the country. As Britain prepares to withdraw its troops next year from its longest war since the Napoleonic wars ended in 1815, it is right to ask exactly what has been achieved—and to acknowledge that, with no hyperbole, the answer may be close to nothing. One former British diplomat in the region said: "No doubt they will redefine the original goals to claim some kind of success, but in my book, this is what failure looks like."

There will be a temptation, as the images of army vehicles burned and twisted by roadside bombs disappear from television screens, to say that we are well out of it, and to leave the question of why it fell so short of its aims to fade in embarrassed silence. That would be an injustice to those who have died, to their families, and to voters, as well as an evasion of the lessons that should be learned.

It is hard to find any aspect of recent foreign policy in which senior diplomats are so incredulous and bitter about the mistakes, the confusions of strategy, the loss of life and the expense of tens of billions of pounds in pursuit of goals that were never clear and mainly never attainable. Sherard Cowper-Coles, UK ambassador to Afghanistan from 2007 to 2009, used to transfix his colleagues and journalists by the fierce candidness of his briefings—startling enough when delivered in Kabul, but prone to leave a roomful of officials in shifting, discomfited silence when beamed back to large screens in the Foreign and Commonwealth Office through the staccato transmission of a satellite video-link. Now he says of Afghanistan's future after the Nato-led coalition forces leave next year: "The picture isn't very good. Helmand province in a year or two is likely to be back to much where it was —apart from a few new roads and schools and clinics—before British forces blundered in there in 2006." Asked whether he thought the 12 years were a waste of time, money and lives, he said: "It has been a good experience for the British armed forces at a tactical level, but on balance, yes."

Another former senior diplomat says: "We achieved the essentials—al-Qaeda routed out of Afghanistan and the Taliban overthrown. But all the rhetoric about founding a democratic country where women would have the same rights—that was never achieveable." And Paddy Ashdown, Liberal Democrat peer and former Royal Marine, declared at the end of last year that "it is now crystal clear that we have lost in Afghanistan" and that staying "is not worth the life of one more soldier."

Yet Afghanistan is not just "Another War Lost," as one headline put it recently. It was a worse failure for Britain than was Iraq. More British personnel have been killed (444 compared to 179 in Iraq) and it cost far more (good estimates put the cost at between £30bn and £40bn by the time troops leave at the end of 2014, compared to about £9bn for Britain's contribution in Iraq). It was also a conflict in which Britain claimed it could demonstrate superior skills. The failure has far more implications for Britain's place in the world than did the setbacks of Iraq.

This is the last war in which Britain will make those claims, not least because the regular army is now being cut to 82,000 (compared to 110,000 at the start of the Afghan conflict). But as the troops come home, there are five key questions that merit an inquiry by parliament that matches the seriousness with which it investigated the misjudgments of Iraq. Two must dominate any investigation: what has been achieved, and at what cost. But Britain made three mistakes above all which deserve particular scrutiny: fighting in Iraq and Afghanistan at the same time; taking on responsibility for combating the drugs trade; and taking on the lethal responsibility for the "hornets' nest" of Helmand province.

Question 1: Did the Iraq war doom the Afghan conflict?

In a word, yes. Of all the UK's mistakes, fighting two wars at once was the biggest. Of course, some say that for Britain to enter the Afghan war at all was a mistake, darkly citing the three failed historic attempts to subjugate the country between 1839 and 1919. Yet that is too dismissive. For Britain to have refused to join the US in pursuit of Osama bin Laden after 9/11 would been a rejection of any alliance with the US, never mind a special relationship. In an impassioned speech on the evening of Sunday 7th October 2001, Tony Blair confirmed that British "assets" were involved in the start of US military action, while acknowledging that "there is at present no specific credible threat to the United Kingdom that we know of." For Britain, entering the war was the minimum price of keeping an alliance with the US. "It was not really a choice, for any politician, to go into Afghanistan," says one former senior diplomat, "whereas Iraq, in a sense, was more a war of choice."

One damaging effect, often overlooked, is that the 2003 Iraq invasion instantly changed the view of Afghans themselves about the foreign forces already within their borders; they suddenly saw them as hostile invaders, and the two conflicts as instigated in parallel by the west against Muslim countries—and (so the accounts often went) in pursuit of their resources.

A second consequence is that governments involved in both conflicts, particularly the US and UK, "took our eye off the ball," as several British officials now put it. From 2005 to 2007, the US regarded Afghanistan as the easier war and already won, while in Iraq, the death count and level of violence were rising sharply. "If we'd got going earlier [in Afghanistan] with a security force, if we'd put in the effort in 2002 that we did in 2008, would the Taliban have regrouped?" asks one former official.

A third result is that UK forces were severely overstretched, a conclusion bluntly reached by the highly critical House of Commons Defence Committee in its 2010-11 hearings on Operations in Afghanistan. General Nicholas Houghton, former chief of operations in Afghanistan, in giving evidence, said that when the government made the decision to commit UK forces to Helmand province in early 2006, "the level of reduction in commitment to Iraq that had been forecast and hoped for in 2005 had not actually materialised." He added: "But I sense there was an irreversibility [about the commitment], given the political and international level of the decision." The committee concluded that: "Given the demanding nature of the situation in Iraq, we do not consider that the implications of the decision to move UK armed forces into the south of Afghanistan in early 2006 were fully thought through, in particular, the risk to UK armed forces personnel."

Question 2: Why did Britain take on the role of quelling the narcotics trade?
In October 2001, giving his reasons for joining the US military action, Tony Blair asserted: "We act also because the al-Qaeda network and the Taliban regime are funded in large part on the drugs trade." In a justification which would cripple and befuddle British policy, he added: "Ninety per cent of all heroin sold in Britain originates from Afghanistan. Stopping that trade is, again, directly in our interests."

Two months later, in the Bonn Agreement, as G8 countries committed to helping in the "reconstruction" of Afghanistan shared out the different tasks, Britain formally assumed the responsibility for combating the opium trade, which had been choked off by the Taliban but was rising fast again. As one former diplomat puts it now, "it sort of made sense for Britain to take it on—the heroin on our streets comes from Afghanistan, and America's drugs wars are fought elsewhere." There was also the desire to cut off funds for drug barons.

Yet Britain's actions were a muddle from the start. At different points, officials set out to eradicate poppies, to pay farmers to destroy crops (problematic because of the perverse incentive it would give to grow them), to give farmers an alternative livelihood, and to tolerate the crop. Frequently, its plans were at odds with those of US officials and commanders.

Some projects, such as the Helmand Food Zone, run by the British Provincial Reconstruction Team, had success, although only in a small area, in persuading farmers to abandon poppies by supplying them with subsidised high-grade wheat and fertiliser. But the yield on wheat is a tenth of that on opium; "The truth is, it is very hard to find alternative crops which give them even a fraction of the income," said one British official.

Overall, the efforts have comprehensively failed. Figures in November from the UN Office on Drugs and Crime projected that opium production would reach almost record levels this year, close to its 2007 peak. In April, the UNODC reported that this year "poppy cultivation is not only expected to expand in areas where it already existed in 2012... but also in new areas or in areas where [it] was stopped." More than 90 per cent of the heroin on British streets still comes from there; the fields of purple, red, and pink-and-white poppies still stretch across the Helmand valley.

A consequence of the British commitment to take on the drugs traffic was that it also lethally complicated the military deployment to Helmand province, earning British soldiers the immediate enmity of the local population who feared that their opium crop was at risk.

Question 3: Why did the UK take on Helmand?

The most controversial decision of all for Britain in the conflict is accepting responsibility for Helmand province in 2005 and 2006. As Michael Clarke, director of the Royal United Services Institute, wrote in the "Afghanistan Papers," the think tank's 2011 report on the Helmand decision: "It was the deployment of a battlegroup into Helmand in spring 2006 that turned the UK's commitment to Afghanistan from a 'military operation' into a 'war.'"

John Reid, appointed defence secretary in 2005, famously said in April 2006 that "we would be perfectly happy to leave in three years and without firing one shot because our job is to protect the reconstruction." Two years later, British forces had fired four million bullets. The UK moved rapidly from having about 1,000 military personnel operating with international forces mainly in Kabul and the north to a combat force of 3,300 in Helmand in the spring of 2006, to 6,300 troops by that summer, and almost 7,600 by July 2007. In 2009, Gordon Brown said that the number would be held at "an enduring maximum of 8,300" the next year, but it quickly rose further. Although David Cameron began to withdraw troops during 2011, the numbers still peaked at more than 10,000.

One senior FCO official now says: "If asked 'Should we go into Helmand again?' I'd say 'No'—but we have done quite a lot of good there." A former official says: "In retrospect, going into Helmand looks like a bit of a mistake."

"I don't blame John Reid—or not entirely," said one of those present as ministers came to the decision. "The question is about the quality of the advice he had." Britain had originally thought it would take on Kandahar province, the Taliban heartland, but Canada claimed that task. Helmand, with its green, central valley, appeared quieter "with a fair degree of law and order," as one official put it. But it was by a long way the largest province, more than three times the size of Wales. Military chiefs did not expect it to be entirely benign—but intelligence was almost non-existent.

As Air Chief Marshal Jock Stirrup put it to the committee: "I can recollect a number of discussions around the Chiefs of Staff Committee table that essentially were along these lines—I have used these very words myself, so I can recollect them well—'we don't know much about the south, but what we do know is that it's not the north; it's real bandit country.'" General Peter Wall, now chief of the general staff, in evidence also said: "I absolutely accept that what we found when we had forces on the ground was starkly different from what we had anticipated and hoped for. We were ready for an adverse reaction but... we did not expect it to be as vehement as it turned out to be."

The argument made at the time by some senior British military officials was that Nato forces needed to take on the south; to leave it alone would leave the Taliban with a zone in which they could operate without hindrance, just what the campaign had set out to deny them. Senior British military officials also argued that there was a need to pull back US attention from Iraq—and to demonstrate, after the humiliations of Iraq, that the UK was a valuable and competent military ally for the US. American military criticism had become openly scathing; "I don't know that you could see the British withdrawal from Basra in 2007 in any light other than a defeat," was one comment, from Colonel Peter Mansoor, executive officer to General David Petraeus, then US commander in Iraq.

But a desire to "do something about the south" does not explain why Britain had to take on Helmand alone and why there was not a more thorough assessment of the strength likely to be needed. "We thought we could do Helmand with 3,000 soldiers, and the Americans later showed that even 30,000 wasn't enough," says one British former official.

The decision to go in was compounded by other misjudgments. Britain pushed for the removal of the province's governor, Sher Mohammed Akhundzada, because of apparent links with the drugs trade, but his replacement, Mohammed Daoud, lacked tribal influence. For his own reasons, Daoud encouraged British forces to adopt vulnerable "forward operating bases" in the north of the province. British planning, government briefings showed clearly, was also suffused with the notion of invaluable skills supposedly acquired through historical experience. The FCO gave many enthusiastic briefings on "ink blot tactics"—building on small pockets of success—by which, officials confidently asserted, Britain had succeded in the 1950s Malay campaign. Equally, there were claims that Northern Ireland had equipped the British army with a special skill in "counter-insurgency"—which it could now teach American forces.

Reid, who says the crucial decisions came after he was redeployed to the Home Office, puts some blame on those who fell for the exhortations of Daoud, such as setting up a forward operating base at Sangin. As he told the Commons committee: "You can imagine that when, five weeks later, sitting in the Home Office, I heard that we were fighting for our lives in Sangin, I could not entirely understand it."

The committee concluded: "We are concerned that the Ministry of Defence did not anticipate that the presence of the armed forces in Helmand might stir up a hornets' nest, especially as much of the intelligence was contradictory." It added: "We believe that such concerns as were raised by the armed forces were inadequate at best and that they were not raised, as they should have been, to the very highest levels of government."

Question 4: What has the conflict cost the UK?

One Conservative MP, on a parliamentary trip to Camp Bastion in Helmand, looking out over the roads, the low apartment blocks, warehouses, shops, and one of the most successful surgical emergency hospitals in the world, said: "Who told us, who asked us, when they set out to build this?" Camp Bastion, which holds 28,000 people and covers an area the size of Reading (and is named after the type of sandbag used to form blockades), is a town within a fortress, not a camp.

Defence accounting is opaque at the best of times, and in contrast to the US, the Ministry of Defence has not been forthcoming with the costs, claiming, in some cases, that it does not have the full figures (such as for the future cost of supporting injured soldiers once they have left the services, or the use of equipment that will not be directly replaced). The MoD's figure for the direct military costs to Britain so far, up to the spring of 2013, is £19.4bn (compared with its figure of £8.3bn direct military costs of the Iraq conflict, within a total cost to Britain of that war of just over £9bn).

However, many estimates reckon that the total costs to Britain of Afghanistan are much higher. Frank Ledwidge, a former military intelligence officer, who has published two detailed books on the mistakes and costs of the war to Britain, suggests higher figures, now widely quoted and regarded as plausible. He argues that the total military costs by the time of the exit at the end of next year could reasonably be estimated at £31.1bn, particularly if the cost of maintaining a larger army than would otherwise be needed is added in. In addition, he reckons, the cost of death and injury to forces, even taking a very conservative approach, could be £3.8bn more. The total of development spending by the FCO and the Department for International Development is a further £2.1bn. His total of the direct costs to Britain, therefore, is more than £37bn. That fits with one informal estimate by a Treasury official that at the high point Britain was spending about £6bn a year.

Question 5: What have we achieved in Afghanistan?

"We arrived with one of the narrowest mandates you can think of—to prevent Afghanistan being a haven for terrorism," says one FCO official. "We ended with a massively complex set of goals—a distortion of how Afghanistan itself worked." He added: "Police, army, courts, education—you name it, we were trying to reform it."

The mission was dogged from the start by a proliferation of goals. That was a reflection of Blair's anxiousness to provide justification, and the US's twin aims of retribution and nation-building—a cause to which the Blair team and Britain's development lobby were initially very receptive. "We thought we were good at it," says one former official. "We really did think we could remake Helmand." Blair and his officials at different times proferred the following justifications for entering the conflict (as well as supporting the US and wiping out the drugs trade): to avenge Britons killed on 9/11; to destroy al-Qaeda; to defeat the Taliban; to protect Britain from future terrorist attacks; to build a new democracy; to improve education and women's rights.

The international effort has had the most success in the most clearly-defined goal: defeating al-Qaeda. Osama bin Laden was killed by US Navy Seals in 2011, and al-Qaeda cannot easily use Afghanistan as a base. Ayman al-Zawahiri, who is believed to have plotted 9/11 and now runs the group, is said by Pakistani intelligence officials to have fewer than 100 operatives at his disposal; others add that al-Qaeda is losing out to newer groups in attracting recruits. However, western intelligence believes that Zawahiri directed Nasir al-Wuhayshi, founder of al-Qaeda in the Arabian Peninsula, to plan the recent attacks which, when detected in advance, caused the closure of 21 US embassies and consulates across the Middle East in late July and early August. That is evidence of the growing strength of the group's Arab affiliates, especially in Yemen, which could become its headquarters if the Taliban is contained or diminished in an Afghan settlement.

The second goal of overthrowing the Taliban has also been achieved, although they are clearly not defeated and no peace settlement is now possible without them. Few expect them to regain their pre-2001 control of Kabul or the country at large, but they have good hopes of strengthening their hold on the Pashtun south, and in the spells when military attacks have driven them from the south they have made inroads to the north, where they had no presence before 2001.

However, other goals have now been set aside or downgraded. Democracy? President Hamid Karzai effectively rigged the October 2009 election; this summer there have been loud calls for him to postpone the elections due next spring, either from his supporters who want him to stand for a third term although the constitution forbids it, or from people warning of Taliban intimidation of those with voting cards. This emphasises that security, outside the heavily fortified zones of the capital and a few other areas, is often non-existent, although the Afghan National Army is now performing far better than many observers had privately feared—and suffering considerable casualties. "The insurgency is as strong as ever," said one former official, even if it is no longer reflected in Nato casualties, and so is less represented in western media. Yet if Nato leaves in 2015 with no elections scheduled, or with Karzai reinstated, it would make a mockery of the attempt to install a democratic government.

It is an understatement to say that relations with Karzai are poor; "It is hard to remember that we thought he was a good guy," says one US official, when he stood in the balcony of the US Capitol in January 2002 to receive a standing ovation. He is determined, it seems, to be seen as the father of Afghanistan, not a puppet of the Americans; President Barack Obama had to call him earlier this summer, according to a senior British official, and remind him that he needed the US security forces more than the US needed them to be there, and that he should stop obstructing the agreement about whether some will remain after 2014. His recent demand that the US pay to take home military kit provoked uproar on Capitol Hill and a move to suspend US aid after 2014.

Other goals, such as education and women's rights, have been downgraded, although there has undeniably been progress. Under the Taliban, only about 1.2m young Afghans were in school, 50,000 of them girls, out of a population estimated to be about 28 million. Now, there are more than six million young Afghans in school (the Kabul government quotes about 10 million but western diplomats disagree); more than a third of those in primary school are girls. There are women in parliament, on television and in the health ministry. "There is a new educated, urbanised generation which didn't exist 10 years ago," says one official—although some with experience of the Soviet occupation argue that the Russians did at least as much, pointing to the hundreds of thousands they set out to train.

However the goal of a significant change in women's rights, cherished by Tony Blair and Hillary Clinton, has largely been surrendered with regret, in the face of resistance from a profoundly entrenched culture, particularly in the Pashtun south. The question is whether even the slender gains that have been achieved will last. Others warn, too, of the sheer disruptive shock of the past 12 years to Afghans. An estimated 12,000 of them have been killed—some put the figure much higher—and, according to the United Nations High Commissioner for Refugees, half a million have left their homes since the US invasion, while the population of Kabul has soared from two million in 2001 to five million now, partly by those displaced.

Most important, perhaps, for the future, is the patchiness of economic development, despite the building of schools, hospitals, roads and a mobile phone network and some successful local projects in job creation. Analysts say that the US has put about $80bn into development, but that much has disappeared into security and defence. True, there are some striking successes; the central province of Bamiyan, largely populated by the Shia Hazaras, who were persecuted by the Sunni Taliban, has flourished, and has been particularly active in opening more schools. Kabul has the trappings of development, with dozens of international flights a week, newish cars, and mobile phones in evidence everywhere. Economic growth reached an estimated 11.8 per cent in 2011; tax revenues have risen steadily.

But Afghanistan cannot support itself without huge, constant injections of foreign aid. A confidential (but leaked) International Monetary Fund report in the spring said that recent improvements were faltering. It added that the government this year was failing to reach even the target of covering 40 per cent of its annual non-security spending of about $5bn, because of "widespread tax evasion abetted by government officials, the increasing theft of customs revenues by provincial governors and softening economic growth," as the *New York Times* put it. To take the most pressing example, estimates of the cost of maintaining the Afghan army range from $8bn a year, if kept at its projected size of 352,000 according to a former US official in Kabul, to half that figure for a smaller force—but the country cannot at present support either sum.

Meanwhile, rights to the country's wealth in mineral reserves assets have been sold at prices that some regard as far too low. In 2007, the Chinese Metallurgical Group and Jiangxi Copper Company bought a 30-year lease on the copper deposits at Mes Aynak for $3bn; they reckoned that the valley held perhaps $100bn worth of copper, "possibly the largest such deposit in the world and potentially worth around five times the estimated value of Afghanistan's entire economy," according to author William Dalrymple.

Diplomats bravely sketch out a more upbeat possible future, in which Afghanistan develops its gas reserves and makes it attractive for foreign investors to develop minerals, but in a way that retains some value in the country, while farmers learn how to add value to their excellent agricultural products (other than opium). But they all point out that "this now depends on the Afghans."

This leaves other countries with a difficult dilemma. Pledges of aid run only to 2016 and are dependent on progress against corruption; pledges of security assistance run only to 2018. Yet if these are cut off, the state cannot function.

The example of the Najibullah government, installed by the Soviets, which crumbled three years after the Russian money ended, is not entirely discouraging. Sherard Cowper-Coles argued recently that "when the last soldier of the Soviet 40th Army marched back into the Soviet Union over the River Oxus on 20th February 1989, the Russians left behind a regime which not only survived but also succeeded in defeating the insurgency which the Americans and British were continuing to support. It collapsed only when, in 1992, the Soviet Union itself collapsed, ending the external subsidy on which every Afghan government in modern times has depended."

The international community is committed to trying to preserve some gains. But the slenderness of those gains, and the difficulty of working with Karzai, means that commitment is in doubt.

The fear is not that without foreign support, the Taliban will capture Kabul again but, more likely, that the army and the country will split into ethnic factions. Each would then find an easy ally in a neighbouring country: Pakistan might step up its support for the Taliban, and Russia and Iran (and India) support the Tajiks and Uzbeks in the north. As William Patey, former ambassador to Kabul, puts it: "There is no guarantee that more money will buy success, but what is certain is that without more, it will all turn to something very bad."

There are many lessons that the UK should learn. One is "that we should think much more carefully about getting involved in other people's countries," says one official, and that if we do "we need to be much more rooted in how that society works—we tried to import too many ideas we thought attractive, sitting in 21st-century Europe or America. We need to be very careful about creating a culture of dependency on aid, and much clearer about what foreign intervention is supposed to achieve."

There are also lessons about the limits on Britain's military capability, which should not be set aside just because the government is in the process of cutting the armed forces and there is little public support for any future conflict. In Afghanistan, even more than Iraq, Britain's mistakes stemmed from a culture of gung-ho grandiosity about national capabilities as well as anxiety about the erosion of its standing in the world. Tony Blair, Gordon Brown, and some of Britain's top generals (although not all) seized the conflict as an arena in which to restore a reputation left shredded by the retreat from Iraq, and a relationship with the US which was diminished as a result. "Our biggest mistake was not to be tougher with the Americans—to say 'If you want us to go on with this, you have to put in place a serious political strategy,'" says one official.

Despite David Cameron's rebuttal of General Carter's remarks this summer, that is a point the prime minister appears to have embraced—and to have made at least twice to Obama. That conclusion—that military effort without a political framework was futile—appears to have underpinned his decision to bring troops home in 2014.

But this exit should not be the excuse to brush aside the biggest miscalculation and outright failure in British foreign policy since Suez. It was worse than that in Iraq, which prompted two parliamentary investigations: the Butler Review into the faulty intelligence on weapons of mass destruction, and the Chilcot Inquiry into lessons learned from the conflict. The lessons of Afghanistan are even broader: they extend from military planning through aid to every part of Britain's role in the world. That is the justification now for a thorough parliamentary inquiry which asks, above all: what did we think we were doing, and why did it go so wrong?

The Huawei story

Hostages, espionage and a global trade war—how a Chinese telecoms company is trying to conquer the world

Isabel Hilton

August/September 2019

On the recently completed Huawei campus in Dongguan, near Shenzhen in southern China, 17,000 employees and three imported black swans enjoy life in 12 "villages" built in ersatz European style and set in a landscape of lakes and greenery. The black swans are there to remind the people working at the world's second largest provider of smartphones and the biggest supplier of networking equipment that nothing is certain, and that it is important to prepare for the unexpected.

That thought was vindicated on 1st December last year, thousands of miles and several time zones away from Dongguan's humid atmosphere, when Meng Wanzhou, Huawei's COO and daughter of the company's founder Ren Zhengfei, was detained in Vancouver en route from China to Mexico. She is now facing extradition proceedings to the United States on charges of bank and wire fraud, and conspiracy to commit both in order to evade US sanctions on Iran.

The controversy around this case underlines how this single firm has become a crucible for the Great Power contest between the US and the People's Republic of China, one that has dragged American allies into the tensions. It raises questions about economic supremacy, defence and security in a world in which China increasingly aspires to the upper hand.

In western capitals, Huawei channels profound anxieties about the motives, strategies and ambitions of the Chinese Communist Party, the Chinese state and the companies it controls. Beijing insists that the suspicion it has built up Huawei to usurp western technological monopolies—and that its telecoms expose customers to risks of espionage or future sabotage—are unfounded. Huawei's supporters, including at the highest levels of the Chinese government, argue that such charges betray a declining power's fear of a rising power's innovative energy. Huawei itself, meanwhile, insists that it is simply a private company owned by its employees, unrelated to government or Party. A long list of intelligence agents and investigative reports have found that claim less than credible.

The imminent deployment of 5G technology—the speed and bandwidth of which promises to be the foundation of transformative AI and the Internet of Things—has brought long-running tensions between China and the US to crisis point. The Washington establishment is alarmed, although Trump himself is characteristically inconsistent.

In other western capitals, leaders grapple with profound conflicts of interest—between long-established relationships with the US and the attraction of new opportunities with China, and between the twin imperatives of economics and national security. In Britain, the leak of the National Security Council's decision in April to allow Huawei to supply some "non-core" 5G technology to British phone companies against the strongly expressed advice of Washington, cost the defence secretary his job. The final shape of Britain's future relationship with China remains in limbo.

The people's champion

The volume of news about Huawei may be recent, but the worries go back to its origin story in the 1980s, when China was beginning its long climb out of the poverty and backwardness of the Mao years. It was a decade of optimism and political liberalisation that would end with the trauma of Tiananmen: rapid growth and globalisation would be China's story for the next three decades.

Back then, China had no global brands or native telecoms producers. A former middle-ranking officer in the People's Liberation Army (PLA), with the support of China's high-level national strategy, would change that.

Ren Zhengfei, a former director of the PLA General Staff Department's Information Engineering Academy, had left the army in 1984, and initially found work with a state-owned electronics company. Three years later and along with 14 colleagues, all with military and some with intelligence backgrounds, and armed with an $8.5m loan from a Chinese state bank, Ren set up a new company to import telecoms equipment for the domestic market. He also set up a unit tasked with reverse engineering, so that Huawei could begin to manufacture the products itself.

Reverse engineering basic components certainly counts as low-level piracy. But by the early 1990s, Huawei reportedly employed 500 research and development staff to only 200 production staff, a ratio that suggested that this young company had big ambitions, as well as deep pockets that were hard to account for in its existing commercial operations. Huawei would prosper through impeccable connections.

Ren reportedly had directed the academy that conducted telecoms research for the PLA during his time in the army, and his military links would prove invaluable: the army was a huge potential customer and one that had a strategic interest in cultivating national champions in key technologies. Today, most consumers know Huawei for its handsets, but the company was built on the basic networking technology of the digital world—the switches, routers and servers that handle the data and keep the world online. In 1993, the company released its first switch—a device that allows data to be routed round a network—and was awarded the contract to build the PLA's new telecoms network. In 1996, when the Chinese government decided to invest in national champions that could liberate the country from its dependency on western companies, Huawei, with its military links, was chosen over several rivals.

With that alignment of national and company strategy came a raft of benefits: military and state research institutes helped with funding and staff; state banks offered virtually unlimited lines of credit; and the state subsidised its research. There was support from the rapidly growing city of Shenzhen, which gave priority to the company's projects, huge state contracts, and the conspicuous blessing of senior Party figures who visited regularly. Being a national champion was like having a continuous adrenaline drip.

In the following three years, Huawei's revenues quadrupled and net profits rose tenfold. When the company exhibited at a Geneva trade fair in 1999, the surprise was not only that the equipment on display was being made in China, but how remarkably cheap it was. Supported by its many state benefits, Huawei could build its international market share by undercutting its rivals, which helped drive some rival western companies, including the UK firm Marconi, into bankruptcy.

By this stage, Huawei employed 12,000 people and had become China's biggest manufacturer of the network switching devices that made its first fortune. It boasted revenues of $1.5bn and had sales offices in 45 countries, including one in Libya that was located inside the Chinese embassy. But for prospective foreign partners there were two nagging questions: who really owned Huawei? And who financed and supported it? Given the security sensitivities of telecoms, the answers affected how closely foreign partners would be willing to collaborate.

Evidence of strong backing by the state was not hard to find: Huawei's contracts for the supply and maintenance of military telecoms made a close relationship with the Party a given. Indeed, as long as the company was mainly operating in China, foreign partners such as Texas Instruments and 3com could see those connections as an advantage in helping them enter this unfamiliar market. But as Huawei began to expand into global markets in the late 1990s, that dynamic changed.

Scrutiny became more intense and doubts about ownership intensified. The company has always claimed to be owned by its employees, but in the latest of several iterations of its corporate structure, Huawei's operating company is listed as 100 per cent owned by a holding company; the holding company in turn is 99 per cent owned by the Union of Huawei Investment & Holdings—which the company says is a trade union—and 1 per cent owned by Ren Zhenfei.

But there are no independent unions in China, and union members have no rights over union assets. Huawei's "employee shares," touted by the company as evidence of ownership, are a profit distribution scheme with no meaningful control. "Regardless of who, in a practical sense, owns and controls Huawei," US scholars Christopher Balding and Donald Clarke concluded after digging into this, "it is clear that the employees do not."

By the end of the 2000s, a report from the European Commission concluded that the China Development Bank's credit lines to Huawei, including a $30bn facility, supported the company to carry out government policy and to consolidate its commercial position by extending financial support to its customers to buy Huawei equipment. To the likes of Ericsson and Nokia, feeling the pressure of

Huawei's aggressive pricing in international markets, this seemed unfair. Then there is a deeper concern: if Huawei depends on the Chinese party-state, can it ever be a trusted supplier of critical infrastructure in the west?

Eyes and ears

By the early 2000s, the UK intelligence services were becoming wary. In 2003, the Blair government tasked BT with the modernisation of the country's telecoms infrastructure. Huawei's bid for the contract to supply switching equipment was substantially lower than Marconi's, and BT signalled to government officials that they planned to accept it. Much to the alarm of MI5, officials did not notify ministers until 2006, a year after contracts had been signed. At that point, it seemed too late and potentially too expensive to unscramble the deal.

In 2013, the Commons National Security and Intelligence Committee published a blistering assessment of the decisions surrounding that Huawei contract, and concluded that penny-pinching had produced "a disconnect between the UK's inward investment policy and its national security policy." As would become a pattern with Huawei, however, the horse had bolted long before alarm about the open stable door was raised.

By now, the Chinese company was supplying BT, O2, TalkTalk and EE with mobile handsets, routers and other equipment, and its equipment was embedded in the UK's fixed and mobile telecommunications infrastructure. Huawei also employed 650 people in the UK with big plans to expand. All this had happened, in the view of the Commons committee, without sufficient attention to the national security implications. With the UK saddled with the relationship, its security services looked for a way to manage the risk.

The bizarre solution they had decided on was the Huawei Cyber Security Evaluation Centre (HCSEC), more popularly known as the Cell. This is a monitoring facility set up in November 2010 in Huawei Technologies UK's headquarters in Banbury, in which personnel from the UK's National Cyber Security Centre (and previously GCHQ), work with the company to monitor the security and integrity of Huawei code, in order to evaluate and mitigate the risks of Huawei's involvement in the UK's critical infrastructure.

The structure is highly collaborative—the deputy chair of the HCSEC Oversight Board, for instance, is a senior executive from Huawei. HCSEC reports to the UK government every year and the company makes much of the fact that GCHQ has not found evidence of back doors that could be exploited for sabotage or espionage. It is like a game where one side agrees to snoop on itself, and the other enlists the help of the subject of its prying.

The board's 2018 report was unexpectedly damning. There were "shortcomings in Huawei's engineering processes" it complained, which "exposed new risks in the UK telecommunication networks and long-term challenges in mitigation and management." These flaws persisted despite repeated requests to the company to address them, leading to the mealy-mouthed but damning conclusion that "the Oversight Board can provide only limited assurance that all risks to UK national security from Huawei's involvement in the UK's critical networks have been sufficiently mitigated."

Back in 2013, however, Downing Street neighbours David Cameron and George Osborne were not inclined to worry about the national security risks associated with China. Osborne in particular was enthusiastically chasing a no-holds-barred pursuit of Chinese investment and Ren Zhengfei found a warm welcome at No 10. Huawei announced a £1.2bn research investment in the UK and the company's press release quoted Ren in saying: "Over the past 11 years we have found [the UK] government to be transparent, efficient and practical. The UK is an open market, which welcomes overseas investment."

Ren was less welcome elsewhere. Australia had long banned Huawei from its own internet infrastructure and in 2012 a US intelligence report had concluded that both Huawei and ZTE, China's second biggest telecoms company, represented major security threats to "multiple critical infrastructure systems (that) depend on information transmission through telecommunications systems." These already included electric power grids; banking and finance systems; natural gas, oil and water systems; and rail and shipping channels. If this growing reliance on digital infrastructure made Huawei's participation in 3G and 4G networks problematic from a security perspective, the promise of 5G—a technology you can run the whole country from—increases that risk exponentially: not only will more key services depend on it, but the field of attack will be hugely expanded.

Developments such as self-driving cars will depend on 5G, in a future where 5G-powered artificial intelligence and big data applications will also loom large. Owning the foundational technology will not only establish the dominant standards, but it will also potentially allow Huawei access to the vast quantities of data that will travel on those networks. Achieving a dominant position at the start of a new technological dawn could give a player like Huawei a 50-year advantage, along with a capacity to disrupt the critical infrastructure of any adversary.

US security concerns might have been managed inside a framework of trust and co-operation between the US and China. But growing nationalism on both sides has eaten away at such trust. The US realised, belatedly, that it had neglected the development of 5G and effectively ceded the territory. Once Washington had woken up to the danger, it fumbled for a response just as long-simmering frustrations with the terms of trade with China, and the Pentagon's alarm at Xi Jinping's move to authoritarian nationalism, were about to erupt.

Enemies of the people

The arrest of Meng Wanzhou in Vancouver last December brought matters to a dramatic head. The charges she faces, if extradited to the US, are that Huawei effectively controlled a company called Skycom, set up to trade with Iran in contravention of US sanctions. The company insists that the case is politically motivated.

In some respects, they are right. The sanctions-busting charges can be viewed as an Al Capone move: prosecuting a mobster for tax evasion because it was easier than securing a conviction on racketeering. Other moves had been contemplated: in 2010, under the Obama administration, US counterintelligence agents and federal prosecutors had explored possible espionage cases against Huawei executives in its American facilities. But prosecuting criminal espionage charges risked exposure of confidential sources and methods and the outcome was never certain. It is much easier to go after them for sanctions busting.

The Chinese government's response was swift—and as a defence of the interests of a private company, unusual. Nine days after Meng's arrest two Canadian citizens—Michael Kovrig, a highly respected former diplomat, and Michal Spavor, a businessman—were detained in China. The Canadian court allowed Meng to live in one of her well-appointed Vancouver mansions and to go shopping as she chose. The Chinese authorities, by contrast, jailed the Canadians in harsh conditions, denied them access to lawyers, and later formally arrested them on vague security charges that could carry heavy sentences. Even more unfortunate were two other Canadians: Robert Lloyd Schellenberg, a 36-year-old who appealed a 15-year sentence on drug charges in January 2019, only to be sentenced to death; and Fan Wei, who was sentenced to death on drug charges in April.

Trump, meanwhile, has hinted that Huawei—and Meng—could be bundled into a larger trade settlement, a suggestion that has caused dismay in Canada for undermining the legal process that Canada has defended at considerable cost, and among hawkish Republicans in Congress who see the security threat as paramount.

While Huawei continues to insist it would never bow to demands for surveillance from Beijing's intelligence services— despite two laws that mandate any Chinese individual or entity to do so on request—the response of the west to the firm illustrates the dilemma democracies face in their dealings with China. How to deal with what the European Commission describes as an economic partner that is simultaneously a strategic competitor, and one that plays to very different rules? Australia, long a hardliner on Huawei, has banned the company from its 5G, as has the United States. The US continues to pressure other governments, including Germany and the UK, to follow suit.

A second strand of US strategy is more complicated and has been inconsistently applied: blacklisting Huawei from buying the technology it needs from US companies. It meant Huawei could no longer buy sophisticated US chips, and Google could no longer supply the Chinese company with updates to the Android operating system. Handset sales—which represented about 50 per cent of Huawei's business—dived as retailers and consumers contemplated the possibility that Huawei phones might slowly die for want of software updates.

Denying Huawei access to the advanced technology that it needed to buy from US companies is a doomsday weapon: it may seriously damage Huawei, but global technological supply chains are so intertwined that there is no cost-free move for US interests. The two sides are linked in a bitter embrace: US manufacturers relied on China to produce their equipment at low cost, while Huawei imported 40 per cent of its advanced chips from the US.

Besides, US policy today is only as consistent as its capricious president. Trump lifted a similar ban on China's second largest tech company ZTE, also imposed by the Department of Commerce as a punishment for sanctions busting in 2018, following a phone call from Xi Jinping. After meeting Xi at the G20 summit in Osaka, Trump suggested that he would lift the ban on Huawei buying US components, only to be contradicted almost immediately by his own officials. The position is as clear as mud.

Huawei, meanwhile, has adopted a tone of resilient defiance: a new image has appeared in its Shenzhen headquarters—a grainy photograph of a Second World War Soviet plane that has been riddled by enemy fire, but still manages to fly. The company claims to have its own operating system, ready to launch, along with stockpiles of advanced imported Intel chips needed for 5G networks, which will see it through until it produces its own.

Officially the skirmishes over ZTE and Huawei have strengthened and justified China's resolve to be self-sufficient in advanced technologies. Practically, its capacity to reach its goal is far from certain. Huawei has filed patents for its own Hongmeng operating system, but building and maintaining an operating system that can compete outside China's protected domestic market is a challenge. An untried system is unlikely to find much favour beyond the patriotic Chinese customer base.

As for the imported chips, Huawei's stockpiles will run down if they cannot be replenished. It will be a long summer for Huawei's staff: all leave has reportedly been cancelled for 10,000 engineers and they have been ordered to work around the clock to produce substitutes for foreign software and circuitry.

5G and five eyes

If America's aim was to prevent China dominating 5G infrastructure, it may have already failed. Huawei claims to have 46 commercial 5G contracts in 30 countries and to have shipped 100,000 5G base stations. The company argues that without its equipment, clients will be seriously disadvantaged. Alternatives may exist but the choice is still, as it was for the UK in 2003, between security and cost. It's a dilemma that the west still gives little sign of knowing how to navigate.

In May, the UK government issued a fence-sitting statement on Huawei and 5G as arguments raged between intelligence officers and technical experts about whether allowing Huawei to install "peripheral" 5G equipment while, somehow, excluding it from "the core" would solve the security problem.

In Washington, the Pentagon insists that it cannot operate within a digital system that is not secure and controllable. If the UK were to choose Huawei, therefore, it would risk being out of established alliances, including the so-called "Five Eyes" Anglosphere intelligence sharing network, which has been one of the cornerstones of UK security since the Second World War.

Ostensibly commercial and technical decisions have huge implications for the UK's future alliances. They are not decisions to be taken lightly, or in the middle of other political distractions, such as a Tory leadership election in which these critical dilemmas have been entirely ignored. Yet, as UK companies announce contracts for Huawei 5G equipment, the government's final decision languishes in the long grass.

For the UK the Huawei dilemma offers a foretaste of the difficulties of navigating the clash between the world's two biggest economies outside the EU. Despite the complexities of their industrial interdependence, the two giants are locked into a deepening confrontation that risks forcing others into unappealing compromises between prosperity and security. We are ill-prepared and ill-equipped to cope with that horrible choice.

Politics

Orwell's heir?

Historian Tony Judt brilliantly dissected the failings of liberalism. But in the end he fell into the same traps

Pankaj Mishra

February 2012

Thinking the Twentieth Century
by Tony Judt (William Heineman)

"The 20th century," Tony Judt asserts in this luminous book of conversations with the Yale historian Timothy Snyder, "is the century of the intellectuals." What does it say about intellectuals, then, that the century in which they exercised so much influence on policymaking and public opinion was also the bloodiest in history? There are some sobering answers—few of them flattering—in *Thinking the Twentieth Century*. Published two years after Judt's death from motor neurone disease, this book contains his final views on politics and economics and on a range of thinkers from John Maynard Keynes to Eric Hobsbawm.

A relatively obscure British academic based in New York, Judt refashioned himself in the last decade of his life into a strikingly bold and prominent public intellectual. Published in 2005, his masterpiece *Postwar*, a panoramic account of Europe after the Second World War, broadened his reputation as a scholar of French intellectual history. But Judt was to become even better known for his eloquent defence of the old values of good governance, social and economic justice, and his attacks on his peers—western liberal intellectuals—for having succumbed to the false consolations of dogma and the blandishments of power.

Judt valiantly tried to resurrect a faded ideal: of the unaffiliated intellectual who told the truth as he saw it, as opposed to those who appealed to the higher "truths" of nationalism, human rights, security interests, neo-imperialism, or some other abstraction. "The distinctive feature," he argued in 2006, "of the liberal intellectual in past times was precisely the striving for universality; not the unworldly or disingenuous denial of sectional interest but the sustained effort to transcend that interest." In the end, Judt himself did not overcome the failings of post-war liberalism that he so brilliantly illuminated. But few of his contemporaries seem to have been as aware as Judt of the many traps—the seductions of higher status as well as of ideology—which the 20th century laid for intellectuals.

As Judt's book relates, the raucously polemical century began with the obviously malign thinkers on the right such as the anti-semitic newspaper editor Edouard Drumant and the fascist Robert Brasillach. These were followed by the idealistic thinkers on the left whose endeavour to make a better world for all of humanity ended in, as Albert Camus wrote, "slave camps under the flag of freedom," and "massacres justified by philanthropy."

After two world wars and the Holocaust came an unprecedented era of peace and prosperity in the west—the perfect interlude, you might think, for intellectuals to uphold their oft-asserted ideals of reason and justice. But the Cold War seems to have enhanced the capacity of writers, academics, politicians and journalists for terrible ideological choices. Stalinism and the gulag did not lack for apologists in the west. Nor did the unconscionable nuclear build-up at home, and the destructive proxy wars abroad for the sake of the "free world."

As intellectual life was professionalised in the post-war period, universities and think tanks expanded, bringing previously unheard-of material rewards for those pursuing the life of the mind. Various "systems analysts" and "game theorists," such as Herman Kahn, a connoisseur of thermonuclear war, proliferated around military-industrial complexes. Many more scholar-experts like Walt Rostow and Henry Kissinger eagerly helped advance and justify American policies in the Cold War.

In a prodigiously successful post-war America, the old notion of the freelance intellectual, who questioned all verities, including his own, was threatened with irrelevance. In his influential book *The End of Ideology* (1960), the American sociologist Daniel Bell proposed that the overwhelming superiority of the American model of industrial capitalism and democracy over communism had rendered intellectual debate moot. According to Bell, there was a "rough consensus among intellectuals on political issues: the acceptance of a Welfare State; the desirability of decentralized power; a system of mixed economy and of political pluralism." Furthermore, Bell added, America's "affluent" society could find a place, even "prestige" for even its most bitter former critics.

Indeed, no one moved faster to realise this possibility, and whisper advice to power, than the ex-Marxist radicals of Bell's own generation: Irving Kristol, Jeane Kirkpatrick and Norman Podhoretz. They were the first neoconservatives and precursors to today's Washington-based intellectuals who derive their salaries from Rupert Murdoch's Fox News and the *Weekly Standard* and affirm their allegiance in turn to the right wing of the Republican Party.

Towards the end of his life, Judt, born in 1948, became queasily aware that many liberals of his own generation—a "pretty crappy" one in his unforgiving assessment—had also followed the neocon trajectory, retreating, as he put it, "from the radical nostrums of youth into the all-consuming business of material accumulation and personal security." Unlike Bell's cohorts, who had their first political awakening in the mean 1930s, Judt's peers "grew up in the 1960s in western Europe or in

America, in a world of no hard choices, neither economic nor political." His generation came to maturity as the bland post-war consensus in favour of the welfare state gave way, after the economic crises of the 1970s, to Reagan-Thatcher neo-liberalism. When the Berlin Wall collapsed, Judt's compatriots were ensconced in universities, the media and think tanks. Having lived with the menace of communism for most of their lives, few were immune to the belief that liberal democracy and capitalism had "won."

Over the following years, from the disastrous social and political engineering in Russia by free-marketeers to the invasion of Iraq in 2003, many intellectuals were to ignore classical liberalism's exhortation to moderation and self-scrutiny. Instead, they became vulnerable to the hubristic ambition that had once flourished among their communist rivals. Many adopted the view that political and economic systems originating in one small part of the world could be exported anywhere with sufficient application of will and resources. The Canadian liberal Michael Ignatieff approvingly described the United States as "an empire lite, a global hegemony whose grace notes are free markets, human rights and democracy, enforced by the most awesome military power the world has ever known."

Thinking the Twentieth Century, incandescent on every page with intellectual energy, recounts how Tony Judt managed to escape the delusions of his pretty crappy generation after a conventional start. He outlines in his conversations with Snyder a fairly orthodox career of an Anglo-American academic: stints at Oxbridge and Berkeley, specialist studies in French intellectual history, which in the 1980s broadened into an interest in east Europe, all of this interspersed with minor marital crises.

There seems something conventional, too, about Judt's early Cold-War liberalism. If he absorbed from the French intellectual Raymond Aron an obsession with Marxism, he took from Camus a broader distrust of vulgar instrumentalists—those who claimed that eggs had to be broken in order to make omelettes. This training made him contemptuous of communism and its variants, such as Maoism, that justified sordid means by positing noble ends.

Yet like many anti-communist liberals, Judt did not apply these principles to the practices of modernisation supported by the west in the third world. Meant to usher rural societies into industrial capitalism with western tools and expertise, these top-down measures were often, as with Iran under the Shah, accompanied by immense violence. Nor did he have much to say about the "free" world's support of fanatical Islamists in Afghanistan.

It was as though Judt could not overcome the partial visions of liberalism—an "ideology of the rich," the Irish critic Conor Cruise O'Brien declared once, "the elevation into universal values of the codes which favoured the emergence, and favour the continuance, of capitalist society."

Liberalism had accumulated its persuasive power in western Europe during the heyday of industrial capitalism and imperialism. Battered and on the defensive during the intra-European conflicts of the first half of the 20th century, it acquired, almost by default, a flattering self-definition during its ostensible struggles with the Third Reich and the miserable utopias of Soviet and Chinese communists. Many liberals came to see themselves as upholding a superior universalist ideology, an attitude that amounted in practice to a parochial disregard, even contempt, for other values and worldviews. Symptomatically, the "east" denoted eastern Europe and the Soviet Union in the mainstream liberal perspective, not the vast unknown lands beyond the Aegean Sea, with whom Europe shared a deeply fraught history, and where the United States had, in the post-war era, picked up the white man's burden.

Until the final decade of his life, Judt never seems to have been a vocal outlier. Before 2000 he had little to say about even decolonisation, which defined the second half of the 20th century, and was often violently resisted by the liberal-democratic west. On French colonialism in Algeria, Judt was prone to give the dithering humanist Camus an easier pass than did other critics. In Israel in 1967, Judt witnessed a country "that despised its neighbours and was about to open a catastrophic, generation-long rift with them by seizing and occupying their land." But if the steady rise of settler-Zionism in Israel in the 1970s and 80s troubled Judt a lot, there is little hint of it in his writings. And Anglo-American Europeanists like himself, generally quiescent on economic issues, were hardly well-placed to take a stand against the neo-liberal orthodoxies that began their long reign under Reagan and Thatcher, or to point out that the Third Way of Clinton and Blair actually denoted, in the absence of a Second Way, a refurbished First Way.

Judt may have taken too seriously Raymond Aron's straitjacketing notion, borrowed from Weber, of the responsibility of intellectuals: that they "must always face the decision of how to act in a given situation." (In the case of Aron, a consummate "insider" in French politics, this meant keeping silent on torture in Algeria.) In any case, before 2000 Judt never seems to have criticised the norms of an intellectual milieu where the concerns of European and American elites were paramount, and philosophy and history appeared essentially western in nature and provenance.

This is partly why Judt's emergence as a critic of regnant wisdom in the wake of 9/11 caught many by surprise—especially those demoralised and depressed by the spectacle of western liberals (mostly American, but also some British and French) lining up to justify George W Bush and Tony Blair's wars with such fig leaves as "humanitarian intervention," "regime change," and "democracy-promotion."

Christopher Hitchens, overwhelmed by some "exhilarating" ideological clarity about "Islamo-fascism" on 9/11, had to dramatically renounce long-held principles and acrimoniously debate old mates. Many liberals of Judt's generation didn't even have to work this hard. For them it was the "good Fight,"—"reassuringly comparable," Judt writes, "to their grandparents' war against fascism and their Cold War liberal parents' stance against international communism." In reality it resembled more the ideological manias of the First World War, which turned a European liberal like Thomas Mann into a chest-thumping chauvinist and the American pragmatist John Dewey into a war-monger.

Eastern European intellectuals ennobled in the 1980s and 1990s—Václav Havel and Adam Michnik—also stood behind Bush and Blair. The temptation to follow his old heroes would have been immense for Judt. And such was the intellectual climate of conformity, particularly in America, that few liberals openly questioned the dominant narrative in which liberal democracy was under siege by "Islamo-fascism." (In Britain, the dissenting voices were relatively conservative figures like Geoffrey Wheatcroft, Max Hastings, John Gray and Simon Jenkins.) Ian Buruma's mild reservations about the Islam-baiter Ayaan Hirsi Ali was to provoke a book-length assault on him by Paul Berman; Martin Amis's sadistic fantasies about Muslims went unnoticed long after he first confided them to the *Times*; and a soft bigotry about Muslims and Islam in general has been the norm among many European and American liberal intellectuals.

Nevertheless, as Judt tells Snyder, "it seemed to me increasingly urgent... that we discuss uncomfortable matters openly at a time of self-censorship and conformity." Judt also recognised his unique freedom and responsibility as a tenured academic. "Intellectuals with access to the media and job security in a university carry a distinctive responsibility in politically troubled times." It helped, too, that Judt also possessed a subtle understanding of the paradoxes of the militant humanitarianism advocated by liberal intellectuals. Liberty is indeed, he tells Snyder, "a universal human value." But "ever since the 19th century, we have moved rather too easily from one man's freedom to speak of collective freedoms, as though these were the same kind of things. But once you start talking about liberating a people, or bringing liberty as an abstraction, very different things begin to happen."

Like Orwell, who did so much to rinse the English liberal-left of its cant and self-righteousness, Judt began after 9/11 to chip away at the mendacities and delusions of his own side. His timing couldn't have been better. The ostentatious moralism of many of his peers stemmed from a growing crisis within liberalism. Deprived of its foil in the "east," after 1989, liberalism had become complacent and directionless, passively endorsing neo-conservative and neo-liberal fantasies of remaking the world. Liberals had come to depend on simple ideological oppositions and the satisfaction of standing with the victors of history. Judt was, as he tells Snyder, "not interested in winners"—an un-American moral and political disposition that allied him with those possessed of a tragic vision of history.

He was not going to follow the example of Isaiah Berlin, who, he tells Snyder in one of the sharp asides that pepper this book, largely owed his success in Anglo-American circles to "his reluctance to take a stand, his unwillingness to be 'awkward' about certain 'controversial matters.'" Judt's own god of Zionism had died in 1967. Performing some delayed obsequies in an article in the *New York Review of Books* in 2003, Judt not only assailed the deceptions of the two-state solution, which, even as it recedes from sight, is invoked piously in liberal intellectual circles. Denouncing ethno-nationalism, he called for a single state that accommodated Palestinians as well as Israelis as full citizens.

Judt probably knew the costs of this: exclusion from at least some Anglo-American circles of influence. Many liberal intellectuals had consistently failed to publicly express any disquiet about reflexive American support for a country where, as Judt pointed out, long before this belief became a commonplace, political power had "shifted toward religious zealots and territorial fundamentalists."

After his article on Israel appeared, Judt faced, in addition to brusquely curtailed friendships, organised boycotts and even some threats. Most members of *homo academicus*, a generally timid species, would have capitulated at this point. To his credit, Judt only grew bolder, using every available platform to amplify his ideas: the *New York Review of Books*, one of the few American periodicals to survive the intellectual fiasco of the last decade, as well as the *Nation*, where he praised such reviled figures as Edward Said and argued for the existence of the then taboo entity, the "Israel lobby."

His prose, shorn of academic orotundity, acquired a sardonic vigour without congealing, like the late Christopher Hitchens's style, into a bullying agglomeration of such adjectives as "sinister," "creepy" and "totalitarian." Judt's review of a book on the Cold War by John Lewis Gaddis is typical of his output during this period, criticising it as "perfectly adapted for contemporary America: an anxious country curiously detached from its own past as well as from the rest of the world and hungry for 'a fireside fairytale with a happy ending.'"

As the global recession deepened, Judt also recognised that the liberals promoting democracy abroad had missed the big ideological shifts at home. The obsession with GDP and the fetishisation of individual wealth had shifted public debate from the moral realm of redistribution and justice to the narrowly utilitarian one of productivity and growth. "I think," he tells Snyder, "we really are the victims of a discursive shift, since the late 1970s, towards economics. Intellectuals don't ask if something is right or wrong, but whether a policy is efficient or inefficient." Judt hoped that the young, forced now to deal with the mess left behind by his generation, would rediscover "the politics of social cohesion based around collective purposes."

This reinvention of social democracy was, as Judt himself probably recognised, too optimistic (and, in America, positively utopian). Proposing it, he seemed to be nostalgic about the immediate post-war era in which a nanny state nurtured middle-class intellectuals like himself. "The great victors of the 20th century," he tells Snyder, "were the 19th-century liberals whose successors created the welfare state in all its protean forms."

His foray into intellectual antiquarianism not only simplified the history of capitalism; it also ignored the extent to which welfare-state liberalism depended on its existential rivalry with communism and the continuing economic somnolence of the "east" beyond the Aegean Sea. Not surprisingly, liberals nowadays offer no real solution, apart from a warmed-over Keynesianism, to the severest crisis of capitalism since the 1930s.

Judt, too, failed to see how liberalism, quietly complicit in the long history of unregulated capitalism outside the west, could not but fail to respond to the inequities of liberal capitalist democracy in the west itself, let alone the new threats of environmental degradation. Still, one cannot point out the limitations of Judt's thought without admiring how intrepidly he, in his last years, pushed its limits—an intellectual journey that promised many more surprises when it was cruelly curtailed.

The liberal delusion

Twenty-five years after the fall of the Berlin Wall, the greatest threat to the west comes from the groundless faith that history is on its side

John Gray

October 2014

In October 1997, at a joint press conference in Washington, then-President of the United States Bill Clinton told China's President Jiang Zemin that he was "on the wrong side of history." In March this year, President Barack Obama displayed the same confidence regarding the future course of humankind: by absorbing Crimea into Russia, Obama declared, Russia's President Vladimir Putin was putting himself "on the wrong side of history."

Few among our leaders have any knowledge or interest in the world as it was before they entered politics. Their concern is with the present, the recent past and the near future as they imagine it is going to be. When they declare that the current regimes in China and Russia have no future, they are invoking the events of the past quarter-century—in the first instance, the fall of the Berlin Wall in the autumn of 1989. For them, the collapse of communism was a victory for values—freedom, democracy, human rights—that have universal appeal and near-unstoppable momentum. When they make such assertions, these leaders do not see themselves as invoking any disputable theory or philosophy. They are articulating what has become the common sense of the age; a set of intellectual reflexes and assumptions they have never thought to question.

This reigning consensus is, in the broadest sense, a liberal interpretation of history. All mainstream parties and sections of opinion in western countries hold to a creed in which tyranny and empire are relics of the past, ethnic nationalism is fading away and the rise of militant religion as a factor in politics and war is a temporary aberration. This need not be a belief in historical inevitability; the role of human decisions may be acknowledged, and the dangers of back-sliding recognised. But all those whose thinking is shaped by this view insist that, in the long run, there is no viable alternative to one world united by the same values. It is a view of things that has informed grandiose schemes of regime change, and shapes western policies towards Russia at the present time. The practical upshot has been a type of democratic evangelism, and the principal legacy a litter of failed states.

The dissolution of Iraq that is presently underway is not unexpected. Even before the American-led invasion and the many bizarre decisions that followed, such as disbanding the army and banning the Ba'ath Party, there were good reasons for thinking that regime change would unravel the state. Saddam Hussein's Iraq was a modern secular despotism in some ways resembling Mustafa Kemal Atatürk's Turkey. Toppling this regime could only mean a long period of intense sectarian conflict, most likely ending with a Shia-dominated government in Baghdad operating in an Iranian zone of influence.

Similarly, the overthrow of ruler Muammar Gaddafi in 2011 has turned Libya into a playground of rival militias, tribal warlords and jihadist groups (one of which has declared a caliphate in Benghazi). Libya is now a country without a state. In yet another case, the result of 13 years in Afghanistan is a pseudo-state funded by western aid, systemic corruption and the drug trade, which will struggle to survive when American and British troops complete their departure and the Taliban try to regain power.

You might suppose some lessons could have been learnt from these experiences. Even considered cynically as exercises in grabbing resources, these regime changes were misconceived. How can resources be secured or exploited in a space that is ungoverned or controlled by anti-western forces? Yet only months ago western governments were attempting to put "moderate rebels" in power in Syria, where the only realistic outcomes of such a policy were an irreversibly fractured state, a radical Islamist regime or most likely a mix of both. Even now the United Kingdom and the US continue to support the rebellion against Syria's President Bashar al-Assad, placing themselves in the position of having the Islamic State (IS) as an ally in Syria and, on the other side of a border that no longer exists, an enemy in Iraq. At the moment it looks as though the jihadist group's rapid expansion could tip the balance in the Syrian Civil War and leave it the dominant force in the country. In that event the west could see the defeat of Assad's forces, with the potential knock-on effect of a boost to the IS and a more far-reaching collapse of government in Iraq.

Further western involvement may now be unavoidable in order to mitigate the chaos that earlier intervention has created. How could the west stand by as the Yazidi community faced extinction at the hands of forces for whose rise the west is partly responsible? To do nothing when it is the west that has created the anarchy in which the IS is free to commit its atrocities would itself be an atrocity.

Not every western intervention over the past quarter-century has lacked attainable objectives. The first Gulf War in 1990-91 was successful because its objectives were limited. So, with some caveats, was western military action in the Balkans. Again, a concentrated campaign of bombing of Taliban bases in Afghanistan may have been justified following the 9/11 attacks. In contrast, the "war on terror" was an exercise in futility. The threat was real enough, but it emanated largely from two countries—Saudi Arabia and Pakistan—which were regarded as the west's allies. Occupying Iraq and Afghanistan did nothing to diminish this danger and in fact increased support for terrorist forces. At the same time the west became complicit in practices of secret rendition and torture that violated not just liberal values but those of any civilised state.

To a greater extent than at any period in the past, the world's conflicts have, since the end of the Cold War, come to be seen through the cloudy prism of the liberal mind. Yet the Soviet melt-down had little to do with the spread of liberal values, or with the failings of central planning, which were a feature of the Soviet system from the start. More than any other factors, it was nationalism and religion that destroyed the Soviet state. Demoralising military failure at the hands of western-armed jihadists in Afghanistan, loss of control to the Church and to the Solidarity movement in Poland and national rebellions in the Baltic states—these defeats for the Soviet state, together with the challenge that seemed to be posed to Soviet security by US President Ronald Reagan's "star wars" (his proposed defence strategy against nuclear ballistic missiles) and the destabilising effects of Mikhail Gorbachev's reforms, were what brought the Cold War to a close. The notion that the fall of communism was a decisive victory for western ideas and values—"the end of history"—is the reverse of the truth.

The Cold War was a quarrel between two western creeds—liberalism and communism. From beginning to end, the Soviet Union was a westernising regime, aiming to wrench Russia from its Eurasian and Orthodox past. The collapse of communism was a defeat for this project. If the Soviet inheritance was a military-industrial rustbelt, environmental devastation and tens of millions of ruined lives, post-communist Russia suffered the effects of another western ideology when neoliberal "shock therapy" was imposed: catastrophic depression, a dramatic fall in life-expectancy and the mafia capitalism of the Boris Yeltsin era. Against this background, the idea that Russia would move into the western orbit was wishful thinking. Instead, positioned uncertainly between Europe and Asia, the country has returned to its historic ambiguities. History has continued, and on traditional lines.

The rise of Putin is often described as a return to tsarist traditions of authoritarian rule, but in some respects the state he has built is extremely modern. At its core is a reborn version of the KGB security agency, which Putin is using to co-ordinate policy on a number of fronts. Economically Russia is weak and set to become weaker as its resource-based model, which is heavily reliant on high oil prices, becomes less sustainable. Putin may well be acting on the basis that he has only a few years in which to avert a cataclysmic decline in Russia's position. His response has been a type of "non-linear" or hybrid warfare, using disinformation and deceptive diplomacy, among other techniques.

In Ukraine, mobilising a sophisticated array of media, Putin created a spectacle that has allowed him to mount a covert invasion of the eastern part of the country. As the downing of flight MH17 demonstrated, these methods—in which lines of control and command are oblique and concealed—carry significant risk. But Putin's neo-Bolshevik political technology was effective in achieving his strategic objectives, which were to annex Crimea and destabilise the Kiev government. He always retained the option of using Russian troops to mount a direct invasion. There was never any prospect of allowing separatist forces to be routed. Whatever the cost, Ukraine would be kept from entering a western sphere of influence.

Western leaders claim that talk of Russian encirclement is delusional. But here it is the west that is deluded. The attempt to bring Ukraine into the European Union made sense only on the premise that Russia was too weak to resist. But by blocking Georgia's membership of Nato in 2008 and backing separatist states in Ossetia and Abkhazia, while mounting cyber-attacks in the Baltics, Russia had already demonstrated the ability and the will to defy the west.

For Putin the loss of Ukraine posed an existential threat. While the west was disarming, Putin spent the years following the Georgian crisis modernising his armed forces. His strategy has been to bring stability to Russia's mafia capitalism through a process of part-nationalisation, and by setting limits to the ambitions of the oligarchs while giving them the state's protection. If the west were to capture Ukraine, this semi-baronial system could break down as the oligarchs looked for another leader to secure their interests. Putin could hardly have ignored the challenge posed by such an incursion. Instead, calculating that the west would not defend Ukraine, he would escalate the war until the danger had been neutralised, producing a frozen conflict in which the state is effectively partitioned and excluded from any closer links with the west.

If these strategic realities were disregarded, one reason was the financial crisis, which shifted human and financial resources away from defence and security. But the chief western deficit is cognitive. In the terms of the ruling liberal consensus, Putin's Russia—a highly popular, hyper-modern despotism—cannot exist. The system remains unfathomably corrupt, gay people and some religious minorities are suffering persecution, while opponents of the regime face life-threatening repression. At the same time, by securing a semblance of order in the country and being more self-assertive in its relations with the west, Putin enjoys greater legitimacy than any Russian ruler since the end of tsardom, together with levels of voter support that no western leader can come close to matching.

For those who hold to the liberal consensus, this situation must be highly abnormal. If Putin benefits from unprecedented levels of popularity, they are adamant that this support is bound to melt away with economic stagnation and falling living standards. If Russia's president has been quoting writers like Nikolai Berdyaev or Konstantin Leontiev, who believed Russia embodies a civilisation distinct from the west, he does so only in order to give a spurious rationale for his arbitrary power. The possibility that this is a view of Russia's place in the world that Putin has come to hold, and one which chimes with a Russian majority, has not been considered. The prospect that if he were somehow to be forced out Putin could be replaced by an ultra-nationalist leader who is more anti-western and less rational is too unsettling to contemplate.

Talk of a "new Cold War" illustrates the unreality of western thinking. If Putin were to launch a campaign of irregular warfare in the Baltic states, like the one he sponsored in Ukraine, there would be little the west could do. Nato divisions could not block the seizure of post offices and town halls by citizen groups formed from the Russian minorities, or deal with the covert forces that animate the protests. Nato's capabilities have been run down by successive defence cuts. But this is nothing like the Cold War. Putin is not promoting any universal ideology or model of society. He is attempting something that, in the terms of liberal consensus, is unthinkable—re-asserting the claims of geopolitics, ethnicity and empire. The west has yet to face the prospect that it is going to have to live with an authoritarian Russia indefinitely.

For much of post-communist Europe this is deeply troubling. In the eyes of many in the region, the Soviet debacle was an opportunity to reclaim a normalcy denied them for over 40 years. A sort of normality has returned; but it is the kind that Europe experienced in much of the first half of the last century, a condition of chronic crisis. Structural flaws in the single currency have left much of southern Europe in permanent depression. Reunited by the fall of communism, the continent has been re-divided by the European project. Across Europe, there has been a resurgence of the far right and the politics of hate.

Post-communist countries are now the last redoubt, outside Germany, of the European project. Promising to entrench liberal democracy, the EU is seen as offering security, first of all against Russia, but also as a protector of liberal values. But this safety is mostly illusory. Who can seriously believe that Germany will go to war with Russia for the third time in a century in order to protect Poland or the Baltic states? Nor is the EU a guarantor of liberal values. Versions of democracy exist throughout eastern Europe, but these democracies vary greatly in the degree to which they respect liberal norms. While it presides over a revival of many of the themes of European fascism—including the demonisation of Jews—Prime Minister Viktor Orbán's regime in Hungary is not a dictatorship of the kind that existed in the interwar period. A more modern development, Orbán's regime has harnessed popular sovereignty to create an illiberal democracy.

That democracy can be a vehicle for tyranny was well understood by an older generation of liberal thinkers. From Benjamin Constant, Alexis de Tocqueville and John Stuart Mill through to Isaiah Berlin, it was recognised that democracy does not necessarily protect individual freedom. The greatest danger for these liberals was not that the historical movement towards democracy would be reversed, but rather the ascendancy of an illiberal type of democracy—a development they saw prefigured in Jean-Jacques Rousseau's theory of the general will. Because democratic regimes have a source of legitimacy that other forms of government lack, liberty might be more threatened in the future than in the past. Legal and constitutional protections have little force when majorities are indifferent or hostile to liberal values. Most human beings in every society, much of the time, care about other things more than they care about being free. Many will vote readily for an illiberal government if it promises security against violence or hardship, protects a way of life to which they are attached and denies freedom to those they hate.

Today, of course, these truisms belong in the category of forbidden thoughts. If democracy proves to be oppressive, liberals insist this is because democracy is not working properly—if there was genuine popular participation, majorities would not oppress minorities or tyrannise over themselves. Arguing with this view is pointless, since it rests on an article of faith: the conviction that freedom is the natural human condition, which tyranny suppresses. But freedom is not the mere absence of tyranny, which may be no more than anarchy. Freedom requires a functioning state, with a competent bureaucracy and a legal system that is not excessively corrupt, together with a political culture that allows these institutions to work independently of government. In the absence of these conditions, human rights—legal fictions created and enforced by well-organised states—are meaningless. Such conditions do not exist in much of the world and will not exist in many countries for the foreseeable future, if ever. Where they do exist, they are easily compromised. Far from being the natural condition of humankind, freedom is inherently fragile and will always be exceptional.

Finding this prospect intolerable, liberals in all parties respond with a liturgy that is repeated incessantly in think tanks and universities the world over: a growing global middle class will secure the future of freedom. The assumption is that by some occult process economic modernisation will promote liberal values; but this sub-Marxian formula has little basis in the historical record. The middle classes have put up scant resistance to the rise of dictatorship; often, as in interwar Europe, they have been among the most enthusiastic and committed supporters of authoritarian regimes. Today they support Orbán, Putin and, in growing numbers, movements such as the Front National in France. The idea that the middle class can act as the saviour of liberal values is not an empirical belief. Like Marx's theory of history, it is secular teleology—a rationalist residue of a religious faith in providence.

The trouble with this liberalism is that it is regularly exposed to unpleasant surprises. When western supporters of the Arab Spring compared it with the revolutions of 1848 in Europe, they forgot that the "Spring of Nations"—as the revolutions were sometimes called—had been succeeded by 1850 by a winter of reaction. Democracy came to much of Europe nearly a century and a half later, following periods of dictatorial rule in many countries, two world wars and a geopolitical convulsion in the former Soviet Union. But it is far from self-evident that the Middle East will repeat this European experience even in the long run. Those who were convinced that liberal democracy could take root in the Middle East had not reflected on the fact that the only secular regimes in the region have been dictatorships. When the dictators have been overthrown they have been replaced by Islamist versions of illiberal democracy or failed states.

In part, this may be a result of colonialism. Most of the states in the region are creations of imperial power; many lack any underlying national culture. But the nation state itself is artificial in much of the region, and so far only the Kurds have demonstrated the internal coherence needed to form a European-style state. Western policy has aimed to keep Syria and Iraq in being, but everything suggests they are well on the way to becoming territories without effective states, ruled by shifting configurations of clans and religious allegiances. The states that were cobbled together during the First World War by European diplomats such as François Georges-Picot and Mark Sykes belong in a post-colonial settlement that is rapidly disappearing from memory. When the IS posted a video celebrating the erasure of the Sykes-Picot line between Syria and Iraq, it showed that it understands this fact, which the west has yet to grasp.

Ironically, it is the west—by creating a failed state in Iraq and backing jihadist rebels against Assad's secular tyranny—that has made the rapid rise of the IS possible. But the west has little understanding of the monster it has helped create. Almost invariably, the IS is seen as a reversion to medieval values. Certainly it has been shaped by the 18th-century Wahhabi movement of Sunni fundamentalism, which played a formative role in the development of the Saudi kingdom. But like Putin's Russia, the IS is also extremely modern—and not just in its sophisticated use of the internet. When it posted a video of the beheading of the American journalist James Foley along with a British-accented voice-over, the IS aimed to show that its reach extends far beyond its immediate battleground in Syria and Iraq. More like the French Jacobins, Vladimir Lenin's Bolsheviks or the Khmer Rouge than the medieval Assassins, the IS practises methodical terror as part of its project of creating a new kind of state. As with the regimes these modern revolutionaries founded, the IS is founded on belief not nationality. Partly for that reason, its ambitions are global.

If the ruling consensus finds the IS hard to understand, it may be because the jihadist group reminds liberals of the persistent use of violence in the service of faith. The core of a liberal interpretation of history is the notion that when they have the opportunity to become modern, most human beings will opt for peace, freedom and prosperity over other goals and values. But there is no hidden mechanism linking modernisation with the spread of liberal values. The modern world has been reshaped again and again by movements that have instead chosen death and destruction for themselves and others. In the 20th century, these movements were driven by secular ideologies such as Nazism and communism. Today, the process continues with the IS.

A factor that is neglected when considering the Arab Spring is the role of the financial crisis. Triggered by the self-immolation of a Tunisian street vendor in December 2010, the revolts began with protests against rising food prices. North Africa and the Middle East are heavily reliant on food imports, and in the preceding years prices had risen sharply. These price rises were fuelled by massive injections of liquidity into global markets by the American monetary authorities. Implemented in order to stave off a 1930s-style economic depression, policies of quantitative easing have had the effect of inflating asset prices. Stoking speculation in commodities, this flood of liquidity contributed to regime change in a number of countries. If American power was instrumental in the overthrow of former Egyptian President Hosni Mubarak, the unintended consequences of policies pursued by the Federal Reserve were more important than anything the CIA may have tried to engineer.

The financial crisis showed that the capitalism whose triumph was celebrated in 1989 was fragile. It was also in some respects criminally corrupt. The causes of the crisis included predatory lending on a vast scale, and it has since become known that banks had been rigging financial markets for years. Yet this louche variety of finance-capitalism has faced no significant internal political challenge. The Occupy movements illustrated the impotence of opposition and the absence of alternatives. Neoliberal capitalism's most immediate vulnerability lies elsewhere. Globalisation has produced greater prosperity, for a great many people, than ever existed before. However, by magnifying demands on the planet's resources, globalisation has also made intensified geopolitical competition a permanent condition. In these circumstances, conventional distinctions between war and peace become blurred. The state capitalism of Russia and China has a systematic advantage over the de-centred capitalism of the west, since a political economy that is state-centric can deploy techniques of hybrid warfare more coherently and to greater effect.

Even more than Russia, China's emergence as a great power poses a challenge to the prevailing consensus. In a generation, China has achieved the largest continuing economic expansion in history—an achievement that enabled it to launch a colossal credit expansion in the wake of the financial crisis. There is some truth in the cliché that it was the Communist Party of China that saved western capitalism. Exponents of the ruling consensus say the Chinese model of development is nearing the end of the road: there needs to be a shift to domestic consumption, and an accompanying expansion of political freedom, if mass unrest is to be averted.

Certainly stability cannot be taken for granted. How can continuing flows of Chinese capital into western property be accounted for, if not as purchases of insurance by the elite against a risk of political upheaval? Again, if the world is moving into a period of slower growth—whether because of tightening environmental constraints, declining technical innovation or the increased burden of debt left by policies adopted to deal with the financial crisis—China will be particularly vulnerable. Whatever its achievements, China is more exposed to political blowback from economic slowdown than many other states. With its pervasive corruption and gangsterish infighting, there is no way the current Chinese regime could weather decades of deflation as Japan has done. Alongside nationalist resentment of the US and Japan and lingering memories of the horrors of the Mao Zedong era, continuing economic expansion is its principal source of popular legitimacy. Even a year or two of sub-par growth would provoke an explosion.

But the consensus prognosis is still misleading. While sections of China's elites may be hedging their bets, there is no sign that its rulers are surrendering their dynastic claim to rule. At present, local protests are often followed by compromise and concessions, but in the event of more widespread and threatening unrest, repression is more likely than capitulation. Whatever happens, China is not going the way of the former Soviet Union. But neither is it going to evolve in the direction of a western market economy. China's state capitalism serves the long-term goals of the Chinese state, which centre round restoring China and its civilisation to its rightful place in the world. (This is not only a Chinese phenomenon. In India, a new government has been elected that is committed to promoting the country's Hindu civilisation.) Even if some kind of regime change were to occur, there is no reason to think China's new rulers would aim for anything different.

Like that which existed in the late 19th century, our world is one where great and medium-size powers jostle for control and resources. This is no post-modern order of the sort that some fancied was being built in Europe. It more closely resembles the world envisaged in the Treaty of Westphalia of 1648 that brought the Thirty Years War to an end and in which sovereign states pursue their own interests and, in some cases, imperial visions. Among these rival states—America, China, India, Germany and Japan—the US no longer figures as a hyper-power. With the worst public infrastructure in the advanced world, a disappearing middle class, a higher proportion of the population incarcerated than in any other country and Washington gridlocked by corporate power, no one outside the US sees the American political system as a model to emulate.

Yet in some ways America is the best placed of the great powers. Unlike China, its political system does not require rapid economic growth in order to retain popular legitimacy. The mythology of American nationalism (otherwise known as "exceptionalism") is a powerful cohesive force. In the Barack Obama administration, as at times in the past, this distinctive brand of nationalism has assumed a quasi-isolationist colouring. Exhausted by years of ruinous war, voters are reluctant to risk further costly entanglements. American resistance to military adventure has been strengthened by developments in the energy market. Expert opinion is divided as to the long-term viability of the shale revolution, but if the US were to become again a major oil exporter the impact could be profound. Countries such as Saudi Arabia and Russia, which need high oil prices in order to sustain their current political systems, would face crisis. But there is little reason for thinking these states would evolve in the direction of democracy. Mass impoverishment would likely produce more virulent types of authoritarianism, or in the Saudi case a break-up of the state with contending varieties of radical Islamism being the main beneficiaries.

A succession of cycles and contingencies, history has no overall direction. But if any trend can be discerned at the present time, it is hardly favourable to the west. In part this is the normal course of history. The western pre-eminence of the past few hundred years was never going to be permanent. But western decline is also a process that has been accelerated by repeated attempts to export western institutions. As the American historian Barbara Tuchman showed in her great 1984 book *The March of Folly*, many of history's catastrophes have been the result not of error but of what she calls "folly"—the pursuit of hubristic policies that could be known in advance to be unworkable or self-defeating. Much that the west has done over the past quarter-century can be described as folly in Tuchman's sense.

In any conceivable future, there will be many different kinds of regime. Tyranny and anarchy will be as common as liberal and illiberal democracy; ethnic nationalism will be a persistent force, while clan loyalties and hatreds will be more politically important, in some countries, than nationality; geopolitical struggle will intensify, war mutate into novel and hybrid forms and empire renew itself in new guises; religion will be a deciding force in the formation and destruction of states. There will be many cultures and ways of life, continuously changing and interacting without melting into anything like a universal civilisation. If values such as freedom and tolerance are to survive, this is the world in which they must somehow live. Coping with this world requires realistic thinking of a kind that the liberal mind, as it exists today, is incapable. But this ruling liberalism gives its believers something realist thinking cannot supply—a story, or myth, in which they can shape the future of humankind. As it faces an increasingly disordered world, the greatest danger for the west comes from the groundless faith that history is on its side.

It could have been great

Tony Blair transformed Britain, but he cared more about the limelight than the Labour Party

Ferdinand Mount

April 2016

Broken Vows: Tony Blair: The Tragedy of Power
by Tom Bowers (Faber)

In history, as in private life, short-term memory is the first thing to go.

How the immediate past slips from our grasp, how hard it is to recapture exactly what it felt like at the time. What were they like to live through, the Tony Blair years, even now not 10 years gone? What I remember is a certain easy-going quality, a genuine public relaxation, along with the silly bits (Cool Britannia, the wobbly bridge, the Dome). The tensions that had racked British society from the late 1960s onwards slackened, if only for the time being. I don't mean just that there were no strikes to speak of, very few riots—though there weren't. Nor that there were no domestic economic crises, though there weren't any of those either. I mean more generally that the problems of governing Britain appeared less daunting and insoluble, that life began to seem a little easier to handle. And this was true for most of us, because while the rich got filthy rich, the poor didn't do too badly either.

This indecently rosy picture is the opposite of the one painted, in big splashy tubes of vermilion, purple and nausea-yellow, in Tom Bower's book, for which the word "extraordinary" seems pitifully mild. *Broken Vows* makes you want to dust down adjectives you haven't used in a while, if ever, such as "rebarbative" and "phantasmagoric." Bower is a serial assassin of reputations, falling with relish on the notable rogues of our day—Robert Maxwell, Tiny Rowland, Mohamed al-Fayed, Richard Branson, Bernie Ecclestone, Conrad Black, Simon Cowell. Now Tony Blair goes into the mincer. What comes out are fragments barely recognisable as human flesh. The book is unfailingly unpleasant, inexcusably unfair and, most of the time, rather irresistible. The truth about Teflon Tony, according to Bower, is that from the start he was a lightweight, a butterfly or a gnat—depending on which species you think has the shorter attention span—a hopeless manager, a vain, ghastly, money-grubbing humbug, utterly unsuited to be prime minister.

How he came to be that way is not revealed to us, which is why you couldn't call the book a biography. We learn nothing about Blair's background, or his childhood, or how he came to be leader of the opposition without ever having had a proper job in politics. His heart trouble is brushed aside in a sentence. His family are scarcely mentioned in the book, except for the occasional slighting reference to his wife Cherie Booth—"she wasn't the outstanding lawyer they proclaimed," "she was undoubtedly intelligent, but she was far from brilliant." Surprising, then, that she came top of the country in her bar exams and was a QC in no time. Anything I have read by her on human rights has struck me as cogent and thoughtful.

But for all its raucous tone and saucy quotes, this is a curiously impersonal book. Almost the only glimpse of *la vie intime* is Bower's account of Blair's close friendship with Wendi Deng, Mrs Rupert Murdoch, after which she so abruptly ceased to be Mrs Rupert Murdoch.

And if this can't claim to be a biography, it can't claim to be a political history of the period either. I was repeatedly struck—no, flabbergasted—by the near-total omission of many of the episodes in those years that seemed to me memorable and significant.

Let's start with the Good Friday Agreement of 1998. In *Broken Vows*, Northern Ireland gets just four sentences—and those are only there to point up how success in Ulster encouraged Blair's vainglory in the Middle East. Yet for those on both sides of the Irish Sea, the Agreement was a blessing, the end of three decades of poisonous strife. It was negotiated with exemplary patience by Blair and his lieutenants, conspicuously Jonathan Powell, his chief of staff, who everywhere else in this book is ridiculed as a self-deluded and over-promoted nuisance. Yes, the Agreement was the culmination of painstaking work by previous governments, and it would not have been possible if the Irish Republican Army had not been fought to a standstill. But it would also not have happened without Blair, at the crucial moment, reassuring the Unionists that nobody present would live to see a united Ireland.

Bower tells us scarcely anything either about the Scottish referendum and the establishment of the Scottish parliament, except to rubbish Donald Dewar, Scotland's First Minister. The constitutional change of the century—and Bower treats it as a minor political embarrassment. True, Blair was not much interested in the subject, but that does not excuse his biografiend. Ditto with the House of Lords reform, which gets a single sentence on p107. An incomplete piece of work, no doubt, but the ejection of hundreds of hereditary peers was a project that had been on hold since 1911, and was surely worth a word more in a book of 600 pages.

Again with the Human Rights Act and the Freedom of Information Act, which are touched on only because they were to give Blair trouble later on. Yet these too represent significant alterations in British politics, just as the Civil Partnership Act represented a significant change in social life. To describe it merely as intended "to rid the country of institutionalised homophobia" undervalues the grand ambition for sexual equality that it embodied.

These bizarre down-playings and outright omissions might be pardonable if Bower were instead concentrating on hard economics. *Au contraire*, there is scarcely any economics to be found here. This is partly because he chooses to begin on day one of Blair's government. Yet a great deal—perhaps the most important bits—of the Tony Blair-Gordon Brown economic policy (at the outset they were a genuine duo) had been settled while Labour was in opposition, especially after the death of their leader John Smith in 1994. Smith (not mentioned by Bower) was a genial and attractive character, but he was old fashioned, if not exactly Old Labour. It is doubtful whether he would have gone along with the modernisation Blair and Brown had in mind, which was, broadly speaking to stick to the Margaret Thatcher settlement. The trade union laws were not to be reversed, income tax rates were not to be jacked up to absurd levels, for the first five years public expenditure would be kept to the levels planned by Ken Clarke, the Tory chancellor, and the British economy was to be kept open to the world. Only by following these crypto-Thatcherite guidelines would the economy prosper enough to afford those improvements in health, welfare and education that everyone in the Labour Party dreamed of.

It worked, more or less, for quite a time—as much as anything does in politics. The only place it didn't work was inside the Labour Party, where thousands of new members allured by Blair's youth and brio were soon as disenchanted as the old Left by the disappearance from the horizon of familiar Labour landmarks. His second and third election victories were greeted without enthusiasm among the faithful. Bower catches something of this. Yes, his large majorities were an amazing statistical achievement, but what were they for? Bower tells us that he voted for Blair in 1997 and excitedly followed his progress from Islington to Downing Street, but he too soon sank into disillusion.

Yet the hollowing out of the Labour Party is another notable absentee from these pages. Bower scarcely dips a toe into the brutal mechanics: how the National Executive Committee and the party conference were drained of influence. Those seaside jamborees might have been rough and tawdry, but they did imbue political life with a genuine vivacity. Worse still was the growing power of the central machine over the selection of candidates (a dismal trend equally apparent in the Conservative Party).

So if we are shortchanged on the constitutional, human rights, economic and party management aspects of the Blair years, what do we get for our money? What we are treated to, *in extenso* and *ad nauseam*, is a series of blow-by-blow accounts of meetings between Blair and his senior ministers and civil servants and, above all, between Blair and Brown. And blow-by-blow is right. The vitriol output would be enough to start an old-fashioned ink factory.

"'Fuck off,' screamed the chancellor, and he stormed out of the room" is a typical entry. "You're a crap prime minister and it's time you moved over and let someone better do the job." Brown's team copied their master's voice. Damian McBride (McPoison to his friends), Ed Balls and Ed Miliband were encouraged to speak to the prime minister "like something on a shoe." Ed Miliband makes a particularly slimy impression. He sidles in from next door to enquire of the prime minister: "What is to be gained by you staying on for another six months?" And he brusquely asks Sally Morgan, Blair's chief adviser: "Why haven't you packed up to go? There's a deal." We should not have been surprised when he so cheerfully stabbed his brother in the front. Edmund the Bastard in *King Lear* was a sweetie by comparison.

No one, however, can outdo the chancellor himself: "Are you fucking going or not?" he asked in 2004. When Blair refused to step aside immediately, Brown responded: "There is nothing you could ever say to me now that I could ever believe." This memorable insult was inserted into Robert Peston's book, *Brown's Britain* (2005), at Brown's own request. What a man.

Deafened by the effing and blinding, I find it hard to get a purchase on exactly when and how it all began to fall apart. There seems to have been little discussion of economic strategy between Blair and Brown at any stage. That didn't matter so much when Brown was sticking to the agreed figures for public expenditure, but when they began to compete in making extravagant pledges, the outcome was both sulphurous and disastrous: "he's stolen my fucking budget," Brown yelled when, in January 2000, without telling him, Blair promised David Frost in a television interview that he would double expenditure on the NHS. Later on, it became virtually impossible to extract figures from Brown. "'You asked for a fucking document, so there it is,' shouted Brown, throwing the review papers on Blair's desk." The consequences of all that overspending are still with us today.

Nor were Blair's own crowd much more delicate of speech. Alastair Campbell was as foul-mouthed as he was overbearing and duplicitous. "Fuck off, Tony," snaps Campbell, pushing the prime minister aside as he tries to brief the press on the plane back from Bosnia, "let Charles do this," then shoving General Charles Guthrie forward to give the sitrep. There seems no limit to the pretensions of this ghastly *consigliere*: Campbell forces Peter Mandelson to resign (twice), he tells Robin Cook to divorce his wife, he persuades John Scarlett, the chief of the joint intelligence committee, to let him sex up the Iraq dossier of February 2003, although Scarlett has already recorded his view that the evidence of Saddam's continued possession of weapons of mass destruction is "sporadic and patchy." Campbell didn't care about the revulsion he inspired, believing that his dark arts were essential to Blair's success. Blair thought so too, and so does Bower to some extent. But I've always thought that Blair's charm and "instinctive savvy" (Bower's excellent phrase), combined with the chaos in the Tory Party, were enough to do the trick.

Not surprisingly, this foul-breathed crew were deeply unpopular with the permanent civil service. The special feature of *Broken Vows* is the huge number of interviews Bower had with retired mandarins, all of them itching to tell their stories of humiliation. Robin Butler and his successor as cabinet secretary, Richard Wilson, were repeatedly shut out of key discussions. When they were present, their advice was rudely dismissed, especially when they suggested that Blair might like to go through the proper processes—submit the issue to cabinet, prepare a paper for discussion, set up a cabinet committee. Everything was settled on the sofa by the gang, which as often as not excluded the foreign secretary or the defence secretary as well as the cabinet secretary. The chancellor tended to stomp out of the meeting halfway through if it wasn't going his way. Meetings of the official cabinet lasted 30 or 40 minutes and decided nothing worth mentioning. Even when they did come overwhelmingly to one conclusion, not to proceed with the Millennium Dome, Blair (who had left the room) later overruled it.

We must not romanticise previous practice. Other prime ministers had bypassed cabinet and settled important matters between a handful of trusted ministers. If Blair brushed aside Butler's suggestion that cabinet ought to discuss the independence of the Bank of England, Margaret Thatcher's cabinet did not get a sniff of the chancellor Geoffrey Howe's decision to abolish exchange controls. Nor was Brown's paranoid secrecy about the contents of his budgets so unusual. Chancellors have always done their best to keep their colleagues, often including the PM, in the dark up to the last minute.

But there was something uniquely dysfunctional about Blair's style of doing business. Visitors to Downing Street wondered at the paucity of cabinet papers and the failure, often wilful but sometimes merely thoughtless, to keep minutes of meetings. Initiatives poured out of Blair's team and then withered into oblivion as soon as his mind skittered on to some other topic. He moaned that he kept pulling the levers but nothing happened. Sometimes he blamed obstructive civil servants, sometimes his useless ministers. Bower goes along with some of this, often describing this or that minister or permanent secretary as feeble, indolent or shy. Yet this book represents the revenge of the mandarins, for it offers abundant evidence that you cannot consistently abuse the processes of government and then complain that the ruddy machine doesn't work however hard you kick it.

Part of the trouble on the home front was that New Labour had no clear idea what it wanted to do, except spend billions more on schools and hospitals. To differentiate themselves from the wicked Tories, they began by sweeping away most of the Tory structures for promoting diversity, competition and devolution within the monolithic state services. Then a few of them, led by Blair, began to twig that the Conservative approach might actually produce better results, and a second wave of "reforms" began that furtively imitated it but without using the dread words "market" or "competition." By the end of the Blair years, they had got back more or less to where they had started. With all the billions showered on doctors, nurses and teachers, the services were probably beginning to work as well as they ever had (certainly that was the view of quite a few consultants and head teachers). Bower ridicules Blair for the chaos, but it has to be said that Blair was at least leading the learning curve, while most of his ministers and civil servants were stuck in the 1940s.

Just how decisive Blair's role was can be seen from the counter-example of immigration. Blair shared the general view of his ministers and the Home Office that immigration was a good thing, and that only Tories and racists would choose to raise it as a political issue. So at every turn, Labour opted to slacken controls rather than tighten them: by abolishing the "primary purpose" rule, by refusing to join other European Union nations in at least delaying free entry for citizens from new member states, by extending the legal rights of asylum seekers while purporting to keep out bogus applicants. Because Blair never understood the public anxiety, New Labour never responded to it.

In foreign affairs, Bower is unremittingly hostile to Blair and contemptuous even of his supposed achievements. In Kosovo, success is due to the Americans; in Iraq, failure is due to his own failure to tell the Americans what to do (the actual military victory disappears without trace from Bower's narrative). He sends too many troops to Sierra Leone, and not nearly enough to Afghanistan. And, of course, the lies that led up to the second Iraq war remain blatant and unforgiveable.

That last verdict is now echoed by almost everyone, including those who were happy to see Saddam Hussein removed. Iraq destroyed Blair's reputation in Britain for ever, just as Suez destroyed Anthony Eden's. And its aftershock was to destroy New Labour too. Which is part of the reason why Blair now wanders the globe in search of fresh despots and billionaires to court, a ghostly *Flying Dutchman* laden with loot. The last 50 pages of *Broken Vows*, describing the post-Downing Street years, are marvellously researched but so depressing that I found them hard to get through. The greed and the humbug are every bit as bad as Bower says, but one is struck too by the unspeakable tedium: the vacuous conferences in cavernous five-star hotels, the fake geniality of the private interviews with sheikhs and shysters, the millions of dollars shunted around the globe for projects which are unlikely ever to happen.

The details of the Iraq story are by now so well known that Bower cannot tell us much that is new and we cannot expect much more from John Chilcot's report into the war when and if that tramp steamer ever makes its home port. But Bower's account does at least remind us of some interesting early steps that led Blair on to this fatal path. We have to go back to 1998, when President Bill Clinton ordered B-52s to bomb Iraq, in order to destroy Saddam's strongly suspected stocks of chemical and biological weapons. Blair spoke in parliament even at that time of "improving the possibility of removing Saddam Hussein altogether." The United States Congress had that year passed the Iraq Liberation Act, which empowered the president to remove Saddam. So the president, whoever he might be, already had a free hand, but the British prime minister, especially a Labour prime minister, did not.

It was in April 1999 that Tony Blair flew to Chicago to deliver his speech in defence of liberal intervention to a ballroom full of whooping Republicans. The speech was drafted by Lawrence Freedman (who is today one of Blair's inquisitors on the Chilcot Inquiry). The speech still reads pretty well. It sets out with clarity how difficult it would be for a British Labour PM to do what Blair did four years later. Yes, the world ought not to tolerate genocide and internal repression, but the United Nation's Charter expressly forbade (in Article 2.7) interference in the internal affairs of a member state. The Chicago speech therefore called for a thorough reform of the UN's role, workings and decision-making processes. That is still a long way off. Without this reform, only a trumped-up excuse such as lurking weapons of mass destruction could hope to secure UN approval, and when the trumping-up was itself trumped up, then the whole expedition was morally and politically doomed. The Chicago speech also warned against the easy option of "exit strategies": "having made a commitment we cannot simply walk away once the fight is over." Blair had only to re-read the words he had uttered in Chicago to realise that, in the eyes of the Labour Party, toppling Saddam could never be acceptable.

There was, of course, the decent alternative adopted by Harold Wilson over the Vietnam War: to have offered the Americans sympathy and covert help but no troops (Bush told Blair several times that he would have understood). In the long run, the value of shoring up a modern, open Labour Party would have outweighed Britain's modest contribution to the war. But that was an option too retiring for Blair's ego.

In any case, reflecting was never Blair's forte. Bower tells us he read little of anything: he never seems to have finished his red boxes, he had read almost no history or politics; he was ignorant of large tracts of recent political events. All politicians have to wing it now and then, but Blair was in perpetual flight, seldom anchored to any solid foundation of research or argument. Ultimately, New Labour slipped its moorings and floated off into the unremembered yonder, and in floated the even less tethered Corbyn balloon. If only Tony Blair had loved the limelight a little less and the Labour Party a little more, it might all have ended so differently.

Crisis: why it's time to rewire British politics

For all its quirkiness, our constitution always used to muddle through. But the Brexit crisis has strained it like never before

Tom Clark

May 2019

"I admit that I wasn't on top of the British parliament's 17th-century procedural rules," Angela Merkel confessed in March. The woman who at that moment probably held more sway over the fate of our nation than anyone else outside it—and possibly inside it too—was being sardonic. She knew perfectly well that neither the British people, their MPs or indeed their prime minister were familiar with the venerable precedents which, with great theatricality, the speaker John Bercow had wielded the previous day to scupper the third "meaningful vote," which Theresa May had been banking on to finally pass her derided Brexit deal.

Standing up from his great green chair, in his long black robe, the speaker told a stunned House of Commons that under a principle established in 1604—and then reaffirmed most "notably" in 1864, 1870, 1882, 1891 and 1912—May's plan to grind the House into submission in successive votes would not be "orderly." And, as a result, it would not be happening, at least until something else changed.

Here, in all its baffling absurdity, was the British constitution in action.

May and her dwindling band of loyalists raged at what they saw as Bercow's manipulations of *Erskine May*. Her detractors, meanwhile, felt embarrassed at being rescued by a bolt from the blue summoned up by one man's whim: they understood why Merkel would take the Mickey. British liberals have long yearned to rationalise the far-flung pieces of parchment and vellum, as well as all the half-forgotten precedents on which our governance often rests. The Brexit crisis ought to be the moment that finally chivvies us into getting around to it.

These somewhat farcical events do not, however, make the case for change self-evident. It needs to be argued for—and with subtlety. Because for all the shambling in the Commons that day, a pathologically stubborn prime minister, who had in effect tried to reduce politics to a staring competition, had been checked, balanced and brought down a peg or two. Within days, she was talking about when she'd quit.

Checking brute power is what constitutions are supposed to do. If quirky old Britain achieves it in a way that also apparently makes for cult viewing in California, then where's the harm in that? Would exposing or tidying up the hidden wiring that connects our disparate constitution have led to better governance through the Brexit emergency, or more generally?

Lesson from America

There is a lot in the argument that writing down the ground rules in one neat document does not guarantee reasonable argument or fruitful debate.

What are the ideal conditions for creating a constitution? You'd obviously want a blank slate—in other words, a new country. You'd want a deep well of ideas to draw on, ideally from polymaths like Benjamin Franklin and Thomas Jefferson. And you'd want brilliant draftsmen, ensuring every line counted and cohered: James Madison and Alexander Hamilton spring to mind. It was with these extraordinary advantages, few of them available to Britain today, that the Founding Fathers were able to create the framework for American governance using roughly as many words as this article. Elegant and durable, it is treated with religious reverence at home, and regarded as *the* paradigm worldwide.

And yet, America is today more dysfunctional than anywhere in western Europe, including Brexit Britain. Today those celebrated checks have made government shutdowns routine, and created what Francis Fukuyama calls a "vetocracy," where all sides can stop anything happening, and nobody can get anything useful done. Even before Washington lapsed into today's poisonously partisan culture, fundamental 20th-century reforms had to be rendered from ingenious reinterpretations of 18th-century propositions: legal abortion continues to rest on a right to privacy, which itself was conjured out of a clause about something else; civil rights relied on some bright spark insisting that smooth "inter-state commerce" required them. The displacement of politicians by smart-alec lawyers is arguably not an improvement, even if it isn't as obviously absurd as Bercow's bellowing.

It may have the orderly minimalism of Marie Kondo's home, but America's constitution has become a prison. Amending it is so difficult it has not been done in 27 years, and not meaningfully in nearly 50. Times change and arguments evolve, and so it is—as the late Bernard Crick warned—unwise to presume you can put power relations and rights "above politics." At the very least, aspiring British constitutionalists should seek to build in more flexibility than the Americans.

Nor should they worry too much about getting absolutely everything into one crisp document. The US president's appointment of Supreme Court justices, and their confirmation by the Senate, makes for a tidy organogram, but—even when US politics is functional enough to fill the bench—it produces a politically compromised judiciary. By contrast, the opaque ways by which the English judiciary replenishes itself are mysterious and less democratic in theory, but in practice work far better.

By this point, you may be beginning to feel the temptations of the conservative argument against change. Rather than coming up with a new paper solution that might not work, wouldn't it be better to work with Britain's sprawling, tried and tested constitutional inheritance? After all, recent history is littered with piecemeal reforms—the steady growth of judicial review, the Human Rights Act and Freedom of Information—through which the constitution has evolved to the good, without being entirely recast.

Not long ago, I might have bought that line. The last few months of Brexit chaos, however, have exposed the frightening frailty of both orderly governance and individual rights. The long story of this country can sometimes incline to complacency. Its latest chapter, however, should put the case for radical surgery beyond argument.

The point is not the merits or otherwise of leaving the EU, but the shambolic and at times dangerous way in which this profound change has been attempted. In most democracies, an overhaul this fundamental would have required super-majorities in parliament or the country, and very often for some account to be taken of the views of devolved legislatures, too. In Britain, none of this was required. The traditional argument for the absence of constraints is that it allows for clarity. Today, however, not even the keenest supporters of Brexit could deny that the sprawling process since 2016 has been dogged not only by acrimony, but also confusion.

Since the referendum, Britain has been struggling unhappily to reconcile the "popular sovereignty" of that result with the parliamentary sovereignty on which our wider system is based. As the former lord chief justice, Igor Judge, wrote on these pages in the last issue, plebiscites can be—and in places like Ireland are—built into a country's decision-making processes. But in Britain they never have been, and so we ended up with the very thick fog in which our politics has been lost ever since.

The politicians said 2016's vote was "once and for all," and that is of great democratic importance. Yet the fact remains that legally speaking, the vote was only advisory. In this, the Brexit vote was different from the only other recent UK-wide referendum, about swapping the voting system to AV: the law would have changed automatically if that had been carried. Given the multi-layered complexities of leaving Europe after so many decades, it would have been impossible to draft all the necessary laws in advance. But some sort of plan about what would follow procedurally from a Leave vote was eminently possible, and would have been a very good idea.

The referendum could have been structured differently, so that the Leavers were required to spell out a precise "change" proposition—like, for example, the Australian republicans who tried and failed to do away with the queen in a 1999 referendum in which they also had to explain and defend how a prospective president would be picked. Alternatively, as prominent Leavers including Boris Johnson, Jacob Rees-Mogg and Dominic Cummings have floated at times, there might have been a case for a two-part vote, separating the questions about whether to leave and how to do so. Again, if we'd only looked round the world we'd have found pointers. In the 1990s and then again in 2011, New Zealanders were asked separate questions about whether they wanted to change their voting system, and then—if so—what to.

But David Cameron was too smug to give advance thought to the technicalities that would flow from losing, and there was nothing in our make-it-up-as-you-go-along constitution to require him to be prepared. During the campaign it was suggested at some times that Brexit would mean hugging Europe close and at others that it would mean breaking asunder, a useful ambiguity for Leavers ahead of the vote, but a huge headache for everyone the moment it came to making sense of their triumph. All anyone knew for sure was that 52 per cent of the votes, cast on behalf of just 37 per cent of potential voters, had plumped for something or other called "Leave."

Irksome May

Although the next prime minister had also voted Remain, Theresa May is by temperament closed and controlling, and so it suited her to take a fairly evenly divided vote and divine from it a unified General Will. We saw that, for example, in her instinct that it should be for her alone and not parliament to trigger Article 50, and in her initial reluctance to cede a meaningful vote on her deal to MPs. We saw it again when, during the heightening crisis this March, a premier who had felt it perfectly appropriate to bring vote after vote, gave a weird televised address to the nation in which she condemned other MPs for tabling "motion after motion and amendment after amendment."

She was often knocked back politically, but constitution and precedent were rarely any constraint at all. She enjoyed an alarmingly free hand to brush parliament out of the way at one especially dangerous moment. Just ahead of the European Council on 21st March, she ruled out requesting a long delay on Brexit although she knew—indeed, *because* she knew—this refusal would resurrect the no-deal scenario which the Commons had repeatedly rejected.

Britain's supposedly sovereign parliament could vote for whatever it liked, but—it transpired, at this dangerous moment—it could not reliably tell a prime minister what to do. Had the Council agreed to her request for a once-and-for-all extension until June, it would immediately have closed down any chance of British MEPs taking seats in the new European parliament in July. British MPs would, at once, have been left with a blunt choice between May's deal and No Deal, despite having previously rejected both. Nothing in the British constitution, and nobody in the UK could rescue MPs from being immediately skewered on that fork. It was the European Council which, ignoring May's request, devised a flexible extension and salvaged at least the possibility of parliament retaking control. As I write, it isn't clear how this great power struggle will play out: but that isn't the point. If we want a sovereign parliament—something many Leavers are particularly insistent on—then we don't want to leave it in a position where it can be even *potentially* usurped by a control freak in No 10.

To the extent that the constitution proved capable of safeguarding parliament's role, it relied heavily on the assistance of a few determined individuals. As the legal commentator David Allen Green tweeted: "Three statues outside Westminster please: Gina Miller, Dominic Grieve, and John Bercow." Without the court case taken by Miller, parliament would have been cut out at the beginning of the Article 50 process. Without an amendment tabled by Grieve, MPs would have been cut out of the Brexit endgame. And, without Bercow, the PM would have enjoyed a free hand to grind MPs into submission. So hats off to this trio! But the point of a constitution—surely—ought to be that one does not need to rely on the right person being around at the right time.

And in many other respects the hidden wiring has blown a fuse. All sorts of supposed fundamentals have ceased to operate. Rigid collective cabinet responsibility is one which, arguably, will not be missed. Whether change was overdue there or not, however, it would have been better to pause and debate reform, rather than just switch off the old rule purely because it was getting hard to make it stick. Other customs swept out of the way had obvious value in restraining the mighty and protecting the vulnerable.

It is a splendid tradition of our system that our legal rights can only be removed when struck out expressly in legislation. But in the Brexit stampede, as constitutional scholar Vernon Bogdanor and lawyer Schona Jolly wrote in *Prospect* last year, important protections derived from Europe have been casually diluted. Politicians like Tony Blair wrapped themselves into contortions to deny it, but the EU's Charter of Fundamental Rights has real bite in British courts. It conferred new rights—regarding, for example, protection and access to personal data—and also new teeth to entrench these extra protections along with all the established ones in the older (non-EU) European Convention.

As it prepared to take the country away from Europe and its charter, the government could point out that it wasn't about to rip up any of these rights. But the issue, as elucidated in Bogdanor's new book *Beyond Brexit*, is giving future governments a free hand to legislate these rights away without worrying about running up against judicial review. In that sense, British citizens are—in a manner unprecedented in the democratic world—set to move from a constitution which offers them more protection towards one that offers them less. Splendid tradition, then, has not proved to be enough.

At the same time as the rights of British citizens were being quietly diluted, residency and other rights of EU nationals, no matter how long they had been here, were turned into bargaining chips. A modern and civilised constitution would not, one might hope, have allowed this.

House of Cards

Disregard for the rights of ordinary people was matched by the indulgence of ministerial privileges, especially over MPs, who were left to fight back with improvised and untested weapons. The supposedly-sovereign parliament had no serious opportunity to test whether it had a much-mooted potential majority for a softer Brexit until two days before we had been originally scheduled to leave. As it turned out, even with no time to organise and an unhelpful No 10, MPs who wanted a permanent customs union found they were only a few votes away from carrying the House.

How could it be that this crucial information could emerge so late, and perhaps too late to count? It is because British MPs are not normally free to set the terms of their own discussion, and this was a debate May wanted to shut down. A cursory look at other parliaments including that in Scotland reveals that a parliamentary government is perfectly compatible with MPs exerting collective influence over how they spend their time. But May warned her MPs that any attempt to loosen her iron grip on the timetable would be the end of civilisation, and until very late she was able to bully them into line.

Members were left scrambling for straws to clutch. Labour's Yvette Cooper produced a plan to commandeer a day or two in order to pass a Bill to instruct the PM to request an extension from Brussels. It was an ingenious long shot—but, before the European Council's own intervention, nobody knew whether things would have gone sufficiently smoothly in the Commons and the Lords to pull it off. The idea that the fate of the nation could turn on a procedural wing and a prayer is disconcerting.

The Brexit legislation handed ministers extraordinary powers to make regulations. The aim was to fill the legal void that quitting Europe would otherwise create, but another effect was to accelerate the established drift away from the requirement that their policies needed to be set out—and scrutinised—in primary legislation.

The government has also dragged its heels on the basic requirement to keep parliament abreast of its plans. It had to produce a rapid update following its big defeats on the floor of the House, but only because of Grieve tabling rebel amendments, and Bercow making the improbable, precedent-defying decision to call them. A constitution defined by traditions was here kept on the straight and narrow only because of an eccentric speaker's willingness to dispatch with them.

Ministers also tried to sit on advice from the attorney general about the risk of being stuck in the "backstop" forever, a matter of keen political interest. It invoked legal privilege, as if it were advice from a solicitor to an ordinary private client, rather than on behalf of the public. It was forced to back down and publish only after being defeated by another rebellion.

Whatever the eventual outcome of the almighty tussle between No 10 and a fractured Commons, it is surely objectionable that any prime minister—especially a minority prime minister—could even try to disdain the elected House to which she owes her legitimacy. It is objectionable, too, if MPs' authority ends up being salvaged by foreign governments, instead of being respected by their own.

When it finally seized temporary control of its own proceedings, parliament had to dream up from scratch the rules for the "indicative votes" on the very same day it was to stage them. This sort of haste must have retarded the chance of a fruitful conclusion emerging. So do some deeper traditions.

The very architecture of the Commons—the two green benches two swords' lengths apart—works against compromise, and indeed the consideration of multiple rather than binary choices.

The palace could have been designed for May's "my way or the highway" mould, and without a clear statement of what Britain's constitution actually requires, the people in office can make up the drill. Having scrapped her own social care plans and grammar schools from her 2017 platform, May knew perfectly well that election manifestos have little constitutional force, and none when they fail to win a majority. And yet the moment it began to look as if parliament might soften the Tories' 2017 Brexit plans, both the prime minister and her Brexit secretary Stephen Barclay, behaved as if any difference between the House and their manifesto would represent a "constitutional clash."

The comforting thought would be that people in power always play a bit fast and loose in a crisis, and that this is a storm our 1,000-year-old constitution will soon enough weather. Sadly, there is reason to think that most fundamental tensions exposed during the Brexit saga will flare up again and again.

Back to basics

Among the first tasks for any functional democratic constitution is to settle who gets to be in charge, when an election is called, and who has to be consulted about major changes. It is not only because of Brexit that the answer to all three of these questions has been getting blurred in Britain.

Devolution has been a deepening fact of life for 20 years, and as they sought to hold the Union together in the 2014 independence referendum, all the UK party leaders made a "vow" that the "people of Scotland will be engaged directly" with changes to "the way we are governed." But London has not seen Scotland's 62 per cent Remain vote as reason to offer it any particular sway over Brexit. Northern Ireland, by contrast, has enjoyed special rights, but only because of May being propped up by the factional, and unrepresentatively anti-European, Democratic Unionists: the province's 56 per cent vote against Brexit actually counts for *less than* nothing. Lacking comprehensive reform, London's attitude to the nations and regions continues to be defined by passing flukes of parliamentary arithmetic, and the Union will never be stable.

As to when elections are called, the partial "reform" embodied in the Fixed-term Parliaments Act has the sort of perverse consequences associated with piecemeal tinkering in the tax system. Fixed terms were meant to shift power out of the hands of the PM by ending their ability to threaten colleagues and opponents with an election. But within a few years of its passage, May was able to short-circuit the law and force an opportunistic ballot. By removing the ability to crystallise "confidence questions," it has removed a traditional means of forcing a crisis to resolution. At the same time, by narrowing the range of motions that can topple a government, it has entrenched a zombie administration in office.

The fixed-term law also introduces dangerous ambiguity on the last of our fundamental questions: who gets to be in charge. In years gone by, the loss of a no-confidence vote triggered an election, and that was that. But now, even if the terms of the Act are fulfilled, there are 14 days for someone else to try and cobble together a majority, but no guidance or precedent about who enjoys this chance. The assumption has been that the first chance would go to the leader of the opposition, but is that necessarily right? Tradition has it that the monarch should send for whoever is best placed to command the confidence of the House—which probably isn't Labour leader Jeremy Corbyn. Just three years ago, his own benches voted for him to quit, and many of them continue to mutter he isn't fit for No 10; Tories who agree on nothing else can all agree on that.

In theory at least, it seems more plausible that someone like an Amber Rudd figure on the Tory left or Yvette Cooper on Labour's centre-right would stand a better chance of securing the cross-party acquiescence required to sustain an administration through the emergency. But who is to say whether they will get a go? In extremis, the decision could fall back on the queen. She would not be amused. She had hoped that she'd finished with picking prime ministers back in 1963, when the palace and the "men in grey suits" controversially settled on Alec Douglas-Home. Soon after that the Conservatives dragged themselves into the 20th century, and allowed their MPs to elect their leader.

But in 2019, neither Conservative nor Labour MPs have the final say on their leader. It has been impossible to disguise the seething mood of mutiny on the Labour side since the selection of Corbyn—and it is much easier to get away with chaos in opposition. But it is on the government side where zealous party activists are—now that May has signalled she'll go—set to pick a serving prime minister for the first time in history. If a Johnson or a Rees-Mogg emerges, as they very well could, moderate Tory MPs could refuse to recognise them, leaving a minority government to crumble away. Under Conservative rules, the parliamentary party could soon table a vote of no confidence in a leader foisted on it by the voluntary party. Who would then get the next go at being PM? Nobody knows.

An ordinary country

Underlying the Brexit impasse in parliament and our constitution, then, is the breaking of the pivot between the parliamentary and membership wings of our political parties. Fixing that pivot looks formidably difficult on both sides, and seeing as parties are fundamental in how any modern constitution operates in practice, this greatly ramps up the chances that the old rule book in Britain will continue to throw up strange and perhaps disturbing results. It is time to rewrite it.

This moment of panic is not the time to finalise all the details—and those details will matter. While their form proclaims permanence, the sad reality is that most constitutions don't last long at all. A tally at the University of Chicago a decade ago calculated that the average constitution to come into force since the French Revolution had lasted just 17 years; only a tiny minority of them endure more than a few decades, with many coming unstuck on small snares in the drafting.

What we should be able to settle soon, however, are the basic principles and processes. This country is lucky in that the fundamental ideas to enshrine are familiar and broadly shared: the accountability of parliament to the country, of ministers to parliament and of everybody to the rule of law. For all the talk of division, it should be possible in a mood of consensus to celebrate these inherited ideals, while acknowledging the traditions and processes we have inherited are inadequate to defend them.

To build a new set of effective ground-rules we must be willing to draw on parliaments and constitutions around the world, whether that is the more collaborative approach to parliamentary timetabling seen in Scotland or the express and proactive role of the Bundestag in Germany in picking a new chancellor. When it comes to the relations between nations and regions, myriad federal states have a great deal to teach us.

An enduring constitution cannot, however, be the preserve of professors of comparative government. It must be rooted in the values of the people it is designed to serve. Traditionally, it has been a struggle to persuade most busy citizens to care about questions of process rather than the substance of policy. But after seeing, with Brexit, just how badly things can go awry without the right rules there is a growing appetite for kicking democracy into shape.

At a recent Oxford conference on "remaking the constitution," seasoned campaigners described the mood as more invigorating than anything they had experienced in Britain. The positive example of Ireland harnessing ordinary citizens' voices in its own constitutional processes has encouraged new faith in the possibility of getting ordinary citizens directly involved in the deliberation. Seeing as virtually nobody, on either side, is happy with the direction of Brexit, virtually everybody should—surely—have a new interest in seeing our politics renewed.

Many Remainers view the prospect of departure from the European Union as an anachronistic statement of British exceptionalism. That is as may be. But it could just be that the convulsions we have experienced along the way will finally persuade this country that its venerable heritage does not exempt it from the usual requirement that modern states run themselves according to a coherent rule book. Should that happen, it will represent the shrugging off of another form of exceptionalism. And be very much to the good.

Society

Too diverse?

Is Britain becoming too diverse to sustain the mutual obligations that underpin a good society and a generous welfare state?

David Goodhart

February 2004

Britain in the 1950s was a country stratified by class and region. But in most of its cities, suburbs, towns and villages there was a good chance of predicting the attitudes, even the behaviour, of the people living in your immediate neighbourhood.

In many parts of Britain today that is no longer true. The country has long since ceased to be Orwell's "family" (albeit with the wrong members in charge). To some people this is a cause of regret and disorientation—a change which they associate with the growing incivility of modern urban life. To others it is a sign of the inevitable, and welcome, march of modernity. After three centuries of homogenisation through industrialisation, urbanisation, nation-building and war, the British have become freer and more varied. Fifty years of peace, wealth and mobility have allowed a greater diversity in lifestyles and values. To this "value diversity" has been added ethnic diversity through two big waves of immigration: first the mainly commonwealth immigration from the West Indies and Asia in the 1950s and 1960s, followed by asylum-driven migrants from Europe, Africa and the greater Middle East in the late 1990s.

The diversity, individualism and mobility that characterise developed economies—especially in the era of globalisation—mean that more of our lives are spent among strangers. Ever since the invention of agriculture 10,000 years ago, humans have been used to dealing with people from beyond their own extended kin groups. The difference now in a developed country like Britain is that we not only live among stranger citizens but we must *share* with them. We share public services and parts of our income in the welfare state, we share public spaces in towns and cities where we are squashed together on buses, trains and tubes, and we share in a democratic conversation—filtered by the media—about the collective choices we wish to make. All such acts of sharing are more smoothly and generously negotiated if we can take for granted a limited set of common values and assumptions. But as Britain becomes more diverse that common culture is being eroded.

And therein lies one of the central dilemmas of political life in developed societies: sharing and solidarity can conflict with diversity. This is an especially acute dilemma for progressives who want plenty of both solidarity—high social cohesion and generous welfare paid out of a progressive tax system—*and* diversity—equal respect for a wide range of peoples, values and ways of life. The tension between the two values is a reminder that serious politics is about trade-offs. It also suggests that the left's recent love affair with diversity may come at the expense of the values and even the people that it once championed.

It was the Conservative politician David Willetts who drew my attention to the "progressive dilemma." Speaking at a roundtable on welfare reform (*Prospect*, March 1998), he said: "The basis on which you can extract large sums of money in tax and pay it out in benefits is that most people think the recipients are people like themselves, facing difficulties which they themselves could face. If values become more diverse, if lifestyles become more differentiated, then it becomes more difficult to sustain the legitimacy of a universal risk-pooling welfare state. People ask, 'Why should I pay for them when they are doing things I wouldn't do?' This is America versus Sweden. You can have a Swedish welfare state provided that you are a homogeneous society with intensely shared values. In the US you have a very diverse, individualistic society where people feel fewer obligations to fellow citizens. Progressives want diversity but they thereby undermine part of the moral consensus on which a large welfare state rests."

These words alerted me to how the progressive dilemma lurks beneath many aspects of current politics: national tax and redistribution policies; the asylum and immigration debate; development aid budgets; EU integration and spending on the poorer southern and east European states; and even the tensions between America (built on political ideals and mass immigration) and Europe (based on nation states with core ethnic-linguistic solidarities).

Thinking about the conflict between solidarity and diversity is another way of asking a question as old as human society itself: who is my brother? With whom do I share mutual obligations? The traditional conservative Burkean view is that our affinities ripple out from our families and localities, to the nation and not very far beyond. That view is pitted against a liberal universalist one which sees us in some sense equally obligated to all human beings from Bolton to Burundi—an idea associated with the universalist aspects of Christianity and Islam, with Kantian universalism and with left-wing internationalism. Science is neutral in this dispute, or rather it stands on both sides of the argument. Evolutionary psychology stresses both the universality of most human traits and—through the notion of kin selection and reciprocal altruism—the instinct to favour our own. Social psychologists also argue that the tendency to perceive in-groups and out-groups, however ephemeral, is innate. In any case, Burkeans claim to have common sense on their side. They argue that we feel more comfortable with, and are readier to share with, and sacrifice for, those with whom we have shared histories and similar values. To put it bluntly—most of us prefer our own kind.

The category "own kind" or in-group will set alarm bells ringing in the minds of many readers. So it is worth stressing what preferring our own kind does *not* mean, even for a Burkean. It does not mean that we are necessarily hostile to other kinds or cannot empathise with outsiders. (There are those who *do* dislike other kinds but in Britain they seem to be quite a small minority.) In complex societies, most of us belong simultaneously to many in-groups—family, profession, class, hobby, locality, nation—and an ability to move with ease between groups is a sign of maturity. An in-group is not, except in the case of families, a natural or biological category and the people who are deemed to belong to it can change quickly, as we saw so disastrously in Bosnia. Certainly, those we include in our in-group could be a pretty diverse crowd, especially in a city like London.

Moreover, modern liberal societies cannot be based on a simple assertion of group identity—the very idea of the rule of law, of equal legal treatment for everyone regardless of religion, wealth, gender or ethnicity, conflicts with it. On the other hand, if you deny the assumption that humans are social, group-based primates with constraints, however imprecise, on their willingness to share, you find yourself having to defend some implausible positions: for example that we should spend as much on development aid as on the NHS, or that Britain should have no immigration controls at all. The implicit "calculus of affinity" in media reporting of disasters is easily mocked—two dead Britons will get the same space as 200 Spaniards or 2,000 Somalis. Yet everyday we make similar calculations in the distribution of our own resources. Even a well-off, liberal-minded Briton who already donates to charities will spend, say, £200 on a child's birthday party, knowing that such money could, in the right hands, save the life of a child in the third world. The extent of our obligation to those to whom we are not connected through either kinship or citizenship is in part a purely private, charitable decision. But it also has policy implications, and not just in the field of development aid. For example, significant NHS resources are spent each year on foreign visitors, especially in London. Many of us might agree in theory that the needs of desperate outsiders are often greater than our own. But we would object if our own parent or child received inferior treatment because of resources consumed by non-citizens.

Is it possible to reconcile these observations about human preferences with our increasingly open, fluid and value-diverse societies? At one level, yes. Our liberal democracies still work fairly well; indeed it is one of the achievements of modernity that people have learned to tolerate and share with people very unlike themselves. (Until the 20th century, today's welfare state would have been considered contrary to human nature.) On the other hand, the logic of solidarity, with its tendency to draw boundaries, and the logic of diversity, with its tendency to cross them, do at times pull apart. Thanks to the erosion of collective norms and identities, in particular of class and nation, and the recent surge of immigration into Europe, this may be such a time.

The modern idea of citizenship goes some way to accommodating the tension between solidarity and diversity. Citizenship is not an ethnic, blood and soil concept but a more abstract political idea—implying equal legal, political and social rights (and duties) for people inhabiting a given national space. But citizenship is not just an abstract idea about rights and duties; for most of us it is something we do not choose but are born into—it arises out of a shared history, shared experiences, and, often, shared suffering; as the American writer Alan Wolfe puts it: "Behind every citizen lies a graveyard."

Both aspects of citizenship imply a notion of mutual obligation. Critics have argued that this idea of national community is anachronistic—swept away by globalisation, individualism and migration—but it still has political resonance. When politicians talk about the "British people" they refer not just to a set of individuals with specific rights and duties but to a group of people with a special commitment to one another. Membership in such a community implies acceptance of moral rules, however fuzzy, which underpin the laws and welfare systems of the state.

In the rhetoric of the modern liberal state, the glue of ethnicity ("people who look and talk like us") has been replaced with the glue of values ("people who think and behave like us"). But British values grow, in part, out of a specific history and even geography. Too rapid a change in the make-up of a community not only changes the present, it also, potentially, changes our link with the past. As Bob Rowthorn wrote (*Prospect*, February 2003), we may lose a sense of responsibility for our own history—the good things and shameful things in it—if too many citizens no longer identify with it.

Is this a problem? Surely Britain in 2004 has become too diverse and complex to give expression to a common culture in the present, let alone the past. Diversity in this context is usually code for ethnic difference. But that is only one part of the diversity story, albeit the easiest to quantify and most emotionally charged. The progressive dilemma is also revealed in the value and generational rifts that emerged with such force in the 1960s. At the *Prospect* roundtable mentioned above, Patricia Hewitt, now trade secretary, recalled an example of generational conflict from her Leicester constituency. She was canvassing on a council estate when an elderly white couple saw her Labour rosette and one of them said, "We're not voting Labour—you hand taxpayers' money to our daughter." She apparently lived on a nearby estate, with three children all by different fathers, and her parents had cut her off. (Evidence that even close genetic ties do not always produce solidarity.)

Greater diversity can produce real conflicts of values and interests, but it also generates unjustified fears. Exposure to a wider spread of lifestyles, plus more mobility and better education, has helped to combat some of those fears—a trend reinforced by popular culture and the expansion of higher education (graduates are notably more tolerant than non-graduates). There is less overt homophobia, sexism or racism (and much more racial intermarriage) in Britain than 30 years ago and racial discrimination is the most politically sensitive form of unfairness. But 31 per cent of people still admit to being racially prejudiced. Researchers such as Isaac Marks at London's Institute of Psychiatry warn that it is not possible to neatly divide the population between a small group of xenophobes and the rest. Feelings of suspicion and hostility towards outsiders are latent in most of us.

The visibility of ethnic difference means that it often overshadows other forms of diversity. Changes in the ethnic composition of a city or neighbourhood can come to stand for the wider changes of modern life. Some expressions of racism, especially by old people, can be read as declarations of dismay at the passing of old ways of life (though this makes it no less unpleasant to be on the receiving end). The different appearance of many immigrants is an outward reminder that they are, at least initially, strangers. If welfare states demand that we pay into a common fund on which we can all draw at times of need, it is important that we feel that most people have made the same effort to be self-supporting and will not take advantage. We need to be reassured that strangers, especially those from other countries, have the same idea of reciprocity as we do. Absorbing outsiders into a community worthy of the name takes time.

Negotiating the tension between solidarity and diversity is at the heart of politics. But both left and right have, for different reasons, downplayed the issue. The left is reluctant to acknowledge a conflict between values it cherishes; it is ready to stress the erosion of community from "bad" forms of diversity such as market individualism but not from "good" forms of diversity such as sexual freedom and immigration. And the right, in Britain at least, has sidestepped the conflict, partly because it is less interested in solidarity than the left, but also because it is still trying to prove that it is comfortable with diversity.

But is there any hard evidence that the progressive dilemma actually exists in the real world of political and social choices? In most EU states the percentage of GDP taken in tax is still at historically high levels, despite the increase in diversity of all kinds. Yet it is also true that Scandinavian countries with the biggest welfare states have been the most socially and ethnically homogeneous states in the west. By the same token the welfare state has always been weaker in the individualistic, ethnically divided US compared with more homogeneous Europe. And the three bursts of welfarist legislation that the US did see—Franklin Roosevelt's New Deal, Harry Truman's Fair Deal and Lyndon Johnson's Great Society—came during the long pause in mass immigration between the First World War and 1968. (They were also, clearly, a response to the depression and two world wars.)

In their 2001 Harvard Institute of Economic Research paper "Why Doesn't the US Have a European-style Welfare State?" Alberto Alesina, Edward Glaeser and Bruce Sacerdote argue that the answer is that too many people at the bottom of the pile in the US are black or Hispanic. Across the US as a whole, 70 per cent of the population are non-Hispanic whites—but of those in poverty only 46 per cent are non-Hispanic whites. So a disproportionate amount of tax income spent on welfare is going to minorities. The paper also finds that US states that are more ethnically fragmented than average spend less on social services. The authors conclude that Americans think of the poor as members of a different group, whereas Europeans still think of the poor as members of the same group. Robert Putnam, the analyst of social capital, has also found a link between high ethnic mix and low trust in the US. There is some British evidence supporting this link too. Researchers at Mori found that the average level of satisfaction with local authorities declines steeply as the extent of ethnic fragmentation increases. Even allowing for the fact that areas of high ethnic mix tend to be poorer, Mori found that ethnic fractionalisation still had a substantial negative impact on attitudes to local government.

Finally, Sweden and Denmark may provide a social laboratory for the solidarity/diversity trade-off in the coming years. Starting from similar positions as homogeneous countries with high levels of redistribution, they have taken rather different approaches to immigration over the past few years. Although both countries place great stress on integrating outsiders, Sweden has adopted a moderately multicultural outlook. It has also adapted its economy somewhat, reducing job protection for older native males in order to create more low-wage jobs for immigrants in the public sector. About 12 per cent of Swedes are now foreign-born and it is expected that by 2015 about 25 per cent of under-18s will be either foreign-born or the children of the foreign-born. This is a radical change and Sweden is adapting to it rather well (the first clips of mourning Swedes after Anna Lindh's murder were of crying immigrants expressing their sorrow in perfect Swedish). But not all Swedes are happy about it.

Denmark has a more restrictive and "nativist" approach to immigration. Only 6 per cent of the population is foreign-born and native Danes enjoy superior welfare benefits to incomers. If the solidarity/diversity trade-off is a real one and current trends continue, then one would expect in, say, 20 years' time that Sweden will have a less redistributive welfare state than Denmark; or rather that Denmark will have a more developed two-tier welfare state with higher benefits for insiders, while Sweden will have a universal but less generous system.

What are the main objections, at least from the left, to this argument about solidarity and diversity? Multiculturalists stress Britain's multiple diversities, of class and region, which preceded recent waves of immigration. They also argue that all humans share similar needs and a common interest in ensuring they are met with minimum conflict; this, they say, can now be done through human rights laws. And hostility to diversity, they conclude, is usually a form of "false consciousness."

Critics of the dilemma also say, rightly, that the moral norms underpinning a community need not be hard for outsiders to comply with: broad common standards of right and wrong, some agreement on the nature of marriage and the family, respect for law, and some consensus about the role of religion in public life. Moreover, they add, there are places such as Canada (even Australia) which are happily combining European-style welfare with an officially multicultural politics. London, too, has US levels of ethnic diversity but is the most left-wing part of Britain.

In the autumn 2003 issue of the US magazine *Dissent*, two academics, Keith Banting and Will Kymlicka, show that there is no link between the adoption of multiculturalist policies in countries like Canada, Sweden and Britain, and the erosion of the welfare state. But many of the policies they describe are either too technical (allowing dual citizenship) or too anodyne (existence of a government body to consult minorities) to stimulate serious tax resistance. They also assume too swift a reaction to growing diversity—these are forces that take effect over decades, if not generations. Similarly, two British academics, Bhikhu Parekh and Ali Rattansi, have offered a critique of the solidarity vs diversity thesis (partly in response to *Prospect* articles) which also assumes an implausibly rapid connection between social cause and effect. They argue that because the expansion of Britain's welfare state in the late 1940s coincided with the first big wave of non-white immigration into Britain, ethnic diversity cannot be a drag on social solidarity. But the post-1945 welfare state was the result of at least 100 years of experience and agitation. The arrival of a small number of immigrants in the 1940s and 1950s was unlikely to have much bearing on that history. Parekh, Kymlicka and others also argue that labour movement strength, not ethnic homogeneity, is the best indicator of the size of a welfare state. But labour movements themselves are stronger where there are no significant religious or ethnic divisions. In any case, we are not concerned here with the formation of welfare states so much as with their continued flourishing today.

A further point made by the multiculturalists is more telling. They argue that a single national story is not a sound base for a common culture because it has always been contested by class, region and religion. In Britain, the left traces democracy back to the peasants' revolt, the right back to Magna Carta, and so on. But while that is true, it is also the case that these different stories refer to a shared history. This does not imply a single narrative or national identity any more than a husband and wife will describe their married life together in the same way. Nor does it mean that the stress on the binding force of a shared history (or historical institutions like parliament) condemns immigrants to a second-class citizenship. Newcomers can and should adopt the history of their new country as well as, over time, contributing to it—moving from immigrant "them" to citizen "us." Helpfully, Britain's story includes, through empire, the story of many of our immigrant groups—empire soldiers, for example, fought in many of the wars that created modern Britain.

I would add a further qualification to the progressive dilemma. Attitudes to welfare have, for many people, become more instrumental: I pay so much in, the state gives me this in return. As we grow richer the ties that used to bind workers together in a risk-pooling welfare state (first locally, later nationally) have loosened—"generosity" is more abstract and compulsory, a matter of enlightened self-interest rather than mutual obligation. Moreover, welfare is less redistributive than most people imagine—most of the tax paid out by citizens comes back to them in one form or another so the amount of the average person's income going to someone they might consider undeserving is small. This, however, does little to allay anxieties based on *perceptions* rather than fiscal truths. And poor whites, who have relatively little, are more likely to resent even small transfers compared with those on higher incomes.

Despite these qualifications it still seems to me that those who value solidarity should take care that it is not eroded by a refusal to acknowledge the constraints upon it. The politician who has recently laid most stress on those constraints, especially in relation to immigration, is the home secretary, David Blunkett. He has spoken about the need for more integration of some immigrant communities—especially Muslim ones—while continuing to welcome high levels of net immigration into Britain of over 150,000 a year.

Supporters of large-scale immigration now focus on the quantifiable economic benefits, appealing to the self-interest rather than the idealism of the host population. While it is true that some immigration is beneficial—neither the NHS nor the building industry could survive without it—many of the claimed benefits of *mass* immigration are challenged by economists such as Adair Turner and Richard Layard. It is clear, for example, that immigration is no long-term solution to an aging population for the simple reason that immigrants grow old too. Keeping the current age structure constant over the next 50 years, and assuming today's birth rate, would require 60 million immigrants. Managing an aging society requires a package of later retirement, rising productivity and limited immigration. Large-scale immigration of unskilled workers does allow native workers to bypass the dirtiest and least rewarding jobs but it also increases inequality, does little for per capita growth, and skews benefits in the host population to employers and the better-off.

But large-scale immigration, especially if it happens rapidly, is not just about economics; it is about those less tangible things to do with identity and mutual obligation—which have been eroded from other directions too. It can also create real—as opposed to just imagined—conflicts of interest. One example is the immigration-related struggles over public housing in many of Britain's big cities in the 1970s and 1980s. In places like London's East End the right to a decent council house had always been regarded as part of the inheritance of the respectable working class. When immigrants began to arrive in the 1960s they did not have the contacts to get on the housing list and so often ended up in low quality private housing. Many people saw the injustice of this and decided to change the rules: henceforth the criterion of universal need came to supplant good contacts. So if a Bangladeshi couple with children were in poor accommodation they would qualify for a certain number of housing points, allowing them to jump ahead of young local white couples who had been on the list for years. This was, of course, unpopular with many whites. Similar clashes between *group*-based notions of justice and *universally* applied human rights are unavoidable in welfare states with increasingly diverse people.

The "thickest" solidarities are now often found among ethnic minority groups themselves in response to real or perceived discrimination. This can be another source of resentment for poor whites who look on enviously from their own fragmented neighbourhoods as minorities recreate some of the mutual support and sense of community that was once a feature of British working-class life. Paradoxically, it may be this erosion of feelings of mutuality among the white majority in Britain that has made it easier to absorb minorities. The degree of antagonism between groups is proportional to the degree of co-operation within groups. Relative to the other big European nations, the British sense of national culture and solidarity has arguably been rather weak—diluted by class, empire, the four different nations within the state, the north-south divide, and even the long shadow of American culture. That weakness of national solidarity, exemplified by the "stand-offishness" of suburban England, may have created a bulwark against extreme nationalism. We are more tolerant than, say, France because we don't care enough about each other to resent the arrival of the other.

When solidarity and diversity pull against each other, which side should public policy favour? Diversity can increasingly look after itself—the underlying drift of social and economic development favours it. Solidarity, on the other hand, thrives at times of adversity, hence its high point just after the Second World War and its steady decline ever since as affluence, mobility, value diversity and (in some areas) immigration have loosened the ties of a common culture. Public policy should therefore tend to favour solidarity in four broad areas.

Immigration and asylum

About 9 per cent of British residents are now from ethnic minorities, rising to almost one third in London. On current trends about one fifth of the population will come from an ethnic minority by 2050, albeit many of them fourth or fifth generation. Thanks to the race riots in northern English towns in 2001, the fear of radical Islam after 9/11, and anxieties about the rise in asylum-led immigration from the mid-1990s (exacerbated by the popular press), immigration has shot up the list of voter concerns, and according to Mori 56 per cent of people (including 90 per cent of poor whites and even a large minority of immigrants) now believe there are too many immigrants in Britain. This is thanks partly to the overburdened asylum system, which forces refugees on to welfare and prevents them from working legally for at least two years—a system calculated to provoke maximum hostility from ordinary Britons with their acute sensitivity to free riding. As soon as the system is under control and undeserving applicants are swiftly removed or redirected to legitimate migration channels, the ban on working should be reduced to six months or abolished. A properly managed asylum system will sharply reduce the heat in the whole race and immigration debate.

Immigrants come in all shapes and sizes. From the American banker or Indian software engineer to the Somali asylum seeker—from the most desirable to the most burdensome, at least in the short term. Immigrants who plan to stay should be encouraged to become Britons as far as that is compatible with holding on to some core aspects of their own culture. In return for learning the language, getting a job and paying taxes, and abiding by the laws and norms of the host society, immigrants must be given a stake in the system and incentives to become good citizens. (While it is desirable to increase minority participation at the higher end of the labour market, the use of quotas and affirmative action seems to have been counter-productive in the US.) Immigrants from the same place are bound to want to congregate together but policy should try to prevent that consolidating into segregation across all the main areas of life: residence, school, workplace, church. In any case, the laissez-faire approach of the post-war period in which ethnic minority citizens were not encouraged to join the common culture (although many did) should be buried. Citizenship ceremonies, language lessons and the mentoring of new citizens should help to create a British version of the old US melting pot. This third way on identity can be distinguished from the coercive assimilationism of the nationalist right, which rejects any element of foreign culture, and from multiculturalism, which rejects a common culture.

Is there a "tipping point" somewhere between Britain's 9 per cent ethnic minority population and America's 30 per cent, which creates a wholly different US-style society—with sharp ethnic divisions, a weak welfare state and low political participation? No one knows, but it is a plausible assumption. And for that tipping point to be avoided and for feelings of solidarity towards incomers not to be overstretched it is important to reassure the majority that the system of entering the country and becoming a citizen is under control and that there is an honest debate about the scale, speed and kind of immigration. It is one thing to welcome smart, aspiring Indians or east Asians. But it is not clear to many people why it is such a good idea to welcome people from poor parts of the developing world with little experience of urbanisation, secularism or western values.

Welfare policy

A generous welfare state is not compatible with open borders and possibly not even with US-style mass immigration. Europe is not America. One of the reasons for the fragmentation and individualism of American life is that it is a vast country. In Europe, with its much higher population density and planning controls, the rules have to be different. We are condemned to share—the rich cannot ignore the poor, the indigenous cannot ignore the immigrant—but that does not mean people are always happy to share. A universal, human rights-based approach to welfare ignores the fact that the rights claimed by one group do not automatically generate the obligation to accept them, or pay for them, on the part of another group—as we saw with the elderly couple in Leicester. If we want high tax and redistribution, especially with the extra welfare demands of an aging population, then in a world of stranger citizens taxpayers need reassurance that their money is being spent on people for whose circumstances they would have some sympathy. For that reason, welfare should become more overtly conditional. The rules must be transparent and blind to ethnicity, religion, sexuality and so on, but not *blind* to behaviour. People who consistently break the rules of civilised behaviour should not receive unconditional benefits.

The "localisation" of more tax and redistribution would make it possible to see how and on whom our taxes are spent. More controversially, there is also a case—as Meghnad Desai has argued—for introducing a two-tier welfare system. Purely economic migrants or certain kinds of refugees could be allowed temporary residence, the right to work (but not to vote) and be given access to only limited parts of the welfare state, while permanent migrants who make the effort to become citizens would get full access to welfare. A two-tier welfare state might reduce pressure on the asylum system and also help to deracialise citizenship—white middle-class bankers and Asian shopkeepers would have full British citizenship, while white Slovenian temporary workers would not. Such a two-tier system is emerging in Denmark. Indeed it already applies to some extent in Britain: migrants on work permits and spouses during the two-year probationary period cannot get most benefits. If we want to combine social solidarity with relatively high immigration, there is also a strong case for ID cards both on logistical grounds and as a badge of citizenship that transcends narrower group and ethnic loyalties.

Culture

Good societies need places like London and New York as well as the more homogeneous, stable, small and medium-size towns of middle Britain or the American midwest. But the emphasis, in culture and the media, should be on maintaining a single national conversation at a time when the viewing and listening public is becoming more fragmented. In Britain, that means strong support for the "social glue" role of the BBC. (The glue once provided by religion no longer works, and in any case cannot include immigrants of different faiths.) The teaching of multi-ethnic citizenship in schools is a welcome step. But too many children leave school with no sense of the broad sweep of their national history. The teaching of British history, and in particular the history of the empire and of subsequent immigration into Britain, should be a central part of the school curriculum. At the same time, immigrants should be encouraged to become part of the British "we," even while bringing their own very different perspective on its formation.

Politics and language

Multiculturalists argue that the binding power of the liberal nation state has been eroded from within by value diversity and from without by the arrival of immigrant communities with other loyalties. But the nation state remains irreplaceable as the site for democratic participation and it is hard to imagine how else one can organise welfare states and redistribution except through national tax and public spending. Moreover, since the arrival of immigrant groups from non-liberal or illiberal cultures it has become clear that to remain liberal the state may have to prescribe a clearer hierarchy of values. The US has tried to resolve the tension between liberalism and pluralism by developing a powerful national myth. Even if this were desirable in Britain, it is probably not possible to emulate. Indeed, the idea of fostering a common culture, in any strong sense, may no longer be possible either. One only has to try listing what the elements of a common culture might be to realise how hard it would be to legislate for. That does not mean that the idea must be abandoned; rather, it should inform public policy as an underlying assumption rather than a set of policies. Immigration and welfare policies, for example, should be designed to reduce the fear of free riding, and the symbolic aspects of citizenship should be reinforced; they matter more in a society when tacit understandings and solidarities can no longer be taken for granted. Why not, for example, a British national holiday or a state of the union address?

Lifestyle diversity and high immigration bring cultural and economic dynamism but can erode feelings of mutual obligation, reducing willingness to pay tax and even encouraging a retreat from the public domain. In the decades ahead European politics itself may start to shift on this axis, with left and right being eclipsed by value-based culture wars and movements for and against diversity. Social democratic parties risk being torn apart in such circumstances, partly on class lines: recent British Social Attitudes reports have made clear the middle class and the working class increasingly converge on issues of tax and economic management, but diverge on diversity issues.

The anxieties triggered by the asylum seeker inflow into Britain now seem to be fading. But they are not just a media invention; a sharp economic downturn or a big inflow of east European workers after EU enlargement might easily call them up again. The progressive centre needs to think more clearly about these issues to avoid

Identity and migration

If our societies cannot assert positive liberal values, they may be challenged by migrants who are more sure of who they are

Francis Fukuyama

February 2007

Modern identity politics springs from a hole in the political theory underlying liberal democracy. That hole is liberalism's silence about the place and significance of groups. The line of modern political theory that begins with Machiavelli and continues through Hobbes, Locke, Rousseau and the American founding fathers understands the issue of political freedom as one that pits the state against individuals rather than groups. Hobbes and Locke, for example, argue that human beings possess natural rights as individuals in the state of nature—rights that can only be secured through a social contract that prevents one individual's pursuit of self-interest from harming others.

Modern liberalism arose in good measure in reaction to the wars of religion that raged in Europe following the Reformation. Liberalism established the principle of religious toleration—the idea that religious goals could not be pursued in the public sphere in a way that restricted the religious freedom of other sects or churches. (As we will see below, the actual separation of church and state was never fully achieved in many modern European democracies.) But while modern liberalism clearly established the principle that state power should not be used to impose religious belief on individuals, it left unanswered the question of whether individual freedom could conflict with the rights of people to uphold a particular religious tradition. Freedom, understood not as the freedom of individuals but of cultural or religious or ethnic groups to protect their group identities, was not seen as a central issue by the American founders, perhaps because the new settlers were relatively homogeneous. In the words of John Jay (in the second "Federalist Paper"): "A people descended from the same ancestors, speaking the same language, professing the same religion, attached to the same principles."

In the west, identity politics began in earnest with the Reformation. Martin Luther argued that salvation could be achieved only through an inner state of faith, and attacked the Catholic emphasis on works—that is, exterior conformity to a set of social rules. The Reformation thus identified true religiosity as an individual's subjective state, dissociating inner identity from outer practice.

The Canadian philosopher Charles Taylor has written helpfully about the subsequent historical development of identity politics. Rousseau, in the *Second Discourse* and the *Promenades*, argued that there was a big disjuncture between our outer selves, which were the accretion of social customs and habits, and our true inner natures. Happiness lay in the recovery of inner authenticity. This idea was developed by Johann Gottfried von Herder, who argued that inner authenticity lay not just in individuals but in peoples, in the recovery of what we today call folk culture. In Taylor's words, "This is the powerful ideal that has come down to us. It accords moral importance to a kind of contact with myself, with my own inner nature, which it sees as in danger of being lost... through the pressures toward social conformity."

The disjuncture between one's inner and outer selves comes not merely out of the realm of ideas, but from the social reality of modern market democracies. After the American and French revolutions, the ideal of *la carrière ouverte aux talents* was increasingly put into practice as traditional barriers to social mobility were removed. One's social status was now achieved rather than ascribed; it was the product of one's talents, work and effort rather than an accident of birth. One's life story was the search for fulfilment of an inner plan, rather than conformity to the expectations of one's parents, kin, village or priest.

Taylor points out that modern identity is inherently political, because it demands recognition. The idea that modern politics is based on the principle of universal recognition comes from Hegel. Increasingly, however, it appears that universal recognition based on a shared individual humanity is not enough, particularly on the part of groups that have been discriminated against in the past. Hence modern identity politics revolves around demands for recognition of *group* identities—that is, public affirmations of the equal dignity of formerly marginalised groups, from the Québécois to African-Americans to women to indigenous peoples to homosexuals.

It is no accident that Charles Taylor is Canadian, since contemporary multiculturalism and identity politics were in many ways born in Canada, with the demands of the francophone community for recognition of its rights. Law 101 of 1977 violates the liberal principle of equal individual rights: French speakers enjoy linguistic rights not shared by English speakers. Quebec was recognised as a "distinct society" in 1995, and as a "nation" in 2006.

Multiculturalism—understood not just as tolerance of cultural diversity but as the demand for legal recognition of the rights of racial, religious or cultural groups—has now become established in virtually all modern liberal democracies. US politics over the past generation has been consumed with controversies over affirmative action for African-Americans, bilingualism and gay marriage, driven by formerly marginalised groups that demand recognition not just of their rights as individuals but of their rights as members of groups. And the US's Lockean tradition of individual rights has meant that these efforts to assert group rights have been tremendously controversial—more so than in modern Europe.

The radical Islamist ideology that has motivated terror attacks over the past decade must be seen in large measure as a manifestation of modern identity politics rather than of traditional Muslim culture. As such, it is familiar to us from earlier political movements. The fact that it is modern does not make it less dangerous, but it helps to clarify the problem and its possible solutions.

The argument that contemporary radical Islamism is a form of identity politics has been made most forcefully by the French scholar Olivier Roy in his 2004 book *Globalised Islam.* According to Roy, the root of radical Islamism is not cultural—that is, it is not a by-product of something inherent in Islam or the culture that this religion has produced. Rather, he argues, radical Islamism has emerged because Islam has become "deterritorialised" in such a way as to throw open the whole question of Muslim identity.

The question of identity does not come up at all in traditional Muslim societies, as it did not in traditional Christian societies. In a traditional Muslim society, an individual's identity is given by that person's parents and social environment; everything—from one's tribe and kin to the local imam to the political structure of the state—anchors one's identity in a particular branch of Islamic faith. It is not a matter of choice. Like Judaism, Islam is a highly legalistic religion, meaning that religious belief consists of conformity to a set of externally determined social rules. These rules are highly localised in accordance with the traditions, customs, saints and practices of specific places. Traditional religiosity is not universalistic, despite Islam's doctrinal universalism.

According to Roy, identity becomes problematic precisely when Muslims leave traditional Muslim societies by, for example, emigrating to western Europe. One's identity as a Muslim is no longer supported by the outside society; indeed, there is strong pressure to conform to the west's prevailing cultural norms. The question of *authenticity* arises in a way that it never did in the traditional society, since there is now a gap between one's inner identity as a Muslim and one's behaviour *vis-à-vis* the surrounding society. This explains the constant questioning of imams on Islamic websites about what is *haram* (prohibited) or *halal* (permitted). But in Saudi Arabia, the question of whether it is haram to shake hands with a female professor, for example, never comes up because such a social category hardly exists.

Radical Islamism and jihadism arise in response to the resulting quest for identity. Those ideologies can answer the question of "Who am I?" posed by a young Muslim in Holland or France: you are a member of a global *umma* defined by adherence to a universal Islamic doctrine that has been stripped of all of its local customs, saints, traditions and the like. Muslim identity thus becomes a matter of inner belief rather than outward conformity to social practice. Roy points out that this constitutes the "Protestantisation" of Muslim belief, where salvation lies in a subjective state that is at odds with one's outward behaviour. Thus could Mohammed Atta and several of the other 9/11 conspirators allegedly drink alcohol and visit a strip club in the days before the attacks.

Understanding radical Islamism as a form of identity politics also explains why second and third-generation European Muslims have turned to it. First-generation immigrants have usually not made a psychological break with the culture of their land of birth and carry traditional practices with them to their new homes. Their children, by contrast, are often contemptuous of their parents' religiosity, and yet have not become integrated into the culture of the new society. Stuck between two cultures with which they cannot identify, they find a strong appeal in the universalist ideology of contemporary jihadism.

Olivier Roy overstates the case for viewing radical Islamism as a primarily European phenomenon; there are many other sources for radical ideologies coming out of the Middle East. Saudi Arabia, Pakistan, Iran and Afghanistan have all exported radical Islamist ideology, and Iraq may do so in the future. But even in Muslim countries, Roy's analysis remains valid because it is the importing of modernity into those societies that produces the crisis of identity and radicalisation. Globalisation, driven by technology and economic opening, has blurred the boundaries between the developed world and traditional Muslim societies. It is not an accident that so many of the perpetrators of recent terrorist plots and incidents were either European Muslims radicalised in Europe or came from privileged sectors of Muslim societies with opportunities for contact with the west. Mohammed Atta and the other organisers of the 9/11 attacks fall into this category, as do Mohammed Bouyeri (the murderer of Dutch filmmaker Theo van Gogh), the 11th March Madrid bombers, the 7th July London bombers and the British Muslims accused of plotting to blow up an aircraft last summer. It should also be noted that al-Qaeda leaders Osama bin Laden and Ayman al-Zawahiri are both educated men, with plenty of knowledge of and access to the modern world.

If contemporary radical Islamism is understood as a product of identity politics and hence a modern phenomenon, then two implications follow. First, we have seen this problem before in the extremist politics of the 20th century, among the young people who became anarchists, Bolsheviks, fascists or members of the Baader-Meinhof gang. As Fritz Stern, Ernest Gellner and others have shown, modernisation and the transition from *Gemeinschaft* to *Gesellschaft* constitute an intensely alienating process that has been negatively experienced by countless individuals in different societies. It is now the turn of young Muslims to experience this. Whether there is anything specific to the Muslim religion that encourages this radicalisation is an open question. Since 11th September, a small industry has sprung up trying to show how violence and even suicide bombing have deep Koranic or historical roots. It is important to remember, however, that at many periods in history Muslim societies have been more tolerant than their Christian counterparts. The Jewish philosopher Maimonides was born in Muslim Córdoba, which was a diverse centre of culture and learning; Baghdad for many generations hosted one of the world's largest Jewish communities. It makes no more sense to see today's radical Islamism as an inevitable outgrowth of Islam than to see fascism as the culmination of centuries of European Christianity.

Second, the problem of jihadist terrorism will not be solved by bringing modernisation and democracy to the Middle East. The Bush administration's view that terrorism is driven by a lack of democracy overlooks the fact that so many terrorists were radicalised in democratic European countries. Modernisation and democracy are good things in their own right, but in the Muslim world they are likely to increase, not dampen, the terror problem in the short run.

Modern liberal societies in Europe and North America tend to have weak identities; many celebrate their own pluralism and multiculturalism, arguing in effect that their identity is to have no identity. Yet the fact is that national identity still exists in all contemporary liberal democracies. The nature of national identity, however, is somewhat different in North America than it is in Europe, which helps to explain why the integration of Muslims is so difficult in countries like the Netherlands, France and Germany.

According to the late Seymour Martin Lipset, American identity was always political in nature and was powerfully influenced by the fact that the US was born from a revolution against state authority. The American creed was based on five basic values: equality (understood as equality of opportunity rather than outcome), liberty (or anti-statism), individualism (in the sense that individuals could determine their own social station), populism and laissez-faire. Because these qualities were both political and civic, they were in theory accessible to all Americans (after the abolition of slavery) and have remained remarkably durable over the republic's history. Robert Bellah once described the US as having a "civil religion," but it is a church that is open to newcomers.

In addition to these aspects of political culture, American identity is also rooted in distinct ethnic traditions, in particular what Samuel Huntington calls the dominant "Anglo-Protestant" culture. Lipset agreed that the sectarian Protestant traditions of America's British settlers were very important in the shaping of American culture. The famous Protestant work ethic, the American proclivity for voluntary association and the moralism of American politics are all by-products of this Anglo-Protestant heritage.

But while key aspects of American culture are rooted in European cultural traditions, by the beginning of the 21st century they had become decoupled from their ethnic origins and were practised by a host of new Americans. Americans work harder than Europeans, and tend to believe—like Weber's early Protestants—that dignity lies in morally redeeming work rather than in the solidarity of a welfare state.

There are, of course, many aspects of contemporary American culture that are not so pleasant. The culture of entitlement, consumerism, Hollywood's emphasis on sex and violence, and the underclass gang culture that the US has re-exported to Central America are all distinctively American characteristics that some immigrants come to share. Lipset argued that American exceptionalism was a double-edged sword: the same anti-statist individualism that made Americans entrepreneurial also led them to disobey the law to a higher degree than Europeans.

In Europe after the Second World War there was a strong commitment to creating a "post-national" European identity. But despite the progress that has been made in forging a strong EU, European identity remains something that comes from the head rather than the heart. While there is a thin layer of mobile, cosmopolitan Europeans, few think of themselves as generic Europeans or swell with pride at the playing of the European anthem. With the defeat of the European constitution in referendums in France and the Netherlands in 2005, ordinary citizens were once again telling elites that they were not ready to give up on the nation state and sovereignty.

But many Europeans also feel ambivalent about national identity. The formative experience for contemporary European political consciousness is the two world wars, which Europeans tend to blame on nationalism. Yet Europe's old national identities continue to linger. People still have a strong sense of what it means to be British or French or Dutch or Italian, even if it is not politically correct to affirm these identities too strongly. And national identities in Europe, compared to those in the Americas, remain more ethnically based. So while all European countries have the same commitment to formal, political citizenship equality as the US, it is harder to turn that into *felt* equality of citizenship because of the continuing force of ethnic allegiance.

The Dutch, for example, are famous for their pluralism and tolerance. Yet in the privacy of their own homes, the Dutch remain quite socially conservative. Dutch society has been multicultural without being assimilative, something that fits well into a consociational society that was traditionally organised into separate Protestant, Catholic and socialist "pillars." Similarly, most other European countries tend to conceive of multiculturalism as a framework for the coexistence of separate cultures rather than a transitional mechanism for integrating newcomers into a dominant culture (what Amartya Sen has called "plural monoculturalism"). Many Europeans express scepticism about whether Muslim immigrants want to integrate, yet those who do want to are not always eagerly welcomed, even if they have acquired the language and cultural knowledge of the host society.

It is important not to overstate the differences between the US and Europe in this regard. Europeans argue, with some justice, that they face a harder problem in integrating their immigrants—the majority of whom are now Muslim—than does the US. Europe's Muslim immigrants tend to come from quite traditional societies, while the vast bulk of newcomers to the US are Hispanic and share the Christian heritage of the dominant culture. (Numbers also matter: in the US there are two to three million Muslims in a country numbering nearly 300 million; were this Muslim population proportionally the same size as in France, there would be over 20 million.)

Whatever its exact causes, Europe's failure to better integrate its Muslims is a ticking time bomb that has already contributed to terrorism. It is bound to provoke a sharper backlash from populist groups, and may even threaten European democracy itself. Resolution of this problem will require a two-pronged approach, involving changes in behaviour by immigrant minorities and their descendants as well as by members of the dominant national communities.

The first prong of the solution is to recognise that the old multicultural model has not been a big success in countries such as the Netherlands and Britain, and that it needs to be replaced by more energetic efforts to integrate non-western populations into a common liberal culture. The old multicultural model was based on group recognition and group rights. Out of a misplaced sense of respect for cultural differences—and in some cases out of imperial guilt—it ceded too much authority to cultural communities to define rules of behaviour for their own members. Liberalism cannot ultimately be based on group rights, because not all groups uphold liberal values. The civilisation of the European Enlightenment, of which contemporary liberal democracy is the heir, cannot be culturally neutral, since liberal societies have their own values regarding the equal worth and dignity of individuals. Cultures that do not accept these premises do not deserve equal protection in a liberal democracy. Members of immigrant communities and their offspring deserve to be treated equally as individuals, not as members of cultural communities. There is no reason for a Muslim girl to be treated differently under the law from a Christian or Jewish one, whatever the feelings of her relatives.

Multiculturalism, as it was originally conceived in Canada, the US and Europe, was in some sense a "game at the end of history." That is, cultural diversity was seen as a kind of ornament to liberal pluralism that would provide ethnic food, colourful dress and traces of distinctive historical traditions to societies often seen as numbingly conformist and homogeneous. Cultural diversity was something to be practised largely in the private sphere, where it would not lead to any serious violations of individual rights or otherwise challenge the essentially liberal social order. Where it did intrude into the public sphere, as in the case of language policy in Quebec, the deviation from liberal principle was seen by the dominant community more as an irritant than as a fundamental threat to liberal democracy itself.

By contrast, some contemporary Muslim communities are making demands for group rights that simply cannot be squared with liberal principles of individual equality. These demands include special exemptions from the family law that applies to everyone else in the society, the right to exclude non-Muslims from certain types of public events, or the right to challenge free speech in the name of religious offence (as with the Danish cartoons incident). In some more extreme cases, Muslim communities have even expressed ambitions to challenge the secular character of the political order as a whole. These types of group rights clearly intrude on the rights of other individuals in the society and push cultural autonomy well beyond the private sphere.

Asking Muslims to give up group rights is much more difficult in Europe than in the US, however, because many European countries have corporatist traditions that continue to respect communal rights and fail decisively to separate church and state. The existence of state-funded Christian and Jewish schools in many European countries makes it hard to argue in principle against state-supported religious education for Muslims. In Germany, the state collects taxes on behalf of the Protestant and Catholic churches and distributes revenues to church-related schools. (This was a legacy of Bismarck's *Kulturkampf* against the Catholic church.) Even France, with its strong republican tradition, has not been consistent on this issue. After the French revolution's anti-clerical campaign, Napoleon restored the role of religion in education and used a corporatist approach to manage church-state relations. The state's relationship with France's Jewish community, for example, is managed by the Ministre des Cultes through the Consistoire Israélite, which served as the model for Nicolas Sarkozy's recent efforts to create an authoritative Muslim interlocutor to speak for (and to control) the French Muslim community. Even the

1905 law enshrining the principle of *laïcité* had exceptions, as in Alsace, where the state still supports church-related schools.

These islands of corporatism where European states continue to officially recognise communal rights were not controversial prior to the arrival of large Muslim communities. Most European societies had become thoroughly secular, so these religious holdovers seemed quite harmless. But they set important precedents for the Muslim communities, and they are obstacles to the maintenance of a wall of separation between religion and state. If Europe is to establish the liberal principle of a pluralism based on individuals rather than groups, then it must address these corporatist institutions inherited from the past.

The other prong of the solution to the problem of Muslim integration concerns the expectations and behaviour of the majority communities in Europe. National identity continues to be understood and experienced in ways that sometimes make it a barrier for newcomers who do not share the ethnicity and religious background of the native-born. National identity has always been socially constructed; it revolves around history, symbols, heroes and the stories that a community tells about itself. This sense of attachment to a place and a history should not be rubbed out, but it should be made as open as possible to new citizens. In some countries, notably Germany, 20th-century history has made it awkward to discuss national identity, but this is a dialogue that needs to be reopened in the light of Europe's new diversity—for if existing citizens do not sufficiently value their national citizenship, then European countries can scarcely expect newcomers to value it either.

And that dialogue *is* being reopened. A few years ago, Germany's Christian Democrats gingerly floated the idea of *Leitkultur*—the notion that German citizenship entails certain obligations to observe standards of tolerance and equal respect. The term *Leitkultur*—which can be translated as a "guiding" or "reference culture"—was invented in 1998 by Bassam Tibi, a German academic of Syrian origin, precisely as a non-ethnic, universalist conception of citizenship that would open up national identity to non-ethnic Germans. Despite these origins, the idea was immediately denounced by the left as racist and a throwback to Germany's unhappy past, and the Christian Democrats quickly distanced themselves from it. But in the past few years, even Germany has had a much more robust public debate about national identity and mass immigration. During last year's successful soccer World Cup, the widespread expression of moderate national feeling became completely normal, and was even welcomed by Germany's neighbours.

Despite its very different starting point, America may have something to teach Europeans here as they attempt to construct post-ethnic forms of national citizenship and belonging. American life is full of quasi-religious ceremonies and rituals meant to celebrate the country's democratic political institutions: flag-raising ceremonies, the naturalisation oath, Thanksgiving and 4th July. Europeans, by contrast, have largely deritualised their political lives. Europeans tend to be cynical or dismissive of American displays of patriotism. But such ceremonies are important in the assimilation of new immigrants.

And Europe does have its own precedents for creating national identities that are less based on ethnicity or religion. The most celebrated case is French republicanism, which in its classic form refused to recognise separate communal identities and used state power to homogenise French society. With the growth of terrorism and urban unrest, an intense discussion has been under way in France about why this form of integration has failed. Part of the reason may be that the French themselves gave up the old concept of citizenship in favour of a version of multiculturalism. The headscarf ban of 2004 was the reassertion of an older concept of republicanism.

Britain has recently been borrowing from both American and French traditions as it seeks to raise the visibility of national citizenship. The Labour government has introduced citizenship ceremonies for new citizens as well as compulsory citizenship and language tests. It has also started citizenship classes in schools for all young citizens. Britain has experienced a sharp rise in immigration in recent years, much of it from the new member states of the EU such as Poland, and—in imitation of the US—the government sees immigration as a key part of its relative economic dynamism. Immigrants are welcome so long as they work rather than draw welfare and, thanks to US-style flexible labour markets, there are plenty of low-skill jobs to take. But in much of the rest of Europe, a combination of inflexible work rules and generous benefits means that immigrants come in search not of work but of welfare. Many Europeans claim that the less generous welfare state in the US robs the poor of dignity. But the opposite is true: dignity comes through work and the contributions one makes through one's labour to the larger society. In several Muslim communities in Europe, as much as half the population subsists on welfare, directly contributing to the sense of alienation and hopelessness.

So the European experience is not homogeneous. But in most countries, the debate about identity and migration is opening up—albeit driven in part by terror attacks and the rise of the populist right.

The dilemma of immigration and identity ultimately converges with the larger problem of the valuelessness of postmodernity. The rise of relativism has made it harder for postmodern people to assert positive values and therefore the kinds of shared beliefs that they demand of migrants as a condition for citizenship. Postmodern elites, particularly those in Europe, feel that they have evolved beyond identities defined by religion and nation and have arrived at a superior place. But aside from their celebration of endless diversity and tolerance, postmodern people find it difficult to agree on the substance of the good life to which they aspire in common.

Immigration forces upon us in a particularly acute way discussion of the question "Who are we?", posed by Samuel Huntington. If postmodern societies are to move towards a more serious discussion of identity, they will need to uncover those positive virtues that define what it means to be a member of the wider society. If they do not, they may be overwhelmed by people who are more sure about who they are.

The good Muslim delusion

Western powers have been trying—and failing—to dictate what Islam should be for centuries

Sameer Rahim

March 2018

After the London Bridge attacks last June, Theresa May told the nation that a purely military response to Islamic State (IS) was insufficient. What was needed, she said, was a battle of ideas. The prime minister added that there was "far too much tolerance of extremism," and that certain communities—for which read British Muslims—weren't doing enough to tackle the problem. They needed to be "made to understand" that "British values" were "superior" to "anything offered by the preachers… of hate."

In the wake of such an attack, few British people—of any faith—would argue with a preference for law-abiding mutual respect over the bloody chaos unleashed by fanatical attackers. But what precisely, beyond rejecting terrorism, did May hope to make Muslim communities "understand"? And how?

Her statement didn't spell out the answer to either question, but it hardly mattered. The words and deeds of British governments over a decade or more show fairly clearly what she had in mind. Under New Labour, the Home Office cultivated links with recovering Islamists keen to promote their newfound love for British values. Back in 2011, David Cameron jetted to the Munich Security Conference, decried "passive tolerance" and avowed a "much more active, muscular liberalism." More recently, Amanda Spielman—the businesswoman the Conservatives controversially brought in as Ofsted chief inspector—also called for a more "muscular liberalism" in the classroom, in a speech whose target was plainly religious Muslims. One narrative runs through these interventions—that the antidote to violent Islamism is western modernity, defined as a particular (and, for Britain, rather recent) form of social liberalism, alongside a religion-free public sphere.

But how would that work? Does it mean that the 2.8 million Muslims who call Britain home have to abandon their faith to properly assimilate? Or does it mean—just as problematically—the state nurturing an Islamic-inflected liberalism, enforced by a centrally-approved religious authority? After the attacks in Barcelona last August, the *Times* columnist David Aaronovitch flexed some liberal muscle. For any Muslim who doesn't want to travel the whole way to atheism with him, Aaronovitch offered a "progressive form of Islam" that throws off the shackles of the past and becomes "British and therefore modern." Like other muscular liberals he wasn't unduly detained by the question of why Muslims would listen to him. But he did acknowledge that the question of who would ordain such Islamic modernity is, to put it mildly, vexed.

Islam, at least its majority Sunni version, has no institution to thrash out theological cruxes and no universally acclaimed figurehead to articulate doctrine. Instead we have a set of diverse sects with aspiring leaders competing for followers. So voluminous are its sacred texts—the Koran and stories from the Prophet Mohammed's life, or *hadith*, add up to many times the length of the Bible—that you can say (pretty much) anything and find justification for it. Historically Islam has moulded itself to the culture in which it finds itself. Medieval Persian artists had no problem depicting the Prophet with his face uncovered, something absent in the Arab tradition. Today, Indian Islam is distinct from the austere Saudi Arabian kind. Visit the Nizamuddin shrine in Delhi and you will find men and women singing together—in stark contrast to Mecca. The remarkable flexibility of the faith—in a way the muscular liberals fail to grasp—is part of its strength.

Thoughtful British Muslims welcome efforts to open up religious discussion, to debate controversial issues ranging from women's rights to sectarianism. They resist the dominance of hardline imams, and the terrorists who bomb Sufi shrines in Pakistan or burn medieval books in Mali. And if you know where to look, you will find emerging organic forms of western Islam. Yet while I'm personally enthusiastic about such innovation—let a thousand flowers bloom, I say—it also seems obvious to me that crude attempts to impose a division between "good, modern, liberal" Muslims versus "bad, old, conservative" Muslims are dangerous and self-defeating. Such simplistic labelling politicises every impulse to reform before it can put down roots, and such politicisation—in this case a western-approved "safe" Islam—will always alienate more than it attracts.

When May and Aaronovitch claim liberal Islam is the *only* way the religion should be interpreted, they trample on the religion's diversity. If imposed liberalism were to succeed in crushing religious variety, it would also damage pluralism—one of the values May has claimed as essentially British. The paradox can be seen in the work of the new counter-extremism head, Sara Khan, a British Muslim who has worked with the government's Prevent programme. Prevent obliges public sector workers—including teachers—to spot signs of radicalisation, policing what Khan calls rather sinisterly in her book *The Battle for British Islam* "the precriminal space." Prevent effectively sets a template for correct thought, something that should worry open-minded liberals.

As well as being conceptually confused, Khan's approach is doomed to failure on the security front. As any criminologist will tell you, there is no single path to violence: for some it's ideology; for others identity issues or the thrill of dominance. Motivations are usually mixed. But for Khan, the root explanation is always cultural-religious. This is a shame because her organisation Inspire does worthwhile campaigns in Muslim communities, especially for women. But the imprimatur of Prevent taints it, and her demands for blanket uniformity—"Muslims must define what Islam stands for in the contemporary era," she says—makes her the mirror-image of the narrow Islamists she deplores.

It is not the rigidity of Islam, as Khan implies, but its flexibility that renders it vulnerable to terrorist ideology. In the early days of the Afghan mujahideen's fight against the Soviet invaders, religious scruples about suicide made it almost impossible to find anyone willing to blow themselves up. After 40 years of war, the Taliban has developed a theological justification for killing yourself and any innocents who get in the way. Context changes everything. And for two centuries, as liberal commentators keen to impose their standards on the religion fail to realise, it is the west which has created much of that context.

Fourteen years after the bloody crushing of the 1857 Indian Rebellion, a colonial civil servant called WW Hunter—the Aaronovitch of his day—wrote an influential book called *The Indian Musalmans: Are they Bound in Conscience to Rebel Against the Queen?* Hunter concluded that with the right education Muslims could be convinced to be peaceable. Not by anything so crude as converting them to Christianity; instead the British would convert—or should we say reform—Islam itself. "In the very process of enabling them to learn their religious duties," wrote Hunter, "we should render that religion perhaps less sincere, but certainly less fanatical." He rounded off his book with fatwas or edicts from handpicked Indian clerics declaring it was forbidden to rebel. Why would they want to? Colonialism meant progress: "The luxuriant religions of Asia shrivel into dry sticks when brought into contact with the icy realities of western science."

By this time, western meddling with Islam was well established. It was back in 1798 that Napoleon had attacked Egypt, after—he later claimed—he had seen the Prophet appear to him in a dream. This most muscular of leaders justified his invasion by claiming he wanted to free the peasants from their Mamluk rulers; in reality, he was more concerned with pressing back against Britain. At the Battle of the Pyramids, the Egyptian army was smashed by the technologically superior French. Napoleon's troops later turned their cannons on Al-Azhar, a great intellectual centre of medieval Islam, ransacking the library and trampling copies of the Koran.

Although the French stayed only three years, they had a profound impact on the development of Egypt. They set up a national institute for mathematics, political economy and the arts; they built mills and improved irrigation; they turned mosques into cafés, or made them fly the Tricolore. Eventually French scholars produced the magisterial 23-volume *Description of Egypt*.

Looking back at this long history of western disruption and influence, Christopher de Bellaigue notes sagely that, "There is something wonderfully earnest and yet wholly irrelevant about westerners demanding modernity from people whose lives are drenched in it." In his impressive book, *The Islamic Enlightenment*, de Bellaigue points out how many Islamic reform movements there have been since the early 19th century. Picking broadly the same figures as Albert Hourani in his classic

Arabic Thought in the Liberal Age (1962), De Bellaigue offers potted biographies of the charismatic thinkers and rulers who desperately wanted their societies to catch up with the western nations that had dominated them. It is this domination, he believes, that has tainted liberalism's appeal in the Middle East: "The violence and ignorance that we often see today being glorified by a minority of Muslims should in fact be seen as blowback from the Islamic Enlightenment." That blowback was against western-style secularism imposed across the Muslim world during the 20th century—from Turkey to Iran to the Ba'athist Arab states.

Muslim reformers such as Rifa'a al-Tahtawi (1801-1873)—born the year the French left Egypt—were awed by the Napoleonic legacy. Tahtawi travelled to France and wrote a memoir in which he praised its cleanliness, education, intellectual curiosity ("they always want to get to the root of the matter") and lack of pederasty—a common problem in the east. But though Tahtawi was enthused by Europe's "pluralism, freedom and rights," writes de Bellaigue—even translating the "Marseillaise" into Arabic—they also gave him an inferiority complex. So he undertook to trace these same ideas back to the Koran and the Prophet's sayings, sketching the template for later liberal Islamic thinkers.

Islam doesn't stand still—and its changes take many, competing forms. In that same year of 1798, while Napoleon was wading into Egypt, another very different reform movement was undergoing a resurgence: Saudi-Wahhabis rebelled against Ottoman rule in Arabia. The alliance was founded in 1744 by the sheikh Muhammad ibn Saud and theologian Muhammad ibn Abd al-Wahhab, who were a bit like Reformation Puritans. Not only did they want to overthrow their Ottoman masters, they also wanted to purge Islam of cultural accretions they regarded as inauthentic. By 1802 they had sacked Karbala, the holy Shia city; they also targeted Sunni sites, pulling down images and shrines as they conquered Mecca. Medieval Islam brimmed with spirits and saints, Sufism and esoteric philosophy. For the Saudi-Wahhabis, all this was to be pruned in favour of a streamlined, singular Islam.

It would be easy to cast these two movements—the west-facing modernity of Tahtawi and hardline Wahhabi conservatism—as the good guys and the bad guys of Islamic reform, whose descendants are battling it out today. In reality, they were two sides of the same coin. Both were formed in response to imperialism and appealed to a supposed Islamic authenticity. Both disliked the free-wheeling world of pre-modern Islam. And both regarded religion instrumentally, as a vehicle for political and social change. Both Islamic liberalism and political Islamism were—and still are—products of a shared modernity.

One can see the overlap in the Arab thinker Rashid Rida (1865-1935). He advocated latitude in religious interpretation, encouraging Muslims to interpret the Koran with their own reasoning. He accepted Darwin's theory of evolution and said the story of Adam and Eve, which appears in the Koran, was allegorical not literal. Yet he supported the Wahhabis and was fiercely sectarian, declaring that Shiism was "full of fairy tales." Like Napoleon, Rida was convinced he could dispel old superstitions. Being modern meant ditching the mystical Islam of the middle ages and pursuing a disciplined, masculine faith tough enough to take on the British.

For that to happen, western ideas needed to be raided. "Jihad is a binding duty on Muslims," he wrote, "but it is a duty which cannot be performed unless they are strong, and in the modern world they cannot be strong unless they acquire the sciences and techniques of the west." Today, Rida inspires both Muslim liberals and jihadis.

That may sound puzzling, but in fact it makes sense. As Faisal Devji argues in the excellent essay collection *Islam After Liberalism*, in the 20th century, modernity in Muslim countries rarely went hand-in-hand with liberal democracy—think of the secular brutality of Saddam's Iraq. Political slogans about dragging Islam into the contemporary world betray ignorance not only of Islam's long exposure to liberal ideas, but also to the recent political history of the Middle East.

The case of Turkey is one which should give the muscular liberals pause—demonstrating how crackdowns on religion often lead to a dangerous backlash. The 19th century saw a host of reforms under the Ottomans—from telegraph networks, to a professional civil service and the emancipation of religious minorities. These measures culminated in the abolition of the sultanate in 1922. But transforming patchwork Ottoman identities into a singular Turkishness was a violent process. There was no place for Christian Armenians, who were massacred in huge numbers between 1915 and 1917; nor the Kurds, who are still fighting for their own nation.

Kemal Atatürk, the country's secular founder, is often credited with pushing religion into the private sphere and supporting women's rights. Yet he was also a strongman who closed Sufi lodges and banned the Ottoman script, cutting his people off from their roots. The contemporary Islamist resurgence in Turkey attempts to reconnect with that lost past. Once secularists decided that religion was a problem to be stamped out, Islamists could counter-claim that Islam was the solution. When the AKP came to power in 2002, with a platform that included some very modern neo-liberal economics, it turned the Kemalist state on its enemies.

IS are the inheritors of modernity, too. Its founders were originally pro-Saddam secularists who took control of the resistance networks in northern Iraq that the dictator had prepared in the event of his downfall; during the US occupation these networks were hyper-charged with religious zeal. Yet the mass public killings and ideological punishments of IS are more reminiscent of the French Revolution than anything in Islamic history. Even its desperation to recruit westerners—and the prominent roles they give them in beheading videos—show a perverse intimacy with the very people they claim to most hate. IS literature seems super-Islamic, but the approach is quite unlike classical commentaries. Instead the articles read like they were written by western-educated engineers doing a bad impression of a humanities essay—which is what they often are. (See the 2016 book *Engineers of Jihad* by Diego Gambetta and Steffen Hertog.) As De Bellaigue writes: "To its intense irritation, Islamism itself was shot through with Enlightenment values."

While it is true that 19th-century Islamic liberalism did go hand-in-hand with some real improvements, it is important not to confuse cause and effect. Most of the time, theological change caught up with societal change, not the other way round. It was certainly not the ubiquity of some "correct" Islam that nudged things forward; rather, it was the flexibility of the faith that allowed it to adjust.

Take slavery. It had long been central to Islamic societies. It isn't forbidden in the Koran, and the Prophet (like Thomas Jefferson) owned slaves. Yet the texts are ambiguous enough to allow new interpretations. The Koran exhorts equality, and so freeing a slave is highly merited. When the Tunisian leader Ahmed Bey closed the slave markets in the 1840s, he could in conscience declare human bondage was "contrary to religion." Yet there is little evidence he was religiously motivated; he was more likely adjusting to a changing agricultural economy, and a desire to present himself as a "civilised" monarch to the French. A few years later, the Ottomans also started to abolish slavery. "It is a shameful and barbarous practice for rational beings to buy and sell their fellow creatures," said Sultan Abdulmecit. "Are not these poor creatures our equals before God?" Note the order: rationalism first, then religion.

Some clerics grumbled while others fell in line. Since there was no central Islamic authority to declare slavery forbidden, each country went at its own pace—the laggard being Saudi Arabia, which waited until 1962. The orthodox consensus today is that the Prophet had wanted to abolish slavery but was stymied by Arab customs. Only now, the argument runs, are we able to fulfil God's original intentions. Rashid Rida explained the shift as being in "the public interest." This idea of the public interest, or *maslaha*, has been a key component of modern Islamic theology. It is a way of sanctioning huge change without acknowledging anything essential has changed at all. You can see the same phenomenon in Christianity as it reconciles itself to social progress, or indeed in the interpretation of the US constitution which, for many years, was read as compatible with slavery.

Islamic abolition required everyone to tactfully ignore Koranic verses that mention slaves. That's why it caused such a moral crisis when IS gleefully smashed the consensus in 2014. To justify its treatment of Yazidis, an IS magazine claimed that slavery "is a firmly established aspect of the sharia that if one were to deny or mock he would be apostasising from Islam." This is an anachronistic and nakedly self-serving interpretation posing as an ultra-traditional one. It doesn't make IS non-Muslims—liberal Muslims also push scripture to its limits—but it does make them callous and unsophisticated ones. What is vital to note, though, is that IS fighters rape women for the same reason Bashar al-Assad's secular army does the same (on a vaster scale): to exert dominance and spread fear. The only difference is the justification. So they will never be convinced by fatwas telling them what they are doing is un-Islamic—no matter how much that makes Muslims feel better, or softens anti-Muslim feeling in the west.

So what can be done about the problems besetting "the Muslim world"? We could start by questioning that sweeping term. As Cemil Aydin points out in *The Idea of the Muslim World*, "Muslim societies are more divided than ever, riven by civil wars and protracted conflicts across borders"; and they are divergent economically, culturally and politically. Looking at them solely through the lens of a shared religion—practised in very different ways, sometimes hardly practised at all—is an error.

There is too much Islam in Muslim studies. Instead, look to bread-and-butter issues: economic problems; blundering interventions; dictatorships; inequality; climate change. All of these contributed to the rise of IS—religion was merely the activating agent. Ameliorate these problems, give people an accountable government and the chance of a job, and violent religious movements that pretend to hold the answers could lose their allure.

Instead of attempting to impose a narrowing uniformity in the name of modernity, some of the freshest Muslim thinkers are looking to the pre-modern past to imagine a different future. Shahab Ahmed's *What is Islam?*, published shortly before the author's death in 2015, is an erudite love letter to borderline practices—poetry and philosophy, miniature painting and wine-drinking—that flourished before Enlightenment reformers tidied up the faith. The book argues that, far from being backwards obscurantists, medieval Muslims were able to accommodate sophisticated paradoxes better than we moderns. Uniformity was much less easy to enforce without the tools available to the modern state. There is, perhaps, a lesson in that. Turning untamed, vast, diverse Islam into attenuated concoctions such as Islamism or western-certified Islamic liberalism is akin to pouring an ocean into a teacup.

Given the variety in its history, there is no reason why an organic westernised Islam cannot exist alongside all the other kinds—and, contrary to the image of their implacable conservatism, many British Muslims are leading the way. Last summer a Leeds-based imam announced he wanted to set up a national council to issue "progressive" rulings on forced marriage and honour crimes. The UK's Inclusive Mosque initiative—inspired by the African-American scholar Amina Wadud—has experimented with female-led collective prayers. During Ramadan, I was invited to break my fast at the Big Gay Iftar held in London—unthinkable a few years ago.

In a recent review of Simon Schama's ongoing Jewish history, the former Archbishop of Canterbury Rowan Williams challenged the idea of eradicating multiple traditions "in the name of absolute public uniformity," and suggested instead that living together must involve "the harder work of managing the reality that people have diverse religious and cultural identities." For British Muslims—and I suspect for some British Christians like former Lib Dem leader Tim Farron—managing that reality is a daily task: compromising here, staying firm there; abandoning rules that don't make sense, keeping others that work. Islam's many strands will either flourish or pass into history as the social circumstances—and the needs of its adherents—determine they should. The clunky interventions of muscular liberals are unlikely to help since British Muslims are already—like everyone else—in a dynamic adjustment with modernity.

Making such adjustments can be an exhausting process, especially under the keen eyes of boundary-policing Islamists or government watchdogs. But it is also exhilarating to see new cultural hybrids being thrown up. The English convert Tim Winter, also known as Abdul Hakim Murad, runs a Muslim choir in Cambridge. One of his songs is an Arabic hymn in praise of the Prophet set to the tune of an old English folk tune. The words and music match with a breathtaking beauty, and transform seeming opposites into a united whole. For me, that sounds like home.

Economics

Where do we go from here?

The markets have ruled for a third of a century, but it has all ended in tears. A return to selfish nationalism is possible. If we are to avoid this sombre outcome, we must find ways to rub the rough edges off globalisation

Robert Skidelsky

January 2009

Any great failure should force us to rethink. The present economic crisis is a great failure of the market system. As George Soros has rightly pointed out, "the salient feature of the current financial crisis is that it was not caused by some external shock like Opec… the crisis was generated by the system itself." It originated in the US, the heart of the world's financial system and the source of much of its financial innovation. That is why the crisis is global, and is indeed a crisis of globalisation.

There were three kinds of failure. The first was institutional: banks mutated from utilities into casinos. However, they did so because they, their regulators and the policymakers sitting on top of the regulators all succumbed to something called the "efficient market hypothesis": the view that financial markets could not consistently misprice assets and therefore needed little regulation. So the second failure was intellectual. The most astonishing admission was that of former Federal Reserve chairman Alan Greenspan in autumn 2008 that the Fed's regime of monetary management had been based on a "flaw." The "whole intellectual edifice," he said, "collapsed in the summer of last year." Behind the efficient market idea lay the intellectual failure of mainstream economics. It could neither predict nor explain the meltdown because nearly all economists believed that markets were self-correcting. As a consequence, economics itself was marginalised.

But the crisis also represents a moral failure: that of a system built on debt. At the heart of the moral failure is the worship of growth for its own sake, rather than as a way to achieve the "good life." As a result, economic efficiency—the means to growth—has been given absolute priority in our thinking and policy. The only moral compass we now have is the thin and degraded notion of economic welfare. This moral lacuna explains uncritical acceptance of globalisation and financial innovation. Leverage is a duty because it "levers" faster growth. The theological language which would have recognised the collapse of the credit bubble as the "wages of sin," the comeuppance for prodigious profligacy, has become unusable. But the comeuppance has come, nevertheless.

Historians have always been fascinated by cyclical theories of history. Societies are said to swing like pendulums between alternating phases of vigour and decay; progress and reaction; licentiousness and puritanism. Each outward movement produces a crisis of excess which leads to a reaction. The equilibrium position is hard to achieve and always unstable.

In his *Cycles of American History* (1986) Arthur Schlesinger Jr defined a political economy cycle as "a continuing shift in national involvement between public purpose and private interest." The swing he identified was between "liberal" (what we would call social democratic) and "conservative" epochs. The idea of the "crisis" is central. Liberal periods succumb to the corruption of power, as idealists yield to time-servers, and conservative arguments against rent-seeking excesses win the day. But the conservative era then succumbs to a corruption of money, as financiers and businessmen use the freedom of de-regulation to rip off the public. A crisis of under-regulated markets presages the return to a liberal era.

This idea fits the American historical narrative tolerably well. It also makes sense globally. The era of what Americans would call "conservative" economics opened with the publication of Adam Smith's *Wealth of Nations* in 1776. Yet despite the early intellectual ascendancy of free trade, it took a major crisis—the potato famine of the early 1840s—to produce an actual shift in policy: the 1846 repeal of the Corn Laws that ushered in the free trade era.

In the 1870s, the pendulum started to swing back to what the historian AV Dicey called the "age of collectivism." The major crisis that triggered this was the first great global depression, produced by a collapse in food prices. It was a severe enough shock to produce a major shift in political economy. This came in two waves. First, all industrial countries except Britain put up tariffs to protect employment in agriculture and industry. (Britain relied on mass emigration to eliminate rural unemployment.) Second, all industrial countries except the US started schemes of social insurance to protect their citizens against life's hazards. The great depression of 1929-32 produced a second wave of collectivism, now associated with the "Keynesian" use of fiscal and monetary policy to maintain full employment. Most capitalist countries nationalised key industries. Roosevelt's new deal regulated banking and the power utilities, and belatedly embarked on the road of social security. International capital movements were severely controlled everywhere.

This movement was not all one way, or else the west would have ended up with communism, which was the fate of large parts of the globe. Even before the crisis of collectivism in the 1970s, a swing back had started, as trade, after 1945, was progressively freed and capital movements liberalised. The rule was free trade abroad and social democracy at home.

The Bretton Woods system, set up with Keynes's help in 1944, was the international expression of liberal/social democratic political economy. It aimed to free foreign trade after the freeze of the 1930s, by providing an environment that reduced incentives for economic nationalism. At its heart was a system of fixed exchange rates, subject to agreed adjustment, to avoid competitive currency depreciation.

The crisis of liberalism, or social democracy, unfolded with stagflation and ungovernability in the 1970s. It broadly fits Schlesinger's notion of the "corruption of power." The Keynesian/social democratic policymakers succumbed to hubris, an intellectual corruption which convinced them that they possessed the knowledge and the tools to manage and control the economy and society from the top. This was the malady against which Hayek inveighed in his classic *The Road to Serfdom* (1944). The attempt in the 1970s to control inflation by wage and price controls led directly to a "crisis of governability," as trade unions, particularly in Britain, refused to accept them. Large state subsidies to producer groups, both public and private, fed the typical corruptions of behaviour identified by the new right: rent-seeking, moral hazard, free-riding. Palpable evidence of government failure obliterated memories of market failure. The new generation of economists abandoned Keynes and, with the help of sophisticated mathematics, reinvented the classical economics of the self-correcting market. Battered by the crises of the 1970s, governments caved in to the "inevitability" of free market forces. The swing-back became worldwide with the collapse of communism.

A conspicuous casualty of the swing-back was the Bretton Woods system, which succumbed in the 1970s to the refusal of the US to curb its domestic spending. Currencies were set free to float and controls on international capital flows were progressively lifted. This heralded a wholesale change of direction towards free markets and the idea of globalisation. This was, in concept, not unattractive. The idea was that the nation state—which had been responsible for so much organised violence and wasteful spending—was on its way out, to be replaced by the global market. The prospectus was perhaps best set out by the Canadian philosopher, John Ralston Saul, in a 2004 essay in which he proclaimed the collapse of globalisation: "In the future, economics, not politics or arms, would determine the course of human events. Freed markets would quickly establish natural international balances, impervious to the old boom-and-bust cycles. The growth in international trade, as a result of lowering barriers, would unleash an economic-social tide that would raise all ships, whether of our western poor or of the developing world in general. Prosperous markets would turn dictatorships into democracies."

Today we are living through a crisis of conservatism. The financial crisis has brought to a head a growing dissatisfaction with the corruption of money. Neoconservatism has sought to justify fabulous rewards to a financial plutocracy while median incomes stagnate or even fall; in the name of efficiency it has promoted the off-shoring of millions of jobs, the undermining of national communities, and the rape of nature. Such a system needs to be fabulously successful to command allegiance. Spectacular failure is bound to discredit it.

The situation we are in now thus puts into question the speed and direction of progress. Will there be a pause for thought, or will we continue much as before after a cascade of minor adjustments? The answer lies in the intellectual and moral sphere. Is economics capable of rethinking its core principles? What institutions, policies and rules are needed to make markets "well behaved"? Do we have the moral resources to challenge the dominance of money without reverting to the selfish nationalisms of the 1930s?

The enquiry must start with economics. If the case for the deregulated market system is intellectually sound, it will be very hard to change. Free-marketeers claim, contrary to Soros, that the crisis is the fault of governments. US money was kept too cheap for too long after the technology bubble burst in 2000 and the attacks of 11th September 2001. The market was temporarily fooled by the government. This is a shaky defence, to say the least: if the market is so easily fooled, it cannot be very efficient.

One can also argue that the problem is not with the market system, but the fact that markets are too few and inflexible. This seems to be the view of Yale economist Robert J Shiller. He likens the financial system to an early aircraft. Just because it is prone to crash doesn't mean we should stop trying to perfect it. Shiller claims that new derivative products will soon be able to insure homeowners against the risk of house prices going down. To my mind, this is an example of trying to cure a state of inebriation by having another whiskey. There are two things wrong with it. First, if financial innovation is, in fact, the route to greater market efficiency, the financial system would have been getting more stable in the last 25 years of explosive financial engineering. Instead it has become more volatile. Second, the assumption that, given enough innovation, uncertainty can be reduced to risk, is just wrong. There will never be sufficient knowledge to enable contracts to be made to cover all future contingencies.

An analogous argument is that there was not enough marketisation in the global monetary system. Instead of the "clean" floating of currencies, "dirty" floating became the rule. Importantly, China and most of east Asia refused to float their currencies freely. China reverted unilaterally to a form of Bretton Woods, deliberately undervaluing the yuan against the US dollar. The resulting imbalances enabled American consumers to borrow $700bn a year from the parsimonious but super-competitive Chinese, at the cost of losing millions of manufacturing jobs to them. The Chinese saved, the Americans spent, and their debt-fuelled spending created the asset bubbles that led to the credit collapse. This source of instability needs no revision of economic theory, simply the establishment of a free market in foreign currencies. However, the assumption that a world in which currencies were allowed to float freely would be immune from the financial storms we have experienced depends on the belief that currencies will always trade at the correct prices—the global version of the efficient market hypothesis.

A different claim, which goes back to Marx, is that certain structures of economy are less stable than others. Globalisation has increased instability by producing a shift in world GDP shares from wages to profits as the release of low-wage populations into the global economy has undermined the bargaining power of labour in rich countries. This has led to a crisis of under-consumption, staved off only by the expansion of debt (as Gerald Holtham points out, in *Prospect*'s December 2008 issue). There is some truth in this. A greater equality of incomes would create more stable purchasing power.

But the main source of instability lies in the financial markets themselves. And here it is clear that the battle of economic ideas still needs to be fought. Keynes is important in this because he produced the most powerful case for supposing that financial markets are not efficient in the sense required by efficient market theory. As he explained in *The General Theory of Employment, Interest, and Money* (1936), classical economics had ignored the two main causes of systemic financial failure: the existence of (unmeasurable) uncertainty and the role of money as a "store of value." The first led to periodic collapses of confidence; the second led investors to hoard cash if interest rates fell too low, making automatic recovery from collapses difficult. The function of government was to remove the depressive effect of both by giving investors continuous confidence to invest.

Contrary to the belief of some recent economic theories, the future is just as unknowable as Keynes thought it was. The mathematical "quants" who set up the Long Term Capital Management hedge fund in 1994 worked to a risk model which showed that the kind of financial meltdown which, in fact, bankrupted them four years later, could occur only once every four million years. This was not a rationalisation of financial interests: it was self-deception.

What economics needs, therefore, if it is to have any purchase on real world behaviour, is a new starting point. It needs to accept that the changing nature of the world precludes people from having enough information to always make contracts at the "right" prices. Such a change is a necessary condition for a permanent change in policy. Each previous crisis has produced a leading economist with the authority to challenge the prevailing consensus. So the call for a new Keynes is not just rhetorical.

Opinion as to the degree of supervision, regulation and control needed to make a market economy well-behaved is to be found along a continuum. At one end are the free-marketeers who believe only the lightest touch is needed; at the other are classical Marxists who believe it requires public ownership of the whole economy. In between are varieties of social democrats and middle wayers, the most famous of whom is Keynes. This territory is sure to be extensively explored over the next few years as the pendulum starts swinging back. For the question of making markets well behaved goes beyond the question of securing their efficiency. It involves making the market economy compatible with other valued aspects of life. The French social democratic slogan of the mid-1990s—"market economy yes, market society no"—encapsulates the idea that limits should be placed on the power of the market to shape social life according to its own logic.

The battleground will be about the role of the nation-state in the globalising economy of the future, for the nation-state is the main repository and guardian of the values and traditions threatened by the disruptive power of the global market. A paradox of globalisation—which was supposed to see a withering of the nation-state—is that it has led to a revival of nationalism. A deregulated world turned out, unsurprisingly, to be one dominated by the strong. This process reached its apogee with the presidency of George W Bush and the Iraq War—which emphasised US determination to act as a free agent. Other states, too, in Europe and elsewhere, are now acting as semi-free agents. The effective choice is between a more regulated global capitalist system and its possibly violent breakup into a menagerie of warrior nationalisms.

But to ensure we have an ordered system requires us to make globalisation efficient and acceptable. In the course of that debate, I expect one crucial point to emerge: the benefits of globalisation are real, but have been exaggerated. Improvements in the allocation of capital and reductions in opportunities for corruption are offset by increased volatility. Globalisation also raises huge issues of political accountability and social cohesion that are scarcely considered by economists, and only lazily by politicians.

There seem to be four main reasons for this blind spot. The first is the intellectual domination of economics in this debate, with its individualistic and developmental perspective. Globalisation—the integration of markets in goods, services, capital and labour—must be good because it has raised many millions out of poverty in poorer countries faster than would otherwise have been possible. Any interference with this process is impious. A second idea is that it is inevitable: technology—most conspicuously the internet—abolishes national frontiers. Technology cannot be undone. So, whether we like it or not, globalisation is our fate, and our morals and social conventions must adapt to it. The third idea is that globalisation is evolutionary; any check would be regressive. Fourthly, globalisation forces us to think of the world as a unit, which is necessary if we are to solve planet-wide problems.

These are powerful propositions, derived from the era of scarcity and not adjusted to the era of partial abundance, nor to the existence of natural limits to growth. Today the benefits of globalisation are much more obvious for poor than for rich countries. In the 1950s and 1960s, the northern hemisphere was for free trade, the southern protectionist. Today the position is partly reversed. Globalisation offers the best hope for poor countries to catch up with the rich. But growth has become less important for rich countries. In the early 1930s, Keynes thought that the international division of labour could be carried too far. "Let goods be homespun," was the title of an article he wrote in 1932. He wanted a "well-balanced" or "complete" national life, allowing a country to display the full range of its aptitudes, and not simply to be a link in a value-adding productive chain spanning the globe. Moreover, the economic benefits of off-shoring are far from evident for richer states. Since 1997, Britain has lost 1.1m manufacturing jobs—29 per cent of its total—many of them to developing countries. The result has been a dramatic deterioration in Britain's current account balance, and a decline into deficit on the investment income balance too, meaning we pay more to foreign investors in interest and dividends than we receive from abroad. This makes it harder for Britons to pay down their huge debts to the outside world.

Keynes's warning that the pursuit of export-led growth is bound to set nations at each others' throats is still relevant. But that does not mean just sticking as we are. Some rowing back of financial globalisation and cross-border financial institutions is required to rebalance market and state. This process is underway, as national regulators take a tighter grip over the financial institutions they are bailing out. Regulators are increasingly sceptical of banks that depend excessively on wholesale funding. Without this, there will be a natural tendency for banks to shrink back within their own frontiers.

One of the biggest problems with the global trading order remains the enormous arbitrages in tax, labour and non-wage costs that exist. These have encouraged companies to relocate operations, and depressed the bargaining power of labour. Companies like WalMart of the US and Nokia of Finland have been huge outsourcers to Asia. The only solution short of raising barriers is for governments to co-operate in flattening out some of these differences—for China, for example, to increase wages. Ralston Saul has noted that the era of globalisation saw "multiple binding economic treaties... put in place while almost no counterbalancing binding treaties were negotiated for work conditions, taxation, the environment or legal obligations." It will be difficult to create new global systems that balance public good and self interest. But the alternative is the beggar-my-neighbour world of protectionism.

Another way to curb outsourcers would be to use antitrust powers. Breaking up megalithic multinationals would at least prevent them enjoying quasi-monopoly rents, and thus reduce the incentive.

Globalisation is necessarily blind to the idea of political accountability because none exists at the planetary level. Yet the crisis has challenged the idea that we should all unthinkingly follow the logic of the bond market. When the crunch came, we discovered that national taxpayers still stand behind banks, and national insolvency regimes matter. A more rules-based exchange rate system is not inconceivable. This might seek to put some curbs on capital movements—especially at times of economic stress.

And, in this new climate, national politicians are likely to reach for ideas and influences that until recently would have seemed exotic. The idea, for example, that economic growth does not, beyond a certain point, make people happier. David Cameron, a market-friendly Conservative, has talked about the importance of general wellbeing as an alternative to the mania for economic growth. Rich countries could probably abandon the globalist project without much damage to their material standards and with possible gain to their quality of life. Rejecting the inevitability of market-based globalisation would not necessarily be harmful—especially if it were accompanied by a reassertion of democracy at a national level. This is not a pipe dream. New Zealand, which was the first country to attempt to become a post-national nation state in the 1980s with a radical programme of privatisation and deregulation, changed tack in 1999. The electorate endorsed an interventionist government devoted to raising taxes, reimposing economic regulations and establishing a stable private sector. It happened because reform failed to deliver the goods. Other countries may follow suit if the political costs of maintaining a global economy are seen as too high. Rich countries surely have a duty to help poor countries, but not at the expense of an awful way of life.

"Well-behaved" markets should not only be more stable, they should be more morally acceptable. It is indefensible for a top American CEO to earn 367 times more than the average worker (against 40 times in the 1970s). Part of the swing-back in political economy will be to use the tax system to redress the balance between capital and impotent labour.

The crisis has rightly led to a revival of interest in Keynes. But he was a moralist as well as an economist. He believed that material wellbeing is a necessary condition

Rise of the super-family

Is there any room left at the top?

Alison Wolf

May 2013

In the old developed world, where middle incomes are stagnant, today's race goes to the super-family. It's a throwback in many ways. It is tight knit, nuclear, husband-wife-and-kids, but with a twist: two successful, two highly educated, two well-paid parents. And it is a key reason why the top section of society is drawing away from the rest.

The 1970s were the start of it. It was when educated women penetrated every part of the professional labour market. They also started to take less and less time out of work when they had children, and began to earn serious money. Across the rich countries of the OECD, the group of leading developed economies, women now hold half of the "Class I" professional and managerial jobs. These are the jobs of the top sixth of society by income: the jobs of the elite.

This can be hard to square with the flow of stories about unequal pay for women. But highly educated women now have work lives that are very like those of highly educated men, and increasingly different from other women's. I became aware of this newly divided sisterhood some years ago and wrote about it in an article for *Prospect*. But only now is it clear how distinctive elite families have also become.

People at the top marry among themselves. Of course, people have always tended to marry their own kind, a process known as assortative mating. Elizabeth Bennet and Mr Darcy were the fairytale exception to this rule of the marriage market, which Jane Austen observed so acidly. But assortative mating has increased of late.

Partly, this is because women are now more educated. In the past, male doctors couldn't expect to marry female doctors as hardly any existed. Male business executives couldn't marry female ones for the same reason. They married nurses and secretaries instead (many of them very able). But that isn't the whole story. Increases in assortative mating go well beyond what you would expect statistically from the rise in female graduation rates. Like is marrying like to an increasing degree.

Women often suspect that men prefer to marry women much less intelligent than themselves. If that were true, they could certainly have gone on doing so—but they haven't. They want to date, and marry, women like them. You can see this clearly from the US Ivy League, where colleges were strong-armed into admitting women by their own students' preferences.

As recently as the late-1960s, Harvard, Yale and Princeton still lacked a single female undergraduate. Their leaders found it increasingly difficult to justify—and besides, being single-sex was bad for business. They were losing many of their best applicants to co-educational rivals. Alpha men, it turned out, wanted to meet, date, and eventually marry highly educated women like themselves. Alpha women were similarly keen to meet their counterparts; as Oxbridge men's colleges progressively turned co-educational, the women's colleges bled top female students.

You can see what has been happening if you look at British politicians. It is not that long ago that John Major was prime minister; but Norma was the last of the traditional Downing Street wives. Since then, the first families of Downing Street have been two-career graduate partnerships, involving women who were lawyers, designers, journalists, senior civil servants and company directors.

But it is not just assortative mating that marks off the elite. Once married, the graduate professionals are much more likely to stay that way. Among the well-off, intact marriages are still the norm.

It's easy to miss this widening gap between elite marriage patterns and those of everybody else. The media reports the break-ups and the huge settlements of the rich and famous. And we also, most of us, know couples where one would love to marry and the other won't (the latter is usually male).

Nonetheless, the statistics are clear. The majority of elite men marry, and marry women very like themselves. Graduate professionals have divorce rates that are much lower than those of other groups. Right across the developed world, graduate fathers are overwhelmingly likely to be married to the mothers of their children at the time their children are born. And this remains true in societies marked by soaring rates of illegitimacy.

In the European Union as a whole, more than a third of all births in 2009 were to unmarried women. In France, it is over 50 per cent, in the UK it is the upper-40s. In the US, the overall figure is about 40 per cent. But less than 5 per cent of births to white American graduate mothers were extramarital in 1965 and that figure remains unchanged.

British graduates are more likely to have children out of wedlock than Americans, but only one British graduate mother in 30 is single and living alone when she gives birth. Among the cohabiting parents, about 85 per cent of graduate fathers and mothers are married. In the US, among people in their late-twenties and thirties, divorce rates are around twice as high for non-graduates as for graduates.

You wouldn't guess this from contemporary language. "Partner" is now the useful, but also the politically correct, non-judgemental word for any long-term relationship. What is striking is how many people now use it even when referring to their own legal spouse. But look at what elites do, not what they say.

The posterboy for marriage as just-a-lifestyle-choice has for many years been Scandinavia. Social scientists describe a Nordic model and the eminent Danish sociologist, Gøsta Esping-Andersen, claims that "in Scandinavia co-habitation is now de facto the same as marriage." Not according to the data, it isn't. In Sweden (where the overall marriage rate is not, by modern standards, particularly low) the highly educated are almost twice as likely to marry as the less educated, and less likely to divorce. As a Swedish friend remarked, "it's nonsense to claim that there's no difference between marriage and co-habitation. I mean, the King got married."

Today, western societies boast a phalanx of affluent, graduate two-career families, determined to advance the interests of their children. And while elite families don't love their children any more or less than anyone else, their increasingly distinctive family lives put them at a huge advantage.

As recently as the late-1970s, having a first child after the age of 30, let alone 35, was highly unusual for women of any class. For the bulk of society, it still is. In Britain about half of all women who were born here and do not have qualifications are mothers by the age of 22. Other, more educated but non-graduate, women also have their children at what used to be a normal age for everyone, with peak child-bearing between 25 and 29.

But live among today's graduate classes and you might get the impression that no one even contemplates pregnancy until 30 looms. In the UK and France, the proportion of graduates having a baby before 30 has halved in the last few decades. Among American female graduates, the years between age 30 and 35 are now the child-bearing peak. The pattern is international, but only for mothers with full bachelors degrees.

By the time elite families have children, they are a good deal richer than other parents. These are, for the most part, families headed by two adults already well into their careers. Most will avoid the financial fallout of a split. Two really can live more cheaply than one.

The last quarter century has been a period of growing inequality in many developed countries. After the Great Compression of the mid-20th century, inequality has grown again, most markedly in the US, pretty markedly in the UK, but in a lot of other countries too. The ones we notice are the super-rich. We are shocked and infuriated by million-pound bonuses. But it's not just 1 per cent cleaning up, while the other 99 per cent do badly. People in the top 15 per cent, people in jobs that today bring in upward of £45,000, have been doing pretty nicely too, both male and female.

Inequality among men has grown. But inequality among women has also been growing fast—and on many measures even faster. The number of women with seriously large incomes has exploded; gender gaps have vanished among young professionals. The much-cited male-female gap in average pay exists because so many women are in low-paid occupations—care, retail and cleaning—often work part-time, and often drop out of work for years when their children are small.

Childcare costs are extremely high in many countries but, for professionals, paying them is conceivable. Two-career families are the main users of formal childcare, of nurseries as well as nannies. Having money to start with makes it easier to stay in well-paid employment and having money makes it easier to help your children. Elite families typically score in having not just two good salaries but two degrees to draw on during their own children's education, and two sets of useful contacts.

The tendency for children born into the top fifth of the income scale in the developed world to be top fifth as adults is high, and surprisingly uniform. At this level it's the same, generation to generation, in Denmark as in the US, and slightly higher in Sweden than in Britain. (Where Scandinavians are more socially mobile is in movement in and out of the middle.) Elite families are doing a good job of keeping their children prosperous.

Yet these parents are also very anxious, and rightly so. Competition is international. Formal education is ever more important as a gateway to the sunny uplands, and finely tuned CVs are passports to the right schools, the right colleges, the right shortlist. Surveying the globe, families are not sure if anything will be enough.

One result is among the more intriguing findings of contemporary social research. Even though far more mothers are employed than in the post-war decades, the average time spent by parents on active childcare has increased markedly since the 1960s. It has done so for all parents, but it has increased most of all for the most educated.

This is not about being in the house while a child plays video games or (heaven forbid) wanders up the street in search of a friend. It is time when doing something with the child is the main activity. University-educated working mothers in the US and UK, for example, have been doubling their active time. Fathers in all social groups have also increased theirs, but graduate fathers have done so almost twice as much as others. And these are not small time commitments. Graduate mothers in Australia spend an average of two hours a day more on direct childcare than mothers with no upper secondary qualifications, even though they are also more likely to be working full time.

Some of the change may be because we won't let kids roam free any more. But a lot of it is surely anxiety about their futures, not their present safety. Children need to do well from an early age, parents conclude. If activities, chauffeuring, tutoring come at the expense of leisure time, then that is the price that today's parents are determined to pay.

In the late 20th century, university education exploded across the globe. A degree brings large benefits in terms of earnings and opportunities, and many jobs have become graduate only. However, in key respects, education is a positional good, meaning that its value lies partly in how it is perceived by others, and there lies the root of professional parents' angst. It is not just about gaining a skill, as it is when you learn to drive. It is just as much about telling the world, through your educational success, whether you are better than other people, or worse; whether you are cleverer or not so bright. It is about competing. And the best way to signal your quality is to get a degree with a brand attached.

As higher education has boomed, top universities have maintained their grip on routes to the top. Take the year 2010. Oxford-educated David Cameron became prime minister. Cambridge-educated Nick Clegg became his deputy. They faced, across the chamber, the winner of the 2010 contest for leadership of the Labour

Party. This contest had involved five candidates and every one of them was a graduate of Oxford or Cambridge. In the same year, Elena Kagan became a Justice of the Supreme Court of the United States. Her confirmation meant that the nine-member Court had three female justices for the first time. It was also the first time the Court was made up entirely of justices who were educated at either Yale or Harvard law schools.

When universities were few and far between, a university and a top university were much the same thing. But today, name recognition matters ever more. In addition, the more global the economy, the more brand recognition comes from international sources and, increasingly, international league tables. Top families have known this for years. Chancellor Helmut Kohl, for example, was leader of Germany for over 15 years. He was the architect of German reunification, the personification of German tastes in food, drink and holidays. He also sent one son to Harvard and one to MIT.

As the world globalises, as English becomes ever more dominant as a global language but wealth moves east, more and more families have the resources to back their children's futures. And they are mostly in a state of stress. The very scope of higher education on offer creates a winner-take-all situation. Our brains can only cope with a limited number of name brand universities; everyone wants their children to go to one of those.

This makes families everywhere education-obsessed. Houses cost significantly more in the catchment area of a good state school. Out-of-school tutoring is booming across the world; what was once seen as a Japanese eccentricity, or even monstrosity, is now a big UK growth industry. But the families that can really spend on education are the elite, the families whose joint incomes let them buy the most expensive commodity of all—other people's time. Including the time of top teachers.

International boarding schools and top UK public schools cost upwards of £30,000 a year and this can stretch most families' finances. The strains are also particularly clear among the independent day schools of the big cities, where so many two-career families live. In New York, the competition to get one's children into the right (private) nursery leading to the right (private) kindergarten, and on through to high school and a top university, leaves parents exhausted and desperate. In the London borough of Kensington and Chelsea, 43 per cent of pupils now attend independent schools, as do half the white children within the city boundaries of Chicago. Families that can't afford the best private schools, but can afford a move to a leafy suburb, do so.

Elite parents worry about anorexia, drinking and drugs; but the vast majority of their children sign up to the rules for doing well in life. It's not just that they clock up the grades their parents are paying for. The real evidence comes from something else: the age when they first have sexual intercourse, for both boys and girls. It is stark and simple. The worse you are doing academically, the more likely you are to have underage sex, and the higher your grades the more likely you are to start having sex only after age 20. Graduates make up for it later, but at 16, or 18, academic grind can have a big influence on your sex life. Ambitious kids wait.

All these changes mean that family income today has a stronger influence on whether you go to university than it did a few decades ago. That is because it is now more or less automatic that a child from a professional family gets a degree; lower down the income scale, it is still only the most academic. And of course it's not just whether you go to university, it is also where.

The most dramatic example of family influence is the favoured access that American private colleges give to legacy students. These are the children of alumni who are, in turn, a major financial support for any private institution. At Harvard and Princeton, legacies have three or four times as much chance of an offer as other comparable candidates. Europeans, when they hear about this, are deeply shocked. But the substance of European advantage is not so different.

In France a very few super-academic secondary schools, in high-income neighbourhoods populated by city super-families, dominate entry to the Grandes Écoles that train the French elite. In the UK, successive governments have put enormous pressure on top universities to increase the number of students they accept from state schools. But their success has been very limited. It is not clear, in any case, that social justice and social mobility are greatly served if the main beneficiaries of government targets are professional families in suburbs and university towns with good state schools. For the children of the poor, the barriers emerge long before university entry.

In this family-driven society of ours, what of the future? Truthfully, more of the same.

When Michael Young wrote *The Rise of the Meritocracy*, he was not just coining a new word, but writing a satire. The book ends with revolution, as the unselected rise up against a state run on strictly meritocratic lines. Any serious change in today's university entry patterns, any serious attack on top schools, would require a revolution in its turn. No government can rule against its elites for more than a very short time. And all the trends that are drawing today's super-families away from the pack look set to continue into the near future.

There is, however, one counterweight. Many high-earning professionals don't have children, and elite families are mostly small. Top people don't have many children, in part because rearing elite children is a super expensive affair. So even with assortative marriage, even with intensive parenting, and all the right education, there will, still, be some room at the top. But only some.

The hidden rewiring

Accounts of the financial crisis leave out the story of the secretive deals between banks that kept the show on the road. How long can the system be propped up for?

Adam Tooze

August 2017

It is a decade since the first tremors of what would become the Great Financial Crisis began to convulse global markets. Across the world from China and South Korea, to Ukraine, Greece, Brexit Britain and Trump's America it has shaken our economy, our society and latterly our politics. Indeed, it has thrown into question who "we" are. It has triggered both a remarkable wave of nationalism and a deep questioning of social and economic inequalities. Politicians promise their voters that they will "take back control." But the basic framework of globalisation remains intact, so far at least. And to keep the show on the road, networks of financial and monetary co-operation have been pulled tighter than ever before.

In Britain the beginning of the crisis was straight out of economic history's cabinet of horrors. Early in the morning of Monday 14th September 2007, queues of panicked savers gathered outside branches of the mortgage lender Northern Rock on high streets across Britain. It was—or at least so it seemed—a classic bank run. Within the year the crisis had circled the world. Wall Street was shaking, as was the City of London. The banks of South Korea, Russia, Germany, France, Belgium, the Netherlands, Ireland and Iceland were all in trouble. We had seen nothing like it since 1929. Soon enough Ben Bernanke, then chairman of the US Federal Reserve and an expert on the Great Depression, said that this time it was worse.

But the fact that the tumult assumed such spectacular, globe-straddling dimensions had initially taken Bernanke by surprise. In May 2007 he reassured the public that he didn't think American subprime mortgages could bring down the house. Clearly he underestimated the crisis. But was he actually wrong? For it certainly wasn't subprime that brought down Northern Rock. The British bank didn't have any exposure in the United States. So what was going on?

The familiar associations evoked by the Northern Rock crisis were deceptive. It wasn't panicking pensioners all scrambling to withdraw their savings at once that killed the bank. It wasn't even the Rock's giant portfolio of mortgages. The narrative of Michael Lewis's *The Big Short*, of securitisation, pooling and tranching, the lugubrious details of trashy mortgage dealing, the alphabet soup of securitised loans and associated derivatives (MBS, CDO, CDS, CDO-squared) tell only one part of the story. What really did for banks like Northern Rock and for all the others that would follow—Bear Stearns, Merrill Lynch, Lehman, Hypo Real Estate, Dexia and many more—and what made this downturn different— so sharp, so sudden and so systemic, not just a recession but the Great Recession—was the implosion of a new system not just of bank lending, but of bank funding.

It is only when we examine both sides of the balance sheet—the liabilities as well as the assets—that we can appreciate how the crisis was propagated, and then how it was ultimately contained at a global level. It is a story that the crisis-fighters have chosen not to celebrate or publicise. Ten years on, the story is worth revisiting, not only to get the history right, but because the global fix that began to be put in place in the autumn of 2007 is in many ways the most significant legacy of the crisis. It is still with us today and remains largely out of sight. The hidden rewiring of the global monetary system provides reassurance to those in the know, but it has no public or political standing, no resources with which to fight back if attacked. And this matters because it is increasingly out of kilter with the nationalist turn of politics.

In the wake of the crash and its austere aftermath, voters in many countries have pointed the finger at globalisation. The monetary authorities, however, have quietly entwined themselves more closely than ever before—and they have done so in order to provide life support to that bank funding model which caused such trouble a decade ago. Ten years on, the question of whether this fix is sustainable, or indeed wise, is a question of more than historical interest.

In 2007 economists were expecting a crisis. Not, however, the crisis they got. The standard crisis scenario through to autumn that year involved a sudden loss of confidence in American government debt and the dollar. In the Bush era, the Republicans had cut taxes and spent heavily on the War on Terror, borrowing from China. So what would happen, it was asked anxiously, if the Chinese pulled the plug? The great fear was that the dollar would plunge, interest rates would soar and both the US economy and the Chinese export sector would crash land. It was what Larry Summers termed a balance of financial terror. America's currency seemed so doomed that in autumn 2007, the US-based supermodel Gisele Bündchen asked to be paid in euros for a Pantene campaign, and Jay-Z dissed the dollar on MTV.

But somewhat surprisingly, like the nuclear stand-off in the Cold War, the financial balance of terror has become the basis for a precarious stability. Crucially, both Beijing and Washington understand the risks involved, or at least they seemed to until the advent of President Donald Trump. Certainly during the most worrying moments in 2008 Hank Paulson, Bush's last treasury secretary, made sure that Beijing understood that its interests would be protected. Beijing reciprocated by increasing its commitment to dollar assets.

In 2007, it was not the American state that lost credibility: it was the American housing market. What unfolded was a fiasco of the American dream: 8.7m homes were lost to foreclosure. But the real estate bust wasn't limited to the US. Ireland, Spain, the UK and the Netherlands all had huge credit booms and suffered shattering busts. As homeowners defaulted some lenders went under. This is what happened early on to predatory lenders such as New Century and Countrywide. Bankruptcy also came to the Anglo Irish Bank and Spain's notorious regional mortgage lenders, the *cajas*. In the fullness of time, it was—perhaps, though not necessarily—the fate that might well have befallen Northern Rock too. But before it could suffer death by a thousand foreclosures, Northern Rock was felled by a more fast-acting kind of crisis, a crisis of "maturity mismatch."

Banks borrow money short-term at low interest and lend long at marginally higher rates. It may sound precarious, but it is how they earn their living. In the conventional model, however, the short-term funding comes from deposits, from ordinary savers. Ordinarily, in a well-run bank, their withdrawals and deposits tend to cancel each other out. Fits of uncertainty and mass withdrawals are always possible, and perhaps even inevitable once in a while. So to prevent them turning into bank runs, governments offer guarantees up to a reasonable amount. Most of the Northern Rock depositors had little to fear. Their deposits were, like all other ordinary savers, guaranteed by then Chancellor Alistair Darling. The investors who weren't covered by government backing were those who had provided Northern Rock with funding through a new and different channel—the wholesale money market. They had tens of billions at stake, and every reason to panic. It was the sudden withdrawal of this funding that actually killed Northern Rock.

As well as taking in money from savers, banks can also borrow from other banks and other institutional investors. The money markets offer funds overnight, or for a matter of weeks or months. It is a fiercely competitive market with financial professionals on both sides of every trade. Margins are slim, but if the volumes are large there are profits to be made. For generations this was the preserve of investment bankers—the ultimate insiders of the financial community. They didn't bother with savers' deposits. They borrowed in the money markets. From the 1990s commercial banks and mortgage lenders began to operate on a similar model. It was this new form of "market-based" banking combined with the famous securitisation of mortgages that enabled the huge expansion of European and US banking that began to crash in 2007.

By the summer of 2007 only 23 per cent of Northern Rock's funding came from regular deposits. More than three quarters of its operation was sustained by borrowing in capital and money markets.

For these funds there were no guarantees. For a run to develop in the money market, the mortgages did not need to default. All that needed to happen was for the probability of some of them defaulting to increase. That was enough for interbank lending and money market funding to come abruptly to a halt. The European money markets seized up on 9th August. Within a matter of days Northern Rock was in trouble, struggling to repay short-term loans with no new source of funding in prospect. And it was through the same funding channel that the crisis went global.

The attraction of money market funding was that it freed you from the cumbersome bricks-and-mortar branch network traditionally used to attract deposits. Using the markets, banks could source funding all over the world. South Korean banks borrowed dollars on the cheap to lend in Won. American banks operating out of London borrowed Yen in depressed Japan, flipped them into dollars and then lent them to booming Brazil. The biggest business of all was the "round tripping" of dollars between America and Europe. Funds were raised in America, which for reasons of history and the nation's sheer scale, is the richest money market in the world. Those dollars were exported to institutions and banks in Europe, who then reinvested them in the US, very often in American mortgages. The largest inflow of funds to the US came not from the reinvestment of China's trade surplus, but through this recycling of dollars by way of Europe's banks. Barclays didn't need a branch in Kansas any more than Lehman did. Both simply borrowed money in the New York money markets. From the 1990s onwards, Europe's banks, both great and small, British, Dutch, Belgian, French, Swiss and German, made themselves into a gigantic trans-Atlantic annex of the American banking system.

All was well so long as the economy was buoyant, house and other asset prices continued to go up, money markets remained confident and the dollar moved predictably in the direction that everyone expected, that is gently downwards. If you were borrowing dollars to fund a lending business the three things that you did not want to have happen were: for your own loans to go bad; money markets to lose confidence; or for dollars to suddenly become scarce, or, what amounts to the same thing, unexpectedly expensive. While the headlines were about sub-prime, the true catastrophe of the late summer of 2007 was that all three of these assumptions were collapsing, all at once, all around the world.

The real estate market turned down. Large losses were in the pipeline, over years to come. But as soon as Bear Stearns and Banque Nationale de Paris (BNP) shut their first real estate funds, the money markets shut down too. Given the global nature of bank funding this produced an acute shortage of dollar funding across the European and Asian banking system. It was the opposite of what the best and brightest in macroeconomics had expected: strong currencies are, after all, meant to be built on thrift and industry, not shopping splurges and speculative debts. But rather than the world being glutted with dollars, quite suddenly banks both in Europe and Asia began to suffer periodic and panic-inducing dollar shortages.

The paradigmatic case of this counterintuitive crisis would eventually be South Korea. How could South Korea, a champion exporter with huge exchange reserves be short of dollars? The answer is that in the years of the recovery from the 1997 East Asian crisis, while Korean companies Hyundai and Samsung had conquered the world, Korea's banks had been borrowing dollars at relatively low interest rates to lend out back home in Won to the booming home economy. Not only was there an attractive interest rate margin, but thanks to South Korea's bouyant exports, the Won was steadily appreciating. Loans taken out in dollars were easier to repay in Won. As such these loans cushioned the losses suffered by South Korean firms on their dollar export-earnings.

By the late summer of 2008 the South Korean banks operating this system owed $130bn in short-term loans. Normally this was no problem: you rolled over the loan, taking out a new short-term dollar credit to pay off the last one. But when the interbank market ground to a halt the South Koreans were painfully exposed. Barring emergency help, all they could do was to throw Won at the exchange markets to buy the dollars they needed, which had the effect of spectacularly devaluing their own currency and making their dollar obligations even more unpayable. South Korea, a country with a huge trade surplus and a large official dollar reserve, faced a plunging currency and a collapsing banking system.

In Europe the likes of RBS, Barclays, UBS and Deutsche had even larger dollar liabilities than their South Korean counterparts. The BIS, the central bankers' bank, estimated that Europe's mega-banks needed to roll over $1-1.2 trillion in short-term funding. The margin that desperate European banks were willing to pay to borrow in sterling and euro and to swap into dollars surged. Huge losses threatened—and both the Bank of England and the European Central Bank (ECB) could not do much to help. Unlike their East Asian counterparts, they had totally inadequate reserves.

The one advantage that the Europeans did have over the Koreans was that the dollars they had borrowed had largely been invested in the US, the so-called "round-tripping" again. The huge portfolios of American assets they had accumulated were of uncertain value, but they amounted to trillions of dollars and somewhere between 20 and 25 per cent of the total volume of asset- and mortgage-backed securities. In extremis the Europeans could have auctioned them off. This would have closed the dollar-funding gap, but in the resulting fire sales the European banks would have been forced to take huge write downs. And most significantly, the efforts by the Fed and the US Treasury to stabilise the American mortgage market would have been fatally undercut.

This was the catastrophic causal chain that began to emerge in August 2007. How could the central banks address it? The answer they found was three-pronged. The most public face of crisis-fighting was the effort to boost the faltering value of the mortgage bonds on the banks' books (typically securitised versions of other banks' mortgage loans, which were becoming less reliable in the downturn), and to provide the banks with enough capital to absorb those losses that they would inevitably suffer. This was the saga of America's Troubled Asset Relief Programme, which played out on Capitol Hill. In the case of Northern Rock this prong involved outright nationalisation. Others took government stakes of varying sizes. Warren Buffett made a lucrative investment in Goldman Sachs. Barclays has now been charged by the Serious Fraud Office with fraudulently organising its own bailout, by—allegedly—lending money to Qatar, which that state is then said to have reinvested in Barclays. Without the bailout, you ended up with Lehman: bewildered bankers standing on the pavements of the City and Wall Street carrying boxes of their belongings. The masters of the universe plunged to earth. It half-satisfied the public's desire for revenge. But it did nothing for business confidence.

With enough capital a bank could absorb losses and stay afloat. But to actually operate, to make loans and thus to sustain demand and avert a downward spiral of prices and more bankruptcies, the banks needed liquidity. So, secondly, the central banks stepped in, taking over the function, which the money market had only relatively recently assumed but was now suddenly stepping back from, of being the short-term lenders. The ECB started as early as August 2007. The Bank of England came in late, but on a large scale. The Fed became the greatest liquidity pump, with all of Europe's banks benefiting from its largesse. The New York branches of Barclays, Deutsche, BNP, UBS and Credit Suisse were all provided with short-term dollar funding on the same basis as Citi, Bank of America, JP Morgan and the rest.

But it was not enough. The Europeans needed even more dollars. So the Fed's third, final and most radical innovation of the crisis was to devise a system to allow a select group of central banks to funnel dollars to their banks. To do so the Fed reanimated an almost-forgotten tool called the "swap lines," agreements between central banks to trade their currencies in a given quantity for a given period of time. They had been used regularly in the 1960s, but had since gone out of use. Back then, the aim was stabilising exchange rates. This time, the aim was different: to stabilise a swollen banking system that was faltering, and yet abjectly too big to fail. At a moment when dollars were hard to come by, the new swap lines enabled the ECB to deposit euros with the Fed in exchange for the dollars that the eurozone banks were craving. The Bank of England benefited from the same privilege.

Not that they were welcome at first. When the Fed first mooted the idea in the autumn of 2007, the ECB resisted. It did not want to be associated with a crisis that was still seen largely as American. If Gisele didn't want to be paid her modelling fees in US dollars, why on earth should the ECB be interested? But as the European bank balance sheets unravelled, it would soon become obvious that Frankfurt needed all the dollars it could get. Initiated in December 2007, the swap lines would rapidly expand. By September all the major European central banks were included. In October 2008 the network was expanded to include Brazil, Australia, South Korea, Mexico, New Zealand and Singapore. For the inner European core, plus Japan, they were made unrestricted in volume. The sums of liquidity were huge. All told, the Fed would make swap line loans of a total of $10 trillion to the ECB, the Bank of England the National Bank of Switzerland and other major banking centres. The maximum balance outstanding was $583bn in December 2008, when they accounted for one quarter of the Fed's balance sheet.

It was a remarkable moment: the Fed had effectively established itself as a lender of last resort to the entire global financial system. But it had done so in a decentralised fashion, issuing dollars on demand both in New York and by means of a global network of central banks. Not everyone was included. Russia wasn't, which was hardly surprising given that it had come to blows with the west over Georgia's Nato membership application only weeks earlier. Nor did the Fed help China or India.

And though it helped the ECB, it did not provide support to the "new Europe" in the east. The Fed probably imagined that the ECB itself would wish to help Poland, the Baltics and Hungary. But the ECB's president Jean-Claude Trichet was not so generous. Instead, eastern Europe ended up having to rely on the International Monetary Fund (IMF).

The swap lines were central bank to central bank. But who did they really help? The reality, as all those involved understood, was that the Fed was providing preferential access to liquidity not to the "euro area" or "the Swiss economy" as a whole, but to Deutsche Bank and Credit Suisse. Of course, the justification was "systemic risk." The mantra in Washington was: you have to help Wall Street to help Main Street. But the immediate beneficiaries were the banks, their staff, especially their highly-remunerated senior staff and their shareholders.

Though what the Fed was doing was stabilising the global banking system, it never acknowledged as much in so many words, certainly not on the record, where it said as little as it decently could about the swap line operation. The Fed's actions have global effects. But it remains an American institution, answerable to Congress. Its mandate is to maintain employment and price stability in the US economy. The justification for the swap lines, therefore, was not global stability, but the need to prevent blowback from Europe's de facto Americanised banks—to avoid a ruinous, multi-trillion-dollar fire sale of American assets. Once the worst of the crisis had passed, Bernanke would assist the European banks in liquidating their American assets by way of the Fed's three rounds of asset purchases, known as quantitative easing (QE).

The swaps were meticulously accounted for. Every cent was repaid. No losses were incurred—the Fed even earned a modest profit. They were not exactly covert. But given the extraordinary extension of its global influence that the swaps implied, they were never given publicity, nor even properly discussed. Bernanke's name will be forever associated with QE, not swap lines. In his lengthy memoirs, *The Courage to Act*, the swaps merit no more than a few cursory pages, though Bernanke as a scholar of the 1930s knows very well just how crucial these instruments were. Is this an accident? Surely not. In the case of the swap lines, the courage to act was supplemented by an ample measure of discretion.

The Fed did everything it could to avoid disclosing the full extent and range of beneficiaries of its liquidity support operations. They did not want to name and shame the most vulnerable banks, for fear of worsening the panic. But there are politics involved too. Given the rise of the Bernanke-hating Tea Party in 2009, the likely response in Congress to news headlining the scale of the Fed's global activity was unpredictable to say the least. When asked why no one on Capitol Hill had chosen to make an issue of the swap lines, one central banker remarked to me that it felt as though "the Fed had an angel watching over it."

One other reason for the tight lips is that the story of the swap lines is not yet over. The network was rolled out in 2007 and 2008 as an emergency measure, but since then it has become the under-girding of a new system of global financial crisis management. In October 2013, as the Fed prepared finally to begin the process of normalisation by "tapering" its QE bond purchases, it made another decision which made plain that the new normal would not be like the old. It turned the global dollar swap line system into a standing facility: that is to say, it made its emergency treatment for the crisis into a permanent feature of the global monetary system. On demand, any of the core group of central banks can now activate a swap line with any other member of the group. Most recently the swap line system was readied for activation in the summer of 2016 in case of fallout from the Brexit referendum.

As the original crisis unfolded in 2008, radical voices like Joseph Stiglitz in the west, and central bankers in the big emerging economies called for a new Bretton Woods Conference—the meeting in 1944, which had decided on the post-war currency system and the creation of the IMF and the World Bank. The Great Financial Crisis had demonstrated that the dollar's exorbitant privilege was a recipe for macroeconomic imbalances. The centre of gravity in the world economy was inexorably shifting. It was time for a new grand bargain.

What these visionary suggestions failed to register was that foundation of the world's de facto currency system were not public institutions like the IMF, but the private, dollar-based global banking system. The introduction of the swap lines gave that system unprecedented state support. The Fed had ensured that the crisis in global banking did not become a crisis of the dollar. It had signalled that global banks could rely on access to dollar liquidity in virtually unlimited amounts, even in the most extreme circumstances. The central banks had, in other words, staged their Bretton Woods 2.0. But they had omitted to invite the cameras or the public, or indeed to explain what they were doing.

The new central bank network created since 2008 is of a piece with the new networks for stress testing and regulating the world's systemically important banks. The international economy they regulate is not one made up of a jigsaw puzzle of national economies, each with its gross national product and national trade flows. Instead they oversee, regulate and act on the interlocking, transnational matrix of bank balance sheets.

This system was put in place without fanfare. It was essential to containing the crisis, and so far it has operated effectively. But to make this technical financial network into the foundation for a new global order is a gamble.

It worked on the well-established trans-Atlantic axis. But will it work as effectively if it is asked to contain the fallout from an East Asian financial crisis? Can it continue to operate below the political radar, and is it acceptable for it to do so? With the Fed in the lead it places the resources, expertise and authority of the world's central banks behind a market-based system of banking that has shown its capacity for over-expansion and catastrophic collapse. For all the talk of "macroprudential" regulation, Basel III and Basel IV, rather than disarming, down-sizing and constraining the global banking system, we have—through the swap lines—embarked on, if you like, a regulatory race to the top, where the authorities intervene heavily to allow the big banks in some countries to continue what they were doing before the unsustainable ceased to be sustained. And without even the political legitimacy conferred by G20 approval. Not everyone in the G20 is part of the swap line system.

The Fed's safety net for global banking was born at the fag-end of the "great moderation," the era when economies behaved nicely and predictably, and when a "permissive consensus" enabled globalisation. Though a child of crisis, it bore the technocratic, "evidence-based" hall marks of that earlier era. It bears them still.

Can it survive in an age when the United States is being convulsed by a new wave of economic nationalism? Is there still a guardian angel watching over the Fed on Capitol Hill? And with Trump in the White House, how loudly should we even ask the question?

Culture and ideas

Wittgenstein and the two cultures

Wittgenstein's philosophy is at odds with the scientism which dominates our times. But his thought is still relevant

Ray Monk

July 1999

Ludwig Wittgenstein is regarded by many, including myself, as the greatest philosopher of this century. His two great works, *Tractatus Logico-Philosophicus* (1921) and *Philosophical Investigations* (published posthumously in 1953) have done much to shape subsequent developments in philosophy, especially in the analytic tradition. His charismatic personality has fascinated artists, playwrights, poets, novelists, musicians and even movie-makers, so that his fame has spread far beyond the confines of academic life.

And yet in a sense Wittgenstein's thought has made very little impression on the intellectual life of this century. As he himself realised, his style of thinking is at odds with the style that dominates our present era. His work is opposed, as he once put it, to "the spirit which informs the vast stream of European and American civilisation in which all of us stand." Nearly 50 years after his death, we can see, more clearly than ever, that the feeling that he was swimming against the tide was justified. If we wanted a label to describe this tide, we might call it "scientism," the view that every intelligible question has either a scientific solution or no solution at all. It is against this view that Wittgenstein set his face.

Scientism takes many forms. In the humanities, it takes the form of pretending that philosophy, literature, history, music and art can be studied as if they were sciences, with "researchers" compelled to spell out their "methodologies"—a pretence which has led to huge quantities of bad academic writing, characterised by bogus theorising, spurious specialisation and the development of pseudo-technical vocabularies. Wittgenstein would have looked upon these developments and wept.

There are many questions to which we do not have scientific answers, not because they are deep, impenetrable mysteries, but simply because they are not scientific questions. These include questions about love, art, history, culture, music—all questions, in fact, that relate to the attempt to understand ourselves better. There is a widespread feeling today that the great scandal of our times is that we lack a scientific theory of consciousness. And so there is a great interdisciplinary effort, involving physicists, computer scientists, cognitive psychologists and philosophers, to come up with tenable scientific answers to the questions: what is consciousness? What is the self? One of the leading competitors in this crowded field is the theory advanced by the mathematician Roger Penrose, that a stream of consciousness is an orchestrated sequence of quantum physical events taking place in the brain. Penrose's theory is that a moment of consciousness is produced by a sub-protein in the brain called a tubulin. The theory is, on Penrose's own admission, speculative, and it strikes many as being bizarrely implausible. But suppose we discovered that Penrose's theory was correct, would we, as a result, understand ourselves any better? Is a scientific theory the only kind of understanding?

Well, you might ask, what other kind is there? Wittgenstein's answer to that, I think, is his greatest, and most neglected, achievement. Although Wittgenstein's thought underwent changes between his early and his later work, his opposition to scientism was constant. Philosophy, he writes, "is not a theory but an activity." It strives, not after scientific truth, but after conceptual clarity. In the *Tractatus*, this clarity is achieved through a correct understanding of the logical form of language, which, once achieved, was destined to remain inexpressible, leading Wittgenstein to compare his own philosophical propositions with a ladder, which is thrown away once it has been used to climb up on.

In his later work, Wittgenstein abandoned the idea of logical form and with it the notion of ineffable truths. The difference between science and philosophy, he now believed, is between two distinct forms of understanding: the theoretical and the non-theoretical. Scientific understanding is given through the construction and testing of hypotheses and theories; philosophical understanding, on the other hand, is resolutely non-theoretical. What we are after in philosophy is "the understanding that consists in seeing connections."

Non-theoretical understanding is the kind of understanding we have when we say that we understand a poem, a piece of music, a person or even a sentence. Take the case of a child learning her native language. When she begins to understand what is said to her, is it because she has formulated a theory? We can say that if we like—and many linguists and psychologists have said just that—but it is a misleading way of describing what is going on. The criterion we use for saying that a child understands what is said to her is that she behaves appropriately—she shows that she understands the phrase "put this piece of paper in the bin," for example, by obeying the instruction.

Another example close to Wittgenstein's heart is that of understanding music. How does one demonstrate an understanding of a piece of music? Well, perhaps by playing it expressively, or by using the right sort of metaphors to describe it. And how does one explain what "expressive playing" is? What is needed, Wittgenstein says, is "a culture": "If someone is brought up in a particular culture—and then reacts to music in such-and-such a way, you can teach him the use of the phrase 'expressive playing.'" What is required for this kind of understanding is a form of life, a set of communally shared practices, together with the ability to hear and see the connections made by the practitioners of this form of life.

What is true of music is also true of ordinary language. "Understanding a sentence," Wittgenstein says in *Philosophical Investigations*, "is more akin to understanding a theme in music than one may think." Understanding a sentence, too, requires participation in the form of life, the "language-game," to which it belongs. The reason computers have no understanding of the sentences they process is not that they lack sufficient neuronal complexity, but that they are not, and cannot be, participants in the culture to which the sentences belong. A sentence does not acquire meaning through the correlation, one to one, of its words with objects in the world; it acquires meaning through the use that is made of it in the communal life of human beings.

All this may sound trivially true. Wittgenstein himself described his work as a "synopsis of trivialities." But when we are thinking philosophically we are apt to forget these trivialities and thus end up in confusion, imagining, for example, that we will understand ourselves better if we study the quantum behaviour of the subatomic particles inside our brains, a belief analogous to the conviction that a study of acoustics will help us understand Beethoven's music. Why do we need reminding of trivialities? Because we are bewitched into thinking that if we lack a scientific theory of something, we lack any understanding of it.

One of the crucial differences between the method of science and the non-theoretical understanding that is exemplified in music, art, philosophy and ordinary life, is that science aims at a level of generality which necessarily eludes these other forms of understanding. This is why the understanding of people can never be a science. To understand a person is to be able to tell, for example, whether he means what he says or not, whether his expressions of feeling are genuine or feigned. And how does one acquire this sort of understanding? Wittgenstein raises this question at the end of *Philosophical Investigations*. "Is there," he asks, "such a thing as 'expert judgment' about the genuineness of expressions of feeling?" Yes, he answers, there is.

But the evidence upon which such expert judgments about people are based is "imponderable," resistant to the general formulation characteristic of science. "Imponderable evidence," Wittgenstein writes, "includes subtleties of glance, of gesture, of tone. I may recognise a genuine loving look, distinguish it from a pretended one… But I may be quite incapable of describing the difference… If I were a very talented painter I might conceivably represent the genuine and simulated glance in pictures."

But the fact that we are dealing with imponderables should not mislead us into believing that all claims to understand people are spurious. When Wittgenstein was once discussing his favourite novel, *The Brothers Karamazov*, with Maurice Drury, Drury said that he found the character of Father Zossima impressive. Of Zossima, Dostoevsky writes: "It was said that… he had absorbed so many secrets, sorrows, and avowals into his soul that in the end he had acquired so fine a perception that he could tell at the first glance from the face of a stranger what he had come for, what he wanted and what kind of torment racked his conscience." "Yes," said

Wittgenstein, "there really have been people like that, who could see directly into the souls of other people and advise them."

"An inner process stands in need of outward criteria," runs one of the most often quoted aphorisms of *Philosophical Investigations*. It is less often realised what emphasis Wittgenstein placed on the need for sensitive perception of those "outward criteria" in all their imponderability. And where does one find such acute sensitivity? Not, typically, in the works of psychologists, but in those of the great artists, musicians and novelists. "People nowadays," Wittgenstein writes in *Culture and Value*, "think that scientists exist to instruct them, poets, musicians, etc. to give them pleasure. The idea that these have something to teach them-that does not occur to them."

At a time like this, when the humanities are institutionally obliged to pretend to be sciences, we need more than ever the lessons about understanding that Wittgenstein—and the arts—have to teach us.

The heroic absurdity of Dan Brown

The less his talent, the more amazing his achievement

Clive James

July 2013

Inferno
By Dan Brown (Bantam)

As a believer in the enjoyably awful, I would recommend this book wholeheartedly if I could. But it is mainly just awful. Nevertheless it is still almost worth reading. In the publishing world they have a term, "pull line," which means the few words of apparent praise that you can sometimes pull out of a review however hostile. Let me supply that pull line straight away, ready furnished with quotation marks: "The author of *The Da Vinci Code* has done it again."

Once again, that is, he makes you want to turn the pages even though every page you turn demonstrates abundantly his complete lack of talent as a writer. The narrative might be a bit less compulsive this time but you still want to follow it, if only to find out whether the hero and the heroine will ever get together. But to do that, they will first have to stop running to escape the heavies.

Discussing Dante even as they run, they are a handsome couple, the hero and the heroine, rather like Robert Donat and Madeleine Carroll in *The 39 Steps*. The hero we already know. He is Robert Langdon, fresh from his activities as the "symbologist" who cracked the code associated with the famous painter whose surname was Da Vinci. (If Dan Brown's all-time bestseller had been about the Duke of Edinburgh, it would have been called *The Of Edinburgh Code.*)

Langdon, though an American, still favours English tailoring. It must be easier to run in. Running beside him is Dr Sienna Brooks, described as a "pretty, young woman," in keeping with Dan Brown's gift for inserting the fatal extra comma that he or one of his editors believes to be a sign of literacy. And indeed I should perhaps have written "the fatal, extra comma," but something stopped me: an ear for prose, I hope.

Dan Brown has no ear for prose at all, a handicap which paradoxically gives pathos, and even tenderness, to his attempts at evoking Sienna's charm. He has no trouble evoking her brains. She has an IQ of 208 and at the age of four she was reading in three languages. You can picture the author at his desk, meticulously revising his original sentence in which, at the age of three, she was reading in four languages. Best to keep it credible. But how to register her beauty as an adult? Here goes: "Tall and lissom, Dr Brooks moved with the assertive gait of an athlete."

Would that be the assertive gait of a Russian female weightlifter? Probably more like the assertive gait of the British pentathlete Jessica Ennis. Anyway, as usual with a bad writer, the reader has to do most of the imagining. A canny bad writer keeps out of the way so that the reader's mind can get to work with its own stock of clichés, but Dan Brown shows deadly signs of an ambition to add poetry to his prose. Take, from quite early in the book, his chilling portrait of the beautiful female assassin who is stalking the heroic couple as they flee from one famous location in Florence to another. Later on they will flee from one famous location to another in other famous cities, notably Venice and Istanbul, but early on they are stuck in the famous city of Florence, being hunted down by the beautiful female assassin whose name is Vayentha. How can she be described, in view of the fact that all the "tall and lissom" adjectives have already been lavished on Sienna? Langdon looks out of the window, and there she is:

"Outside his window, hidden in the shadows of the Via Torregalli, a powerfully built woman effortlessly unstraddled her BMW motorcycle and advanced with the intensity of a panther stalking its prey. Her gaze was sharp. Her close-cropped hair—styled into spikes—stood out against the upturned collar of her black leather riding suit. She checked her silenced weapon, and stared up at the window where Robert Langdon's light had just gone out."

That counts as a long paragraph for Dan Brown. Generally he believes that a short paragraph will add pace, just as he believes that an ellipsis will add thoughtfulness. Groups of three dots appear in innumerable places, giving the impression that the narrative ... has measles. This impression is appropriate, because the famous symbologist and the pretty, young woman are actually impelled by their mission to save the world from plague. It isn't just because the heavies are after them that they are always in such a hurry.

In fact the heavies turn out not to be so heavy after all. They, too, are out to save the world, which must surely soon die unless its population is drastically reduced. How this can be done is the central question raised by the book, unless you think that the central question raised by the book is how it ever got published. Dan Brown and all his characters take it for granted that a Malthusian interpretation of earthly existence must be correct. The fact that Malthus turned out to be wrong doesn't slow them down for a moment. They just keep running, always one step ahead of whichever panther-like assassin is unstraddling herself from her BMW just behind them.

Eventually they get to where they would never have thought of running to if it had not been for Robert Langdon's skills as a symbologist. I had better not reveal how it all comes out: there might be a few readers of this review who have not already read the book. But just in case you haven't, let me suggest that it ends the way it began, as a fizzer. Your enjoyment will eventually depend on how much you, in your role as a symbologist, can revel in the task of decoding the text to lay bare the full extent to which the author can't write.

The less he can write, of course, the more admirable his achievement. As well as the heroism of Robert Langdon, we must think of the heroism of Dan Brown. This is a man who started out with such a shaky grasp of the English language that he still thinks "foreboding" is an adjective meaning "ominous." I also relished "Sienna changed tacks." Read aloud, these three words would suggest that the pretty, young woman had altered her arrangement with the Internal Revenue Service. But Dan Brown has never read one of his own sentences aloud in all his life; and why, now, would he need to? He can buy and sell all the pedants in the world.

On top of the shaky language are piled the solecisms. "Pandora is out of her box." (Dan, she was never in it.) Piled on top of the solecisms there are the outright mistakes. The C-130 in which the World Health Authority task force travels is called a "transport jet." It should be a turboprop. In Istanbul, "the Bentley roared away from the curb." The last Bentley that ever roared was racing at Brooklands before the Second World War. But at least he tried to tart up his text with the occasional everyday fact.

More questionable is when the fact is from a higher realm of experience and comes accompanied by a judgment. Brown has put prodigies of effort into mugging up the scholarly background of his story, but the laborious deployment of learned lore is too often undermined by signs that he can't tell one painting or piece of sculpture from another, even though he knows all the names and has seen every masterpiece from close up. (Some of them are probably hanging in his house by now; he must have the purchasing power of the Metropolitan Museum.) He uses the word "masterpiece" when referring to Vasari, who never painted a masterpiece in his entire career: even at the time, it was well known that Vasari's gigantic pictures were mainly of use in order to cover walls.

On the subject of Michelangelo, who really did create masterpieces, Dan Brown has admirably taught himself every name and date, but can still refer to "the sombre phalanx of Michelangelo's crude Prigioni." Actually the term "sombre phalanx" is quite good, but the word "crude" won't do at all, because the unfinished look of those sculptures is the sculptor's dearest effect. Throughout the book, the reader will find evidence that the writer's learning has been hard won. It must have been hard won because it is so heavily worn. Langdon will engage in private speculations about Dante while he is running flat out, the pretty, young woman matching him stride for stride.

Do they get together in the end? Alas, or perhaps hooray, he realises that he is too old for her. But hooray, or perhaps alas, she offers herself anyway. There is something ... irresistible about the tall symbologist. He is a bit like a wildly successful American author of brain-teasing thrillers, but he has taken another course.

As for the author himself, he will probably go on taking every course there is, in his heroically studious search for a new subject. Dante was a bad choice, I think. Most of Brown's huge audience won't have a clue what he's talking about. If they want to find out, I recommend my new translation of *The Divine Comedy*, which Brown was mischievously shown by the American newspaper *USA Today*. The author of *Inferno* said of my translation that it was "kind of clever." I want you to know this because if even a tiny percentage of the audience of *Inferno* chooses my translation to find out more about Dante, I might come closer to being rewarded for years of labour.

So I have no reason to begrudge Dan Brown his universal success. But I wouldn't begrudge it anyway. I am an old man: old enough to find pretentious absurdity a diverting spectacle. There is not enough of it in this book, but its author will return, undaunted. Meanwhile he leaves us with a scene in which Robert Langdon puts on Sienna's wig—she's bald, I forgot to say—and she helps him to secure it into place with his tie. The scene comes about half way into the book and it proves beyond question that Brown can't picture what he himself is describing.

Unfortunately, however, he also shows evidence that he is learning from his mistakes. We don't want him to. We want him to give us everything he's got, and in his case a kind of exalted stupidity is an essential part of it. Should you read this book? Of course you shouldn't. Will you read this book? Of course you will. As Sienna puts it: "The mathematics is indisputable."

Love, factually

Many have thrown off the God delusion. The romance delusion has us in a firmer embrace

Will Self

November 2016

At my own first wedding—as at the first weddings of so many others—the principal Bible reading was from St Paul's First Epistle to the Corinthians. You know the one, all about faith, hope and love: "Love is patient and kind; love does not envy or boast; it is not arrogant or rude. It does not insist on its own way; it is not irritable or resentful; it does not rejoice at wrongdoing, but rejoices with the truth. Love bears all things, believes all things, hopes all things, endures all things."

Actually, the version read out at our own rather traditional service was from the King James translation, which renders the original as "charity" rather than "love"—a semantic shift of some significance, because what we contemporarily understand as the love between committed sexual partners is quite different to any form of beneficence. When the priest intones—"So now faith, hope and love abide, these three; but the greatest of these is love"—we tend not to think of selfless acts of giving. Instead, looking to the couple standing hand-in-hand before the altar, we meditate on the comparative ephemerality of the phenomenon we call romantic love—ephemeral, even by the increasingly short standards of duration of most marriages. We wonder: Will theirs last? Do they love each other enough? Will the memory of that love (if not the love itself) sustain them when things get rough?

A Church of England marriage is an odd thing—true, the modern service has jettisoned the stern injunctions that prefaced my own first (and lamentably brief) union. No longer are the congregation told marriage was ordained firstly for "procreation," and secondly as "a remedy against sin, and to avoid fornication; that such persons as have not the gift of continency might marry, and keep themselves undefiled members of Christ's body." Instead, we have a touchy-feely, tambourine-tapping, guitar-strumming substitute: "The gift of marriage brings husband and wife together in the delight and tenderness of sexual union and joyful commitment to the end of their lives." A charmingly naive estimation, I'd say, of the ability of us contemporary, spoilt, sexually sophisticated instant-gratifiers to stay the mortal, marital course.

Underlying this shift from a view of marriage as a *de jure* bromide, to one which joyfully acknowledges human concupiscence are all sorts of factors, not least the changing status of women in our society. However, I'd suggest that still more significant has been the changing perception of romantic love. It's perhaps a little too trite to suggest that as we've lost our religious impulse, our urge for transcendence (and by extension personal immortality) increasingly takes the form of romantic longing, but the parallels between the two states of feeling are legion.

To assert that romantic love has a history at all may seem absurd to many. After all, whatever else we can say about our strange and delusory existence one thing seems certain: human nature. If, by this we mean qualities hard-wired into us, it has no history, given our gross anatomy has remained unchanged for pushing a quarter of a million years. But our perception of that nature constantly, quicksilverly shifts. To say that romantic love is an invention of the medieval era—a culturally-productive mode of human-being carried, castle-to-castle, by the touchy-feely lute-strummers of that time—would seem to deny any of the finer feelings to the myriad who came before. Did Cleopatra not love Antony, and Eve, Adam? We feel it in our marrow, this wild and improbable love we have, on occasion, for one another. And part of that feeling is the overpowering sense that such romantic yearnings are fundamentally constitutive of who we are, and who we've always been.

Which brings us, logically enough, to everyman's psychosis. Freud's bleak view of romantic love is that it is a delusionary state, perpetrated on us poor phenotypes by geno-typically insensitive and inexorable evolutionary processes. In this he was only following Schopenhauer, who, with his bracing cynicism sees the prettiest and most alluring of women as furnished with the "weapons and implements necessary for the protection of her existence, and for just the length of time they will be of service to her... Just as the female ant after coition loses her wings, which then become superfluous, nay, dangerous for breeding purposes, so for the most part does a woman lose her beauty after giving birth to one or two children; and probably for the same reasons."

Any number of sociobiological accounts, from the eugenicists of the late 19th and early 20th century to the evolutionary psychologists of our own era, will display this elasticised reductionism: snapping the animal facts of sexuality back in our faces, no matter how carefully we try to ease off our beloved's underwear. But really, socio-biologists are in accord with that traditional, King James's version of the Anglican wedding service, which also shouts down our billing and cooing with its stern insistence on "procreation" and "continence." Indeed, a lot of the problems we have with our collective love life derive from our unwillingness to accept our own embodiment. The gossamer robes with which we clothe our love, and the airiness of the sentiments with which we propel it, suggest the dangerously superfluous wings not of ants, but angels.

But Manichean as the Christian analysis of romance may be, dividing us all into fornicating apes and procreating demigods, it at least provides a viable metric by which to regulate our lives. Too much fornication? Better get continent—a few trips to church will probably help keep you in check—unless, that is, you find the idea of Mary's swollen belly and ghostly donor-insemination arousing. Too much continence? Better get procreating for a few years until natural increase puts paid to her allure...

That sounds pretty bleak, but switching to the perspective of the atheistic Freud hardly lightens the mood. The idea seems to be that romantic love is a kind of fetishisation—dripping our polymorphously perverse drives safely into the parsimonious marital loving cup. Fair enough. But while other neuroses can at least, in theory, be dissolved simply by hauling them to the surface of consciousness, it's not at all clear that a deep acceptance of our animality will really help us to be more humane. Arguably, the greatest victims of the 1960s sexual revolution were vulnerable young women, forced to be promiscuous in the name of equality, just as patriarchy had sequestrated them in support of its opposite. Freud was particularly taken by the way dogs sniffed each other's genitals and anuses; if I read him rightly, he proposes in *Civilisation and its Discontents* that every instance of so-called human progress, from bipedalism to the Brooklyn Bridge, is the result of our overwhelming urge to cease with this awful sniffing.

I don't know about you, but after a number of years on this broad, green, ceaselessly generative planet, I've begun to have difficulty suspending disbelief in sex, let alone romance. Put that in there? Let her do that to this? Make such a noise? I don't think so... it all seems preposterous, not in the least bit natural.

I'm not saying I've developed repression to the proportions of Ruskin, who was so appalled on his wedding night by his young bride's pubic hair that he recoiled back into lifelong celibacy. But the contemporary fashion for baldness in the youthful female pubis should give us all cause for deep thought. In biology the retention of childlike features into adulthood is seen as potentially adaptive: instead of being hard-wired, individuals have the capacity to learn. What, however, does the wilful and mass retention of pubic hairlessness into adulthood suggest, if not that young women are teaching each other that men, in essence, are all paedophiles?

Maybe that's right, because when you stop to think about it the entire panoply of behaviours we consider as romantic, from sending little billets-doux, to developing a shared vocabulary of pet names, are equally infantile. What's romance, then, but a kind of childish make-believe?

I've been romantically in love six times in my life, three times with women, twice with a man, and once with a dog. I'll return to the instructive canine affair, but first, let us try and analyse this "being-in-love" thing a little more intensively. The Ancient Greeks made a distinction between the erotic and the pacific forms of love, between *eros* and *agape*. *Agape*, while referring in the first instance to all affection, also came to mean a sort of unconditional and universal love, and in this respect it sounds pretty close to the charitable form of love praised by St Paul. Neither *agape* nor *eros* exactly corresponds to our ideas of either selfless Christian devotion, or madly self-seeking passion. But what I'd suggest is that any kind of clear distinction between *agape* and *eros* becomes quite impossible in a human emotional world characterised by multiple shorter-term relationships, whether consecutive or concurrent. Whether, that is, in our modern, dry-as-Tinder world, the Grindr of ubiquitous congress carries an ever-present danger of a friction-induced conflagration. Both *eros* and *agape* could go up in smoke.

Richard Wagner's opera *Tristan and Isolde* is often cited as the pinnacle of Romanticism. The star-crossed, and effectively adulterous, lovers take their own lives rather than face separation by the bounds of conventional morality. It's a familiar enough trope. Familiar, then as now, from a thousand different forms of representation—folk songs and ballads and poems, seamlessly merging with pop hits and television dramas. For Tristan and Isolde, their extinction is a matter of little import. In the realm of the night—and death—they're fated to be together for all eternity, so why not realise and transcend that eternity in a consummation that's at once their dissolution? The inexorable logic of full-blown romantic love demands nothing else. For just as your life will have been a tragic waste—emotionally, spiritually, physically—if you, and the one-among-the-eight-billion you are fated to be with do not coincide, so it can be accorded the greatest success if you can be assured of their undying love, even if it takes a suicide pact to secure that.

Preposterous, no? It is ridiculous that anyone in this day and age, with its copious amounts of relationship advice, and its rational, cost-beneficial conception of human interactions, should maintain such a destructive and self-sabotaging view of the meaning of life. Can that really be all there is to it? Can it truly be the case that anyone—let alone everyone—was put on earth with the sole objective of finding another, particular individual, ordained obscurely for them, and thereafter, in some equally obscure fashion, merging with them to form a sort of trans-temporal gloop of feeling?

If only this were all there were to modern romance—if only it were still just this Wagnerian self-abnegation shtick, so easy to see through for people raised to understand themselves as the masters of their own fate, then I suspect we'd have been able to shrug off its delusions by now. But romance, like all the best ideologies, has adapted. Romance has globalised. Romance has received its own equivalent of the Universal Declaration on Human Rights.

The militant wing of the romance party commit what are known as, and half-excused as, *crimes passionnel*. We would never condemn two lovers whose togetherness was fated, so we find it hard to censure them when they attack anything—from marital bonds to their own pesky and kingly spouses—that jams the clockwork of kismet. The harshness with which we judge those who err in most fiduciary matters is never, and I mean never, extended to adulterers: judge not, lest ye be judged! And the odds are—given the astonishing improbability of anyone ever truly winning the romance lottery—that those in a position to judge will be feeling pretty lovelorn themselves. Still plaintively waiting for their own amorous conflagration, even while they nonetheless enthusiastically fornicate.

So, romance warps our moral judgments in this way: ever requiring us to make and mend the monogamous fences, sectioning off new fields within which new family-crops can be raised. Demography and technology go hand-in-pipette here. With people living longer and longer, while conception can be assisted later and later, we have the difficult task of convincing ourselves that this late-blooming romance really is the one, when more than likely we've told ourselves this several, perhaps many, times before. There is no lover but you, and a thousand plays and films and books prophesy your coming.

If romantic love was passionately unprincipled in the past, nowadays it has to be in conformity with human rights legislation. That's right: you should treat this witch, or warlock, who's ensorcelled you, with the same slightly aseptic respect with which you treat your colleagues. Wildly passionate and improbable affairs must be Kitemarked, so conforming to best practice. It's often noted that in the age where serial monogamy exists alongside the nuclear family, too much pressure is placed on our partners—we want them to be both continent and abandoned, a good friend and a demon lover. Actually, the situation is far worse even than that. We demand of our intimate relationships that they be both grand enough for eternity and sufficiently paltry to sustain the quotidian. We want our lovers to die with us as we mutually gain the very peak of sexual ecstasy—yet then arise and make us a soft-boiled egg with toasted soldiers.

It's a recipe for failure, and that's what I feel: a failure. As I said above, I've been in love with three women in my life, two men and a dog. I'll say nothing of the human relationships—decency demands nothing less. But my dog days were instructive. Obviously the relationship wasn't physically consummated —except with cuddles—although we slept in the same bed. No, it seems to me it's precisely because, to paraphrase Wittgenstein, that if a dog lover could speak, we wouldn't understand its endearments, that we can remain so perfectly in love with them, and they with us. The species-barrier is all we can erect in lieu of the convent walls that kept Abelard and Héloïse apart. Indeed, I can't see how anyone facing contemporary terms of endearment doesn't feel as if they've failed. We fail in making our choice, which, given our belief that partner-choice is sidereally pre-ordained is really no choice at all. And we fail repeatedly in the very act of loving itself, which requires us to simultaneously be selfless and egoistic to the point of self-annihilation.

Romantic love has always been the sort of hit-man of monogamy: once the contract on you has been fulfilled, you cannot stray—the chubby demigod with the bow has put an arrow in your heart. After that a ring on your finger seems a mere formality: what's "till death us do part" compared to eternity? The problem, however, is that the new technologies, and the social media that they support lead us, using a golden thread of machine code, through a labyrinth of possible encounters, towards people who we're encouraged to feel should be not just compatible but ideal. Rationally, we know in our heart-of-hearts that there are indeed scores, nay, millions, of potential partners who might well become our long-term lovers, and happily so. But if there's one thing we understand about everyman's psychosis, it's that it isn't remotely rational. Moreover, its very irrationality seems connected to that idea of ourselves as being in a very important sense unique.

I too, believe everyone is unique, but only by reason of occupying unique spatial-temporal co-ordinates. When it comes to our personalities I'm afraid our individuality is more apparent than real: and the great paradox of the web is that we're ever-trying to convince each other of how particular we are by sharing information about our mass pursuits. Perhaps that's what romantic love is really all about. It's a longing, a desire, a passion, for a state of absolute particularity, a state to which the human condition, with its all too common instinctual drives, doesn't really obtain. No wonder we're all either disappointed or unrequited.

Love that's unrequited is the most perfect as, by definition, it affords no opportunity for disillusionment. I've a friend who's nursed an ungovernable passion for a woman for years now. Repeated sallies have availed him naught—she rejects, and rejects again, but he remains undaunted. After about three years of this he won a concession. She's a musician, and she allowed him to come to her performances on the strict understanding he doesn't try and speak to her; instead of speaking he's permitted to write, once a week, which he does, copiously, although he never gets a reply. I suppose looked at through the lens of contemporary psychologising this is at best neurotic, and at worst looks like a mutually-agreed stalking pact. I've no idea what the object of his desire gets out of it. Perhaps it's simply her way of containing someone she believes to be dangerous. I hope not.

My friend's predicament, reminds me of the idea in Jewish mythology of the Tzadikim Nistarim, or 36 righteous men. These individuals are not known to us, nor to themselves. When one dies, he is replaced by some occult operation. The role of the Tzadikim Nistarim is to justify humankind in the eyes of God, a task they fulfil merely by the fact of their existence. And we believe in romantic love—believe in it more fervently than we do in the utopia of communism or the hidden hand of the market—believe in it as if there were 36 unrequited lovers in the world, whose role is to justify humankind's unquenchable longing in the eyes of... Cupid.

Only unrequited lovers will do—why? Why can't the example of those perfect, loving couples serve to inspire us? Well, for obvious reason: their love for each other is exactly that. They are vessels which ever refill one another without spilling a drop, so there's nothing there for the rest of us.

But I think it's a mistake to imagine that the religiously committed can't make their own accommodation with both romantic and sexual love. Rowan Williams, the erstwhile Archbishop of Canterbury, wrote a beautiful essay in 1989 called "The Body's Grace." It was his response to conflicts in the Anglican Communion over gay priests. In it Williams advances a view of marriage as the best possible vehicle within which to arrive at a perfect union—spiritual, emotional, and most crucially, physical. Williams writes of sexual love: "For my body to be the cause of joy, the end of homecoming, for me, it must be there for someone else, be perceived, accepted, nurtured; and that means being given over to the creation of joy in that other." For Williams, allowing ourselves to be made in the image of our lover's love is a scary business; only long-term committed marriage can give us the confinement within which we can be this abandoned.

It's an attractive—moving, even—prospect, but of course what makes it truly viable for Williams is that it's a synecdoche of God's love for all of humankind.

Recall, God loves us completely and unconditionally—that is the nature of the grace he bestows on us. In turn, our lovers, little gods that they are, bestow grace on us by adoring even those aspects of ourselves and our bodies with which we aren't at all comfortable.

Our problem is that very many of us, myself included, who chose that reading from St Paul's First Epistle to the Corinthians, do not believe in God at all; for us it is love alone that "bears all things, believes all things, hopes all things, endures all things," which is why, I'd wager, that semantic shift occurred between the King James and the New English versions. We worship not at the altar of a beneficent and all-powerful deity, but bow down before a capricious one who taunts us with the very fact of our unassuageable yearnings. There is indeed a rose in the fisted glove and I'm sure you'll agree: all too often the eagle flies with the dove.

All of which should lead us to conclude: if you can't be with the one you love, love the one you're with. Because let's face it, the one you love is just that: the one—the impossibly unique individual, who is nevertheless moulded entirely to the lineaments of your very particular desire. While as for the one you're with, well, I'm sure you agree—you may not love them that much, but they're entirely deserving of your charity.

Science

Life, but not as we know it

Thanks to the new science of synthetic biology, it will soon be possible to create living cells in a laboratory. This could bring big benefits—from medicine to combating global warming—but potential dangers too. I went to Greenland to find out more

Philip Ball

August 2007

I have just spent a week 120 miles above the Arctic Circle listening to a hand-picked group of 17 scientists discuss how to make synthetic life forms. Like it or not, this is going to happen, possibly in the next few years. Some will find that shocking, even blasphemous. To others it will seem a tremendous opportunity, scientifically and economically. Some hope it will help to solve urgent global problems. In any event, there is clearly some explaining to be done.

We are not the first to imagine making life anew to our own design. In Francis Bacon's *New Atlantis* (1627), the scientist-priests who rule the technological utopia of Bensalem on a Pacific island reveal how life has become clay in their hands:

> We make by art, trees and flowers to come earlier or later than their seasons: and to come up and bear more speedily than by their natural course they do. We make... their fruit greater and sweeter and of differing taste, smell, colour and figure... We have also parks and enclosures of all sorts of beasts and birds... By art likewise we make them greater or taller than their kind is, and contrariwise dwarf them and stay their growth. We make them more fruitful and bearing than their kind is, and contrariwise barren and not generative...

It is barely possible to read this today without revulsion, although Bacon deemed these dreams to be a good thing. His vision of a research programme that might lead to such "art" served as a template for the formation of the Royal Society in London in the mid-17th century.

Nearly 400 years later, Bensalem's mastery of life is nigh. Of course, selective breeding can already make beasts "greater or taller," and genetic engineering has produced plants that grow faster, or out of season, or altered in taste and colour.

But this is mere tinkering, often slow or unpredictable. The new life forms now being reported are decidedly more Baconian in their artificiality: bacteria that pulse on and off with light, or that act as photographic emulsion, or that "count" the number of times they divide, or that enact computer logic.

These are the products of synthetic biology, an emerging science that breaks down life as we know it into its component parts, and then reassembles them into something new. The size of these biological parts is typically a few to a few hundred nanometres (millionths of a millimetre). That is also the scale on which physicists, chemists and engineers are now designing ultra-small devices, which is why synthetic biology overlaps with nanotechnology: each can supply components and ideas for the other. This convergence, and the resulting prospect of "cyborg cells," was the subject of our Arctic workshop. It was funded by a philanthropic foundation in California and by research institutes in Delft and Cornell, all established with the backing of physicist and businessman Fred Kavli. Partly as a ploy to ensure that those who attended would stay put, the organisers, Paul McEuen at Cornell and Delft's Cees Dekker, decided to hold it in the town of Ilulissat in Greenland.

There are some obvious reasons why conferences aren't often held in Greenland. It is not an easy place to get to: until May, the only flights came out of Copenhagen, although the Americans attending this workshop took advantage of a newly opened route from Baltimore. Outside the capital of Nuuk, there is nowhere capable of hosting a meeting of any significant size, and in any event Greenlandic travel is not for people on a tight schedule. The introductory session, scheduled for Monday evening, had to be abandoned when the Americans got stranded by fog after landing at Kangerlussuaq (population: 600). Greenland, we are told, is the land of waiting: flight cancellations are routine.

Ilulissat has a population of about 5,000, making it the third biggest town in Greenland. It is unapologetically functional, a perpetual building site perched awkwardly on rocks. There has been no attempt to prettify its gas tanks and container crates—lifelines shipped at much expense from Denmark. It was overcast when we arrived but it felt like we were on the edge of everything. The grey haze where the sea vanishes has a bizarre and frightening quality, a sort of pitiless infinity.

Mindful of the event's resonances, I had packed a copy of *Frankenstein*, and I could see what Mary Shelley's Arctic explorer Captain Walton meant by being "surrounded by mountains of ice which admit of no escape"—especially when the weather closes in. But when, after an extravagant dinner of juicy scallops, smoked whale and roast musk ox, we went for a walk, the absence of even a hint of dusk was invigorating. Our scramble over ancient granite and through mossy bogs was punctuated by the distant cracks of calving ice.

The fog was back on Tuesday morning, coming and going. They say the weather here can change every 15 minutes. We were tense at breakfast, fearing further delay to our tight schedule. The flight had left Kangerlussuaq, we were told, but would it get in? We rejoiced to hear the aircraft whining low over the hotel. Now we could get down to business.

When, some time soon, bacteria are created with DNA made in a laboratory rather than in some parent cell, like every other cell since the dawn of life, it will be one of the most extraordinary developments of modern science. Yet despite the Faustian overtones, this fresh beginning for life on earth will initially cause few ripples outside the science press.

Why do I predict this muted response? Partly because scientists are unlikely to say that they have "made life"—they will accept, I hope, that such a claim is largely meaningless. But also because, outside science, few people give a damn about bacteria. Philosophers and theologians, ever ready to pronounce on the spiritual status of a single human cell, have no yardstick for evaluating the implications of a synthetic bacterium—and show no signs of acquiring one. The first break in a great chain of being that led from pools of primordial slime to Gordon Brown will prompt little more than the question of whether this stuff is safe.

That is a reasonable, but nonetheless parochial, question. Synthetic life is a technology with the potential to raise, and perhaps answer, issues of genuine philosophical standing. Until the early 19th century, many natural philosophers thought that living matter was different in kind from the fabric of the inorganic world. This so-called "vitalism" was slowly eroded by discoveries in organic chemistry and microbiology. But the idea has by no means disappeared from everyday culture: it can be discerned in the common view of life's sanctity and in the belief in a "divine spark" that somehow transforms a fertilised human egg into a human being. George W Bush's recent second veto of a bill lifting restrictions on US federal funding of stem cell research, on the grounds that it would permit the destruction of "human life," has echoes of this sort of modern-day vitalism.

But anyone who researches the mechanics of life—who grapples with the question of how a bunch of molecules co-ordinate themselves into an entity that can reproduce, extract energy from its environment, and evolve—is forced to recognise that there is a hazy boundary between the living and the non-living. At this level, the question "What is life?," which has preoccupied scientists from JBS Haldane to Erwin Schrödinger, ceases to have any meaning. Ticking boxes on a supposed list of criteria for "life" is at best an arbitrary process that exposes our inability to think outside the terms of reference we already know. In the end, the argument becomes circular: life consists in all those characteristics we can identify in things we call living. One of the exciting prospects for synthetic biology is that it might permit the exploration of these boundaries, for example by generating "living cells" with non-natural DNA or with some of the protein machinery replaced by designed non-carbon-based devices made with nanotechnology. In any event, the workshop attendees decided rather quickly that the "What is life?" question was a blind alley. They were keen to get on to the issue of how to redesign it.

Of all the smart things one might think of doing with tailor-made microbes, two leap out as urgent: energy and medicine. There is no better location than Greenland for focusing the mind on the need for alternatives to fossil fuels. The north polar region has experienced more warming than most other places on the planet, and it shows. In our village of Ilimanaq, where we were ferried by fishing boat through a frigid sea of blue-green icebergs, we were told by a local schoolteacher that the village hunters find the glaciers more distant every year, and that the thaw water that gushes between the houses each spring has been coming ever earlier. Later, we hiked along the side of the spectacular Jakobshavn glacier, which has retreated many kilometres since the late 19th century. Our guide, a young woman named Vilhelmina, said that the ice floe in the fjord, which produces 10 per cent of all of Greenland's icebergs, had been much thicker when she was a child.

What can designer cells do about this? One of the prime ambitions is to create microbes that will convert plant matter into chemical substances that can serve as fuels. In essence, this is a kind of brewing. Using brewer's yeast to turn grapes into ethanol isn't yet a cost-effective way of making a fuel you can burn in your car, but it might become so if the conversion can be made more efficient. An engine that burns ethanol, or some other biofuel derived from vegetation, still produces carbon dioxide. But this is reabsorbed from the atmosphere when the feed crop is regrown the next season. So you don't get the steady accumulation of atmospheric CO_2 that comes from burning fossil fuels. The viability of biofuels is fiercely debated—providing transportation fuel for a large industrialised nation would require vast tracts of land to be given over to fuel crops, and the energy costs of getting the fuels to the pumps are troubling. But the balance sheet can only be improved by making the conversion of plant mass to fuel as efficient as can be. The trouble is that plants resist being broken down—some of the fibrous material is hard for organisms to digest. Yeast or bacteria with fibre-busting genetic machinery borrowed from termites could make better use of the raw material. Steven Chu, a Nobel laureate physicist from the Lawrence Berkeley National Laboratory in California who is immersed in the prickly politics of new energy technologies, claimed that hardy and quick-growing switchgrass could satisfy half of US fuel needs if only it was easier to decompose.

A species of bacterium of the *Clostridium* genus contains a multiprotein machine that degrades cellulose (a key component of plant cell walls) into glucose. Scientists at the J Craig Venter Institute in Rockville, Maryland, set up by genomics pioneer Craig Venter, want to engineer a species of cellulose-digesting *Clostridium* that instead generates alcohols like ethanol. John Glass, from the institute, was at the Greenland meeting—a last-minute stand-in for Venter himself, laid low by illness in Costa Rica. Glass suggested that there was no reason to restrict ourselves to ethanol: perhaps we can invent new enzymes that make, say, high-octane hydrocarbons instead.

Giving organisms a suite of genes that allow them to churn out chemical compounds they don't make naturally is a familiar objective in biotechnology, where it is known as metabolic engineering. But with the exception of some relatively simple products such as insulin, cells have not been much exploited as "living factories" for pharmaceuticals. Jay Keasling at Berkeley has spent several years tooling up yeast and bacteria to produce the anti-malarial drug artemisinin, currently extracted at great expense from an Asian shrub. This is one of the most effective drugs on the market, but its prohibitive cost means it has virtually no impact on the formidable death toll from malaria (more than one million a year worldwide).

Making cells that produce artemisinin means giving them over 40 new genes. These have to be synchronised to avoid bottlenecks in the molecular assembly line, which could cause accumulation of substances toxic to the cells. That means the new genes can't simply be slotted into the cells' genomes: Keasling has to grapple with the genetic "circuit diagram" that determines when and how genes are switched on and off. This is one of the issues that distinguishes synthetic biology from traditional genetic engineering: it involves intervening with the genome, the cell's operating system, as if rewiring a complex electrical circuit. There are feedback loops, amplifiers, switches and control circuits that ensure genes operate in synchrony. But the understanding of this systems-scale cell logic is still rudimentary.

Yet Keasling's work shows that the problem isn't intractable. He has now created forms of yeast that make large amounts of artemisinic acid—just a few simple chemical steps away from artemisinin itself—and pump it out of the cells for easy extraction and purification. He hopes to see an industrial process up and running by 2009, making the drug at the affordable cost of ten cents per gram.

The artemisinin story is a reminder of how the pharmaceutical industry still depends on so-called "natural" products—chemical compounds made in nature. Despite grand talk of "drug design" and the promise of new technologies such as antisense therapy, in which problematic genes are "silenced" by DNA-like molecules, most drugs now in use are natural products or compounds derived from them, such as aspirin. Yet the drug pipeline is drying up: fewer are approved now than 30 years ago. One of the hurdles many drug candidates fail to clear is that, even if they work well for most people, there may be small subsets of the population whose genetic make-up will make them prone to nasty, even fatal, side-effects. At the moment, such would-be drugs are binned. But they might be rescued by a quick, easy and reliable means of spotting individuals with the "wrong" genes. These genes can potentially be identified from the proteins they encode, present in blood samples, say. But that's a classic needle-in-haystack affair. Nanotechnology promises to deliver sensors that detect biochemicals highly selectively at very low levels. Scott Fraser of the California Institute of Technology talked about sensors that work like miniature tuning forks set ringing by laser beams: if just a few of the right molecules stick to their surface, the ring changes pitch. This, he said, was what the much-hyped "personalised medicine" should really entail. Decoding individual genomes so as to prescribe drugs tailor-made to our personal genetic constitution is impractical economically and perhaps even scientifically. But screening for common genetic conditions that make good drugs do bad things would at least reduce the crippling rate of attrition in drug discovery.

Things were warming up. Throwing a hugely diverse bunch of scientists together in an isolated outpost on the edge of the world was a risky experiment, not least because they might lack a common technical language and culture. But despite the awesome specialist knowledge in attendance, no one was an expert on how to "make life." "We are all bozos on this bus," was how biophysicist Bob Austin of Princeton put it. By Wednesday night, everyone had begun to shed the burden of expertise and let their imaginations roam. Sadly, the Americans were leaving for Baltimore after lunch the following day.

There are two ways of approaching synthetic biology. One works from the bottom up: starting with chemical reagents taken from the lab store, can you make something that behaves even a little like a living cell? The other is top-down: you take the parts and design principles from natural organisms but then put them together differently. Many regard the first approach as far too difficult, a little like trying to make a computer from wire, solder and a high-school understanding of electronics. All the same, the bottom-up synthesis of living things from crude ingredients must be possible, since it happened of its own accord around 3.8bn years ago—an event for which the earliest evidence comes from rocks just south of Ilulissat. Attempting to generate lifelike systems chemically, however ambitious, might at least address some of the big questions about that event. Which environments are most fecund? What building blocks do you need? Where does the organisation come from? Which comes first: replication or compartmentalisation? Were the earliest cells "garbage bags," as veteran physicist Freeman Dyson put it, containing an uncoordinated mix of stuff, or were they pared-down entities with nothing superfluous?

The top-down approach tends to the view that simplification is a good strategy for designer cells, regardless of whether early terrestrial life showed such economy. We still have little grasp of the rules that govern networks of gene interactions even in rather "primitive" bacteria, but the best hope of untangling them, and thus of exercising rational design, comes from identifying the "minimal cell": the smallest subset of genes needed to sustain a viable organism. The notion of "minimal" is treacherous here, because it depends on context. If you provide a cell with all the amino acids from which proteins are made, say, it no longer needs enzymes for synthesising them. But then it wouldn't live long in the wild. The same is true of genes for coping with temperature changes or attacks by other organisms. Evolution depends on stresses like these which weed the strong from the weak. That's why so much of an organism's genome is devoted to coping with them.

If your designer bacteria that chew up grass and generate fuels are bred in carefully regulated isolation, that may not matter. But it might be best to make them at least heat-tolerant, so that they thrive while contaminating microbes get boiled. In any event, scientists at the Venter Institute are so confident they have identified a set of "minimal genes" that they have applied for a patent. (I'm told it's unlikely to be granted.) This set comprises 381 genes in the genome of a bacterium called *Mycoplasma genitalium*, a parasite of the human genital tract with a remarkably small genome of just 485 protein-coding genes. If Venter's team is right, the stripped-down *M genitalium* genome will be the chassis on which new bacteria will be designed and built more or less from scratch.

How do you build a bacterium with a redesigned genome? DNA—the genetic material—can now be made in long lengths in the lab using chemical methods, with a precisely specified genetic message defined by the sequence of its four chemical building blocks (bases) along the chain. Around 40 companies now supply tailored DNA at around $1 per base—a cost that has been halved each year for the past decade or more. Making a chain as big as an entire bacterial genome remains challenging, but it should be possible to build it in segments and join them together.

Yet a genome is no more an organism than a CD of a computer's operating system is a laptop. How do you reincarnate a naked genome as a living bacterium? In the meeting's most dramatic revelation, John Glass explained how. He and his colleagues have performed the first whole-genome transplant: removing the genome of one species of mycoplasma and inserting it into another. The recipient cells can be "booted up" with the new operating system, and begin behaving just like the donor cells. It's a little like creating an acorn that grows not into an oak but a willow. This surely presages the insertion of a wholly synthetic genome: the Venter Institute scientists will try to use their technique to make cells containing their putative minimal mycoplasma genome and see if they survive.

One might imagine that using nature's tricks to make stuff has a green tinge to it, but there's no telling where the ethical arguments might end up: Angela Belcher of the Massachusetts Institute of Technology, who adapts viruses to make nanotechnological machines, said she has been denounced for "cruelty to viruses." It is proper, however, that the imminence of the first human-made organisms should give us pause. Paul McEuen, a specialist in nanoelectronics, confessed that his sleep was disturbed more by what he had heard than by the midnight sun. The risk of mistakes—of synthetic microbes escaping into the environment or mutating uncontrollably—is bad enough. Yet one can imagine giving an artificial genome a variety of safety features—for example, making the organism dependent on a nutrient that doesn't exist in nature, or giving it a "fail-fast" genetic code different from the one natural DNA uses, such that every mutation proves fatal and evolution is consequently proscribed.

But the thought of bacteria and viruses being deliberately concocted by people wanting to wreak havoc is alarming. Drew Endy of MIT pointed out that making the genome of the Ebola virus now costs about as much as a new Volkswagen. In three years it might cost the price of a laptop, and in five to seven years, that of an iPod.

Yet shelving synthetic biology on the grounds that it is too dangerous simply isn't an option. Now that the technologies exist to reinvent what an organism is, the real question is how we can best ensure that they are used safely and with good intent. Of course, it would be hard to identify a useful technology that has not been militarised (many began in defence labs), and fledgling synthetic biologists are undoubtedly already at work in military establishments. Endy admitted that he knew no more than anyone else about what transpires in the US National Biodefense Analysis and Countermeasures Center at Fort Detrick in Maryland, even to the extent of whether its research is solely defensive. Meanwhile, *Make* magazine, the bible of American home inventors, has already shown its readers how to do "backyard biology," and the idea that inventing your own biological virus might become as easy and attractive to disaffected technophiles as devising computer viruses is obviously disturbing. While it makes sense to insist that DNA-synthesis companies vet their orders, and perhaps that access to pathogen genome data be restricted, that can't close every leak.

Such broader questions benefit from historical perspective, and few scientists can provide as much of it as Freeman Dyson. One of the most influential and politically aware of the post-Manhattan project physicists, he is now 83 but still game for a freezing midnight ride through icebergs. For all its genius, his generation failed to forsee the technological future, he said: "We totally missed all the important things." He recalled how his former Princeton colleague John von Neumann, one of the founders of computer science, estimated that the US would only ever need 18 computers. Dyson himself confessed to once trying to persuade Francis Crick against moving into biology.

It was too early to leave, but time had run out. Another day, we suspected, and the discussion would really have kicked into gear. But if you don't get out of this place on Friday, you're there for the weekend. The organisers and I have drawn up a declaration—the "Ilulissat statement"—to which all the attendees subscribe, proposing in broad outline how we think the field should develop. It's a useful exercise, yet I can't help thinking of Dyson's words. Far from being disheartening, however, I find them rather exciting.

Medicine in black and white

You want your doctor to treat you as an individual. But clinical practice is warped by dubious—and sometimes outright dangerous—ideas about race

Angela Saini

July 2019

When I was pregnant some years ago, a friend of mine—a doctor at a busy London hospital—told me that South Asian women tend to give birth earlier than other women. That passing comment was enough for me to begin cheerfully planning around the likelihood that my baby's arrival was more imminent than I had thought. I prepared the nursery ahead of time. I confidently told my brother-in-law, who was visiting from overseas, that his nephew would be born long before he had to return home. In the event, my son came two weeks late and my brother-in-law missed the birth.

I recalled this when I started researching the use of race in medicine. I remembered how unquestioningly I had accepted my friend's assertion. This wasn't just because I trusted her medical expertise, but also because it slotted neatly into a wider story we have been told: that certain ethnicities and racial groups have different propensities to illness, from diabetes to heart disease to schizophrenia. These assumptions have been creeping into diagnostics and drug evaluation for years, in different ways. But they are assumptions which, as my own pregnancy taught me, can often be misleading. Indeed, in some circumstances, fatal.

On the surface, there are of course average physical differences between populations, most obviously in skin colour and facial features. A handful of inherited diseases also show up in higher frequencies in certain communities than in others: the serious blood condition sickle cell, for example, occurs at greater rates in black Americans than white Americans. There are those who also like to point to the possibility of deeper variations, including in "build." Reviewing Kenya's phenomenal success in long-distance athletics a few years ago, the *Atlantic*'s Max Fisher speculated that the local population's shape, lungs and muscles might give them some "genetic" edge.

But the truth is more complex than it might seem. Scientific reality almost always defies our crude categories of race, which are themselves byproducts of recent human history. Yet claims about "racial difference" reflect and reinforce the widespread belief that race matters in some deeper, visceral way. On far-right websites, I have seen supposed medical differences cited as positive proof of this. Yet most of the apparent differences are illusions, which can lead both doctors and patients down dead ends.

Type caste

For 70 years, most biologists and geneticists have been telling us that race has no basis in biology, that it is a social construct and we are all essentially similar underneath. Yet we continue to hear doctors confidently advise us that race *does* matter in diagnosis and treatment—that diabetes, say, is simply more common in South Asians, or that this treatment might work better in "black" patients. So which one is it? Is race biologically meaningful or not?

Race, if it sits anywhere, lies at the margins of our genomes, manifesting itself in superficial ways such as skin colour. And then only along gradients, which themselves begin to disappear in our deeply intermixed world. The genes for light skin are, for example, found in the oldest communities in Africa, as well as in Europe and Asia. Other measurable traits, such as height or "build," have a hazier connection with race, and possibly no genetic connection at all. Some researchers have reasoned that it may well be lifestyle, training and ambition—rather than anything in the genome of entire populations—that have in recent years history pushed certain Kenyan athletes to the top of those running medal tables. Just the same explanations for why white British athletes have, at times in history, been exceptionally successful, too. As for sickle cell, it is found in all ethnic groups. While it may be rare in white Americans, it is not absent—and this is because it's linked not to skin colour or ethnicity, but to malaria. It's found in peoples of all complexions with roots in regions of the world in which malaria is common, because those with the sickle cell mutation enjoy some protection against that other disease.

Individual differences within the racial categories we commonly use far outweigh group differences, and especially so if the categories are scientifically arbitrary. Historically, in the United States, anyone with the smallest degree of African ancestry has been considered black, a definition since embraced by racist and anti-racist politicians alike. Whatever the politics, though, if a person can have three white European grandparents and still be black, how much genetic meaning can the label really retain?

The conflation of social and seemingly biological categories in medicine can sometimes take a turn for the bizarre, especially when money is involved. Take the American marketing claim that popular blood pressure drug Bystolic works especially well in "Hispanic patients." This implies that there might be some distinct Hispanic ethnicity, causing drugs to act differently in this group. But "Hispanic" encompasses people with native American, black African and white European ancestry—the idea of some distinct biological "Hispanic-ness" makes no sense.

The more fundamental problem is that even when groups are defined with more precision in terms of ancestry, they *still* don't explain much physical variation of any importance. Genetics does not, of course, say that every single person on the planet is different to or the same as the next. What it does say is that we are genetically more similar to people we are related to, and that this similarity tails off as the closeness of that relationship gets weaker. This means that communities of people who have lived near each other for a long time will inevitably be a little more alike, because their ancestors will have bred with each other. But humans have moved around a lot throughout history, so beyond our immediate families, these genetic commonalities tend to be weak.

The result? However racial groups are defined, physical variation within them will, for nearly anything we can measure, overwhelm any average difference that might be observed between them. As far back as 1972, the Harvard biologist Richard Lewontin established that almost all difference sits within populations, and this has since only been vindicated by further genetic evidence.

There are no discrete "types" of people and no hard boundaries around any population groups. There is no gene that exists in all the members of one racial group and not another. Being of the same race doesn't mean two people will necessarily have more in common genetically. Such is the fuzziness that, statistically speaking, it is possible for my genome to be more similar to a randomly-chosen white Briton than to a randomly-chosen Indian.

Do no harm?

Medicine is supposed to be the application of good science, including genetics. Yet the truths of that science are not always reflected in how any of us—patients and, more disturbingly, often medics too—tend to think about human difference when it comes to health. What science has taught us about human variation seems to disappear out the window in the doctor's surgery.

In my case, I didn't pause to ask myself whether South Asian women do tend to give birth early. The scientific jury is out on that "fact." If it were true, it would still be rash to assume it has a genetic basis. There is a markedly raised risk of prematurity and associated problems among African Americans, too, but when Tyan Parker Dominguez of the University of Southern California reviewed the literature on this a few years ago, she noted that black *immigrant* women in the US had "significantly better pregnancy outcomes" than their black American counterparts. More strikingly, "the US-born daughters of black immigrant women" ran into "a significantly higher percentage" of problems than their foreign-born mothers, suggesting that those problems are "likely a function of their experiences in the American social system," such as the stress of growing up in a racist society, "rather than an expression of genetic vulnerability."

We all know, or should know, that we are each individuals, with our own unique physiology, and particular medical profiles. So while there may be *average* differences in early births between one group and another, I might have stopped to ask myself whether or not I would be typical of my group. And yet, such is the collective preoccupation with "stock" that I didn't do that. So where does this obsession come from?

The largest factors that make people within races seem more similar than they are biologically are language, culture and—in racially-divided societies—also class.

Both that and culture certainly impact on diet, lifestyle and health. But it is this trick of the eye, conflating superficial physical difference with deeper cultural or social differences, which makes us believe that race has biological significance. In any society where race has importance, all of us will be susceptible to this illusion, and doctors are not immune.

The modern-day use of racial categories in medicine has been fuelled in part by the habit of collecting racial demographic data when conducting clinical research. Since 2000 the NHS has recorded patients' ethnicities, ostensibly to measure discrimination. But in practice doctors also use this kind of information in diagnosis and treatment.

Very few scientists would pretend that race is an infallible way of making sense of human variation, but some might defend it as a bit of a fudge—a way of lumping together people who share some possible statistical similarity, an average gene frequency for certain diseases. In an imperfect world race can feel at least a little useful. If we knew, for example, that a certain socially identifiable group of people responds to a drug slightly differently on average than another group, then might that not be useful in assigning treatment?

In theory, maybe. In practice, we need to analyse the statistics with care. Suppose that at a population level, scientists spot some marginal difference in a health outcome between two groups—let's say that British Chinese people had been shown to have on average somewhat higher rates of asthma—that doesn't mean you can then diagnose or treat on the assumption that every British Chinese patient will be predisposed to asthma. Each person is too different from the next.

This is true with categories that have *much* more underlying medical meaning than race—such as age ranges, for example. Overlaps and fuzzy boundaries inevitably come into play. There is always debate, for instance, about which ages should be covered by a cancer screening programme.

Sticking too rigidly to certain categories can blind doctors to thinking beyond them. This is also true when it comes to sex which, unlike race, is a category with some obvious biological basis. But it does not extend to making all women different to all men in every way. While women are more likely to get breast cancer, it does—albeit more rarely—strike men, too. A failure to imagine men with breast cancer is one reason why it goes under-diagnosed in them. The British Heart Foundation co-funded a 2016 study which found that women were 50 per cent more likely than men to be given the wrong diagnosis after a heart attack. While women do sometimes present with different symptoms from men, one of the authors, Chris Gale, a professor at Leeds University, concluded that there was a need to "shift the perception that heart attacks only affect a certain type of person… a middle-aged man who is overweight, has diabetes and smokes."

Coming back to race, the dangers are all the greater because—with very rare exceptions, such as sickle cell—innate differences tend to be both small and statistical. And when it comes to those rare -exceptions, relying on race as a diagnostic short-cut can have devastating consequences. American paediatrician Richard Garcia describes the case of a friend who as a child repeatedly failed to receive a correct diagnosis for the serious genetic condition cystic fibrosis because it is known to be more common among white Americans, and she was black. Only when a passing radiologist happened to spot her chest X-ray, without knowing to whom it belonged, was her condition instantly spotted. She had to wait until she was eight years old—shockingly late for a cystic fibrosis diagnosis—and her colour had to be invisible, before she was correctly diagnosed.

Retrofitting race

Where race does matter for health is in the social consequences of discrimination, and in cultural habits. Diabetes has become epidemic in South Asia, for instance, not just because there may be some underlying susceptibility, but also because economic growth has thrust millions of Indian families into both greater prosperity but also more unhealthy diets and sedentary lifestyles.

Another important example is raised blood pressure, something which the World Health Organisation estimates contributes to nearly 13 per cent of deaths globally. Hypertension, persistently high blood pressure, is strongly associated with being black—or at least, it is in the US and the UK: American studies have suggested that it is twice as common in black Americans. A huge difference, no doubt. But is it all down to some innate racial difference in physiology? No. Being "black" is certainly not a reliable indicator of the risks globally if the extremely low rates of hypertension in Africa are anything to go by.

Something else is going on. Living in an urban environment is associated with higher blood pressure, as is having fewer years in education. But the most significant risk factor is salt. "Diet is the underlying cause of hypertension," says Richard Cooper, of Loyola University Medical School in Chicago. It is why he has seen some of the highest adjusted global rates of hypertension in Finland. Most of the population is ethnically Finnish and "white," but their diets have traditionally been lower in fruit and vegetables and higher in fatty meat and salt than those elsewhere in Europe.

Black Americans tend to be poorer than white Americans, which makes it likely that, on average, they will have poorer diets featuring cheaper processed foods with more added salt. So here perhaps we begin to solve the riddle of black Americans and higher blood pressure. Diet, in both Finns and black Americans, is the key—not ancestry or skin colour.

The danger for researchers—and regulators—is that when they approach real gaps between social groups with some notion of race at the front of mind, this distracts from stronger contributing factors. In 2005 the US Food and Drug Administration went so far as to approve Bidil, a drug used to treat heart failure that can develop from hypertension, as the world's first drug to be marketed solely to black patients. In the UK, guidelines issued by the National Institute for Health and Care Excellence recommend that "black people of African or Caribbean family origin" under the age of 55 be given a different drug for hypertension to patients belonging to other groups. From what we know to date about the underlying genetics of human variation, these groups are highly unlikely to be different enough to warrant this kind of racialised healthcare. Yet here it is being used on both sides of the Atlantic.

The use of race might still be defended as a practical proxy—a way of getting at important variation between groups, even if it isn't rooted in any genetic difference. To understand whether it may be warranted in this case, Richard Cooper, along with Canadian epidemiologist Jay Kaufman, at McGill University, crunched the numbers. They discovered that assigning a drug by race for hypertension actually makes very little difference. Combing through published studies on common hypertension drugs, they did find some small statistical gaps, but none of them profound.

In the UK, ACE-inhibitors are recommended as a drug of first choice to white patients under the age of 55 but not recommended for black patients under the age of 55. Kaufman and Cooper's data showed that for 100 white people given this drug, only 52 would respond as hoped. Meanwhile, if 100 black people were given this drug they are usually denied, 41 of them would benefit from it. The gap might be real, but it is modest. According to Cooper, it would be more fruitful for researchers to look at other factors, such as class, education and diet. Giving race more weight creates the illusion that hypertension is down to some innate difference.

So why do we persist with race? Maybe because all of us—medics included—have become so deeply attached to the racial categories we see on census forms that we cannot believe they don't have more biological meaning. We latch on to any scrap of evidence that might give them significance. Cooper, who has looked at hypertension all over the world, describes the science around it as being "retrofitted to accommodate race."

Walls and bridges

Medicine, I have come to realise, is a bit like engineering, the subject I studied at university. Although doctors draw heavily from the sciences to guide them in their diagnoses, and although pharmaceuticals are designed using cutting-edge molecular methods, when it comes to any one patient, there is much art and guesswork involved. It's about getting that person fixed, by hook or by crook, whether that means prescribing a painkiller or a sugar pill. There are thousands of ways to build a bridge and there are almost as many to treat a patient for a -common illness.

Lumping people into categories, especially those that might appear to be "natural," is a tempting way to narrow down the options and reach quicker conclusions. Not every patient will fit the group profile, but it's assumed that the proxy is good enough for most. Race becomes a shorthand in a cash-strapped, time-poor real world in which medics must diagnose and treat.

What is forgotten is that building medical walls between races inadvertently biologises race. It is dangerous if not handled with care because it leads patients—let's face it, all of us at one time or another—to believe that there is more to race than there really is. I have seen racists invoke supposed differences in health to argue that there could well be cognitive differences between races as well. Their logic is that if one set of physical differences exists, why not another?

The lingering presumption that racial gaps in health must be innate also conveniently allows society to wash its hands of the real causes of the disparity. The US is a perfect case in point. Life expectancy at birth of a black American is today three and a half years lower than for white Americans. Black Americans are hit by almost every cause of death at higher rates than white Americans. When medical researchers look for genetic explanations for these gaps, they neglect how unlikely it would be for an entire racial group to be so deeply biologically disadvantaged. They neglect that, in countries like the UK, gaps like these are seen between deprived and wealthier regions.

According to Dorothy Roberts of the University of Pennsylvania, there's zero logic in expecting black Americans to be so medically unusual: to be more susceptible to everything. "How could it possibly be that a group called black people," an arbitrary group which includes individuals with significant Asian and Native American ancestry, could "for an innate biological reason... have a particular health outcome? That just doesn't make sense," she says. "The most plausible, to me the only possible explanation could be because of inferior social conditions." As the social conditions of black Americans have improved, unsurprisingly, so too, and markedly, has health inequality on race lines—although there remains a long way to go.

But race divides in health, even if overwhelmingly not rooted in genes, remain a social reality. So what alternative is there for busy and under-resourced doctors to using race as a medical shortcut?

It may lie in speeding the move towards personalised medicine, where each person's unique health profile, determined by genetic factors as well as non-genetic ones, will guide doctors to the best possible treatment. This would require collecting information on every patient's lifestyle and diet, perhaps also on socioeconomic and environmental factors such as air quality, alongside biology. Under this system—if it can be created ethically and effectively—there would be fewer drugs that don't work, fewer adverse reactions, and hopefully no need for inaccurate proxies. Until then, clinical researchers could improve things by ceasing to search so compulsively for innate racial differences, and instead collecting more data on the other social, cultural and environmental factors that we know globally have a strong bearing on health.

None of this means that genetics or ancestry are disregarded. There will be communities, especially close-knit ones, who may share some disease traits in higher frequencies than others. Very rarely this difference is large. There is, for example, Tay-Sachs, a genetic nerve disorder that is more common than average among Ashkenazi Jews and in non-Jewish French Canadians living near the St Lawrence River. Such instances are few and far between.

But race has a power to make us believe things that lie beyond the facts. Take schizophrenia. In recent years it has been described by some as a "black disease," given that people of black Caribbean ancestry living in the United Kingdom receive proportionately more diagnoses than other groups. Although it is understood to have some heritable component, environmental risk factors, such as living in an urban environment and being an immigrant, have also been shown to be at least as important as genetics. One study published in *Schizophrenia Bulletin* in 2012 found that patients with psychosis were almost three times as likely to have been exposed to adversity as children.

Framing schizophrenia as a "black disease" contrasts, then, with an observation made by Nazi scientist Otmar von Verschuer a year before the outbreak of the

Second World War. Looking at patient data, he wrote, "Schizophrenia is strikingly more frequent among Jews. According to statistics from Polish insane asylums, among insane Jews schizophrenia is twice as common as among insane Poles." He concluded that it must be viewed in Jews as "a racial characteristic." At that time and in that place, then, schizophrenia wasn't a "black disease," but a Jewish one.

Secrets in stereo

Mathematics has been able to predict real-world phenomena with astonishing accuracy. But how that link works is still a mystery

Marcus Chown

October 2019

The Universe Speaks in Numbers: How Modern Maths Reveals Nature's Deepest Secrets
By Graham Farmelo (Faber & Faber)

Galileo was one of the first to realise a profound truth about the Universe: mathematics expresses perfectly the behaviour of the physical world. "Philosophy is written in the grand book (I mean the Universe) which stands continually open to our gaze," he wrote. "But it cannot be understood unless one first learns to comprehend the language and interpret the characters in which it is written. This book is written in the language of mathematics, and its characters are triangles, circles and other geometrical figures, without which it is humanly impossible to understand a single word of it."

Since the 17th century, mathematics has time and time again demonstrated that Galileo was right—it is indeed the unique language of the Universe. Among its spectacular successes have been the predictions of the existence of radio waves, black holes, antimatter, the Higgs boson and gravitational waves. In 1960, the Austrian physicist Eugene Wigner articulated what many had been thinking since the time of Galileo when he remarked on "the unreasonable effectiveness of mathematics in the natural sciences."

So why *is* mathematics so effective in distilling the essence of the world? How is it possible that someone sitting at a desk can write down an arcane mathematical formula that predicts the existence of something previously unsuspected—something that people later discover actually exists in the real world? To put it more bluntly: why does the Universe have a mathematical twin that appears to mimic it in every way? "The astonishing effectiveness of mathematics in physics has enthralled me since I was a schoolboy," says the former scientist and science writer Graham Farmelo. And now it has prompted him to explore the connection in his book *The Universe Speaks in Numbers*.

Perhaps the most striking example of mathematics predicting things in the real world was provided by the British physicist Paul Dirac, the subject of Farmelo's best-selling biography *The Strangest Man* (2009). The thought processes of most great physicists are essentially like those of normal people (though souped-up). They seek everyday mechanical analogues of the Universe, which they can then describe mathematically.

Famously, this was the method of James Clerk Maxwell, a Scot who in the 1860s created a model of electricity and magnetism in which the Universe was filled with turning, toothed, invisible cogs. Once mathematised, the model became "Maxwell's equations," which predicted the existence of a vast array of invisible "electromagnetic waves" that have made possible the ultra-connected world of the 21st century.

Dirac's thought processes, however, were not like Maxwell's, or indeed like those of any normal human being. He believed, at least metaphorically, that "God is a mathematician of a very high order," and that the best way to describe the Universe was to try and concoct a beautiful mathematical equation.

The big problem in the late 1920s was uniting the two towering achievements of early 20th-century physics: Einstein's 1905 theory of special relativity, which describes things moving close to the speed of light; and quantum theory, which describes the world of atoms and their constituents. In the lightest atom, hydrogen, the solitary electron orbits a proton at only about one per cent of the speed of light. However, in the heaviest atoms, the electric pull from large numbers of protons whirls an electron around at close to the speed of light, making a relativistic description essential. And it was just such a description that Dirac plucked from thin air while sitting at his desk in his spartan rooms in St John's College, Cambridge, in November 1927.

The Dirac equation is inscribed on a flagstone near the memorial to Isaac Newton in Westminster Abbey. It perfectly describes everything that was then known about the electron. But when Dirac wrote it down he noticed, to his dismay, that the machinery of the equation was duplicated. It appeared to describe not only a negatively charged electron but a particle with the same mass as the electron and a positive electric charge. In August 1932, 6,000 miles away in Pasadena, California, Carl Anderson, completely unaware of Dirac's prediction, stumbled on the "positron." It was the first particle of antimatter discovered.

Dirac's formula, concocted for its self-consistency and beauty, had predicted the existence of a previously unsuspected Universe in which every subatomic particle has an oppositely charged doppelgänger. The Dirac equation is arguably the most productive equation ever devised, with the most wide-ranging and startling consequences.

Einstein was actually a pioneer of Dirac's mathematical approach. His main motivation for both the special theory of relativity and the general theory of relativity of 1915—also known as Einstein's theory of gravity—was not any experimental result or observation, but the requirement of mathematical consistency. In particular, he realised that the laws of physics are uniquely determined by the fact that they must appear the same to all observers moving at uniform speed with respect to each other (special relativity) and to all observers no matter what their point of view, or "co-ordinate system" (general relativity).

The central importance of "mathematical symmetries" in the Universe was recognised in 1918 by the German mathematician Emmy Noether. She discovered that simple "global" symmetries of space and time are actually the wellspring of the great "conservation" laws of physics such as the one that dictates that energy can neither be created nor destroyed.

Other physicists, following her lead in the second half of the century, discovered that nature enforces a more restrictive symmetry, known as "local gauge symmetry." This led directly to the Standard Model, which describes all of the fundamental building blocks of matter plus the non-gravitational forces that glue them together, and which is widely regarded as the crowning achievement of 350 years of physics.

Farmelo covers all of this with his characteristic clarity, having carried out comprehensive research and personally interviewed many of today's front-rank physicists. They include Edward Witten, often compared with Einstein, and Nima Arkani-Hamed, one of the world's most energetic and imaginative physicists. The result is a book which, with its bird's-eye view of the panorama of modern physics, is as authoritative as it is fascinating.

Einstein, though a pioneer of the idea that mathematics might illuminate the deepest laws of physics, made a fatal wrong turn, refusing to incorporate quantum theory into his worldview with the dismissal that "God does not play dice with the Universe." Einstein's failure inaugurated a period when physics and mathematics, according to Farmelo, went their separate ways. Now, thankfully, he says, they are back together again.

One thing that has been largely responsible for the rapprochement has been "string theory." String theory is the only mathematical description of the world of fundamental physics that unifies both quantum theory and special relativity and which, as a spin-off, predicts the existence of gravity. One drawback, which critics rightly point to, is that the theory, which views the ultimate building blocks of matter not as tiny point-like billiard balls but tiny vibrating "strings" of so-called mass energy, works only in 10 dimensions of space-time. The problem is that we appear to live in a Universe with only three dimensions of space and one of time. Oh, and there is the little matter that string theory has yet to make any testable prediction about the real world. The jury is still out on whether string theory is a mirage or a tantalising glimpse of the fabled "theory of everything" that Stephen Hawking boldly predicted.

String theory is the ultimate embodiment of Galileo's idea that mathematics is the language of nature. However, not everyone believes that it is. Stephen Wolfram, the creator of the computer language Mathematica, thinks that Wigner's "unreasonable effectiveness" is an illusion. Imagine, Wolfram says, a drunk man looking for his dropped car keys on a city street at midnight. The man searches under a street light not because that is the best place to look, but because it is the only place illuminated. Similarly, Wolfram thinks that mathematics illuminates only the bits of the Universe that mathematics is able to illuminate.

Physicists are perfectly happy to accept that they cannot describe many things in the Universe. However, they would say this is simply because our current mathematical tools are inadequate and, in the future, maybe in the 22nd century, we will obtain better tools. Wolfram, however, believes we will never obtain such tools because most of what the Universe is doing is not mathematical (he believes it is computing things—shades of *The Hitchhiker's Guide to the Galaxy*).

Farmelo does not cover Wolfram's views. However, he points out an extraordinary and under-appreciated thing that appears to bolster the view that the connection between mathematics and physics is more than an illusion. The extraordinary thing is that mathematics is not only effective in physics but that physics is also effective in mathematics. When, in the 1970s, the British mathematician Michael Atiyah saw the mathematical potential of local gauge theories, says Farmelo, he inspired a generation of mathematicians to work with physicists on a joint enterprise that has been dubbed "physical mathematics." Since then, whole new fields of mathematics are being opened up, with gauge theory and string theory spawning insights into topology, the study of geometrical shapes.

The fact that the mathematics-physics connection is a two-way street is remarkable and something I have not seen emphasised in any other popular science book. In a way, it compounds the puzzle of the unreasonable effectiveness of mathematics in the natural sciences. Now we also have to explain the unreasonable effectiveness of the natural sciences in mathematics. The mystery is even bigger and even more intriguing than Wigner suspected.

I, for one, am not disappointed that the central mystery of the unreasonable effectiveness of mathematics remains a mystery—and, in fact, is now an even deeper mystery. What excites me about science is not that we know so much but that there is still so much more to find out. But although the mystery of the mathematics-physics connection is unsolved, Farmelo reminds us that the immense practical consequences of this symbiosis should not be overlooked. "Physicists have not one but two ways of improving their fundamental understanding of how nature works by collecting data from experiments and by discovering the mathematics that best describes the underlying order of the cosmos," he says. "The Universe is whispering secrets to us, in stereo."

Stranger than fiction

Marriage for a night

Under Islam, a woman can get married for an hour. The *sigheh* is a Shia solution to a physical need. In Iran, it is an anomaly—a sexual freedom sanctioned by religion but taboo in society

Wendell Steavenson

October 2002

On my first day in the Islamic Republic of Iran, all I could think about was my hijab, the Islamic covering which I was required to wear as a matter of law whenever I was in a public space. My headscarf itched under my chin; my coat felt tight under my arms. I worried about the inch of hair that was showing; I reached up constantly to adjust it, smoothing, checking. I felt oppressed. I saw how men walked and worked, wearing trousers and shirts just as they liked. Watching the women, I noted the variations of hijab: trousered legs and thigh-length jackets, sheer, flowered headscarves, blue headcoverings with a hole for the face that came down to the breast bone, knee-length manteaus and black *chadors*—tents of sheer rayon that fell from the forehead in a mass of folds to the ankle. They seemed difficult to control. The women who wore them were constantly hitching a fold under an arm, grasping a hem with their fingers, drawing it close in around the eyebrows.

Then, after a few days, I got used to the headscarf. I stopped fidgeting and felt normal. As Iranian women often reminded me, "Hijab! It's nothing. In Iran, we have much more important battles to fight."

In Iran, two women are the equivalent to one man as witnesses in a court of law. A woman must have permission from her husband if she wants to leave the country. Men can take up to four wives, but a woman must have her father's permission to marry. Men are granted divorces relatively easily; a woman has to prove abandonment, addiction or impotence. After a divorce, women have custody of boys only until the age of two and girls until they are seven.

However, Iran is also a country where 62 per cent of university students are women, where women work in ministries, schools and hospitals, where they can run their own businesses, drive and vote. There are several female MPs and a female minister of the environment. Iran is a country where, professionally, women can do almost anything.

I was new and confused, a western woman trying to unravel law from religion from culture. I came up with a Venn diagram of three intersecting circles: one for the Islamic Republic and the laws of the mullahs, one for the Koran and its directives from the Prophet Muhammad, and one for the culture of the Iranian people—customs and traditions that stretch back millennia, long before Islam came to Persia.

Iran is full of anomalies. In the Tehran bazaar I saw women covered in flapping black *chadors* shopping for short-sleeved, bare-shouldered white wedding dresses. Eminem is predictably outlawed and predictably popular. But Dariush, a banned Iranian singer who lives in LA and sings traditional Iranian songs backed with drum machines, is more popular. The 14th-century poet Hafiz, who praises women and wine, is so much a part of the national soul that even clerics recite him. At a party, my host offered me a glass of smuggled Australian Shiraz (the fabled Persian grape) and told me that he had paid off the police not to harass female guests for scant hijab and being seen with men who were not of their immediate family. Yet more than half of Iranian women choose to wear the unwieldy *chador*, even though a full length manteau is acceptable to the authorities.

In the midst of all of this, at the heart of my western questions about sex and freedom, religion and female independence, I found the strangest anomaly of all: the *sigheh*.

The *sigheh* is a form of temporary marriage peculiar to the Shia branch of Islam. In its fundamentals it is just like a regular marriage, a contract in which women are entitled to a *mehriyeh*—an amount of money—and in which any children born of the union are considered legitimate. The only difference is that the *sigheh* has a time limit that may be as long as many years or as short as a few hours.

This sounds like an excellent way to avoid the illegality of adultery and sex outside marriage, punishable by stoning (though this almost never happens), lashes and fines. In reality, the practice of *sigheh* is the ultimate oddity in Iran—a sexual freedom sanctioned by the religious establishment but taboo in society.

"In Iranian society, women do not like to admit to *sigheh*," Shirin Ebadi, a specialist in family law, explained. A married man may take as many women as *sigheh* as he likes. Married women, however, may not enter into a *sigheh*. A divorced woman may arrange a *sigheh* freely; an unmarried woman must have the permission of her father.

Ebadi has several certificates from foreign human rights organisations in her office as well as a green, flowery towel framed and hanging on her wall—a souvenir from her 25 days detained in prison for defending a group of students who had been assaulted by vigilantes after student unrest in 1999. She is as outspoken as any woman I spoke to in Iran. "Our problem is not religion, it is the ruling male chauvinist culture," she told me.

I was continually impressed in Iran by women who had stuck their heads above the parapet and suffered the consequences. One afternoon I met Manijeh Hekmat, a director who had recently finished a film entitled *Women's Prison*, in which the prison warden was characterised as a dictator, inmates were shown without hijab and there was a lesbian subplot. Unsurprisingly, the film was banned. Hekmat was tired of her failed efforts to get through the censor. "Prison conditions are the reflection of society," she said, planting her red Doc Martens squarely on the floor and pulling her long hijab coat over her knees.

Ebadi and Hekmat are at the forefront of feminist argument. The more conservative women I met attending Friday prayer were not so concerned with reform. These were the traditional women of south Tehran, wives and mothers of the workmen and small shopkeepers. When they learned that I was a journalist, they crowded around me. One wanted me to know that her daughter was a doctor, but that she also knew the Koran by heart. A robust middle-aged woman told me she studied at a theocratic school, another that she had been illiterate before the revolution, "but now I have a high school diploma." "We go swimming twice a week," announced a younger woman.

This was the biggest surprise of all. Far from repressing women, the revolution freed them from the seclusion of their homes. Traditional families began to send their daughters to school and university—because they would be in hijab, and because in the Islamic Republic there were no discos, no alcohol.

In some respects, what Iranian women have gone through in the last 20 years is much the same as western women over the last 50. Education has brought women into the workforce and given them financial independence. The difference in Iran is the lack of an accompanying sexual revolution. Women are still not supposed to have sex outside marriage. Virginity is highly valued in a bride. Divorced or widowed women entering into *sigheh* are viewed as something between a prostitute and a mistress. For unmarried girls, *sigheh* is completely unacceptable.

"Men are obsessed with the blood. Our boys expect to see blood when they sleep with their wives for the first time," Massey Shiravi told me, pouring more tea, proffering another chocolate. She is a gynaecologist, sympathetic and practical. She sees women before the wedding and the day after, with parents and husbands. Always there is the question of blood. Often girls beg Shiravi to repair a hymen and, illegally, she does so. If there has been no blood on the wedding night the husband will be furious, the girl humiliated. Shiravi gives the girl a private consultation, takes a napkin, puts a spot of blood at its centre and shows it to the husband. "Men are really stupid. I make up all sorts of stories about a bruise or a blood blister, explaining why he could not produce the blood but I was able to. They believe it."

I asked her if things had changed over the 40 years she had been practising. She said no. She told me about 14-year-olds beaten by their fathers because a government pathologist—the doctor who determines virginity—had found a damaged hymen; of husbands' families coming to her house in the middle of a wedding night screaming, "no blood!"; of incest cases thrown out of court...

"The trouble with Iran is that when you scratch the surface you find a lot of nasty tales," Pari told me me. Pari, a freelance journalist, had been educated in Britain and had returned to Tehran recently. She was my bridge between worlds. We were discussing things in a tea house in Tajrish. "So what do people do?" I asked, "What do girls and boys do?" "They play around," Pari said, at ease with western curiosity. "They play with it, but don't penetrate."

Sigheh is a Shia solution to a physical reality. It's a way of trying to organise sexual relations and the need for them within Sharia law. There are many women, for example, who hover around the religious shrines of Qom and Mashhad offering *sigheh* for a couple of hours to travelling clerics and pilgrims. During the war with Iraq, the government encouraged *sigheh* for war widows on the grounds that they could form relationships and receive some money to relieve their plight. More recently, elements in the government have even tried to suggest that *sigheh* could be a way for girls and boys to get to know each other before marriage. "It's a way of trying to control what is already happening," explained Parvin Ardalan, a journalist specialising in women's issues. "They used to arrest a boy and a girl found together. They might say that they were *Sigheh Mahram*, which meant they were legally engaged. They would then have to go before a judge. The girl's hymen would be checked and, if she was not a virgin, she could be lashed. Nowadays there is not so much of this harassment; there are new cafés opening all the time where boys and girls go together."

The Koran is like a handbook; its directives for how to live a good Islamic life are specific. It is not like the Bible, which is full of stories and allegories to interpret. In the holy city of Qom, the intellectual cradle of the revolution, the Grand Ayatollah Sanei explained to me, "Islam is a religion which comes as advice for the human being and there are laws which should be based upon those principles... The principles are of justice, equality and freedom and of easiness." Sex is a part of life and the Prophet is clearly in favour of it. "Islam is a very sexual religion," declared Parvin, as we sat in a kebab place one night, "it allows sexual relations for men in many cases, but the problem is women. Women are supposed to control and guard their sexuality."

Sigheh's tacit nod at sex—at women having sex—is at the nub of the ambivalence. Zahra Mostafavi is the head of the Women's Society of the Islamic Republic of Iran, an organisation which acts as a sort of think tank advising the government on women's issues. Mostafavi's conservative Islamic credentials are impeccable; she is the daughter of the late Ayatollah Khomeini. "It's a natural thing for both sexes to have sexual tendencies," she admits. For Mostafavi, and for other conservatives, *sigheh* is justified on two grounds: that men have these urges and they should have some legal outlet, and that women are, in fact, protected in a *sigheh* because they take on the rights of a real wife—albeit temporarily. "*Sigheh* is actually beneficial for women because it makes the man not take the relationships lightly," she says.

But for many in the clerical establishment, the reality of the arrangement remains distasteful. Grand Ayatollah Sanei is known for his liberal views on women; he talks openly about the need for reform on issues like unequal blood money, women as valid witnesses, and getting women on the national jurisprudence committee. "I believe *sigheh* is a spare tyre," he told me, "really it should only be used in cases of emergency. Problems cannot be solved by *sigheh*; it can in fact ruin lives."

I heard many different stories about *sigheh* situations. They were seldom happy tales of sexual freedom; mostly they were sordid extra-marital complications. Pari told me about her neighbour who lived upstairs. A very traditional woman, she hardly left her apartment, and depended on her husband even to do the shopping.

The woman could not have children, but her husband stayed with her anyway, perhaps because the apartment was in her name. One day she found a small repair in one of her husband's underpants; she knew it wasn't her repair. It turned out that he had had a *sigheh* with another woman for some time and had a daughter from the relationship. Pari's neighbour was distraught, but still she didn't throw him out of the house—not even when the daughter turned seven and came to live with them. "Effectively, she is bringing up this child who is not her own; it's a disaster for her," Pari said. "What about the daughter's natural mother?" I asked. "Apparently she has several other children, by other men she has had *sigheh* with—she was happy to have someone else bring up this child."

The emotional toll of *sigheh*, often just a sanctioned infidelity, is hidden. I found it almost impossible to find women who had had a *sigheh* to talk about it. I went to see a male notary. "Not so many *sighehs* are registered here," he told me. "They prefer to keep it quieter and go through a mullah. I register only about six or eight a month." There are many circumstances in which a couple might get a *sigheh*: young, liberal people who fancy each other, a divorcee trying to shore up her finances, or even people who work in the same office. But in practice, most *sighehs* occur between older men and divorced woman. "Usually the woman is having some kind of family problem," the notary told me. Legally, men must have permission from their first wife in order to get a *sigheh*, but we usually give it to them without this because in Sharia law it is not required."

I leafed through photocopies of *sigheh* registrations. There was definitely a norm: almost three quarters of the couples had stipulated a contract for one year and the price, the *mehriyeh* due to the woman, was 14 gold coins. One gold coin is worth about $80. "That's not bad money," I remarked.

Finally, on my last day in Tehran, I met a woman who had had a *sigheh* and was willing to talk about it. Feri was not what I expected. She decanted herself from a sheer black headscarf and a slinky black coat. She had a swathe of blonde hair, high-arched tweezered eyebrows and endless legs. She was 26. "I consider it a duty as a woman to explain these things," she said. Feri was divorced and had a baby son. She was not a typical Iranian woman, but she was at the vanguard of something, young and angry. "A girl in this country has no rights," she said. "She is either under the protection of her father or her husband. She just goes from one man to another."

After her divorce, Feri had a boyfriend of whom her father disapproved. Their *sigheh* had been an arrangement for legal purposes only ("it didn't change anything between us," she said) but it also served as a slap in the face for Feri's father. He was furious. "He didn't want me with any man," she told me, describing him as a "savage dictator" and saying that she thought he was a typical father. "But he has made *sigheh* a hundred times. My mother knows this quite well. But, no, it's not allowed for his daughter."

Such double standards are manifold. They are there in the shrines where mullahs preach family values but sign short-term *sighehs* for travelling colleagues. One young university professor I talked to said that he understood the theory about boys and girls and free relationships, but he admitted that when he applied it to his own possible future wife, he didn't like the idea at all.

The Koran, on the other hand, is in this respect without hypocrisy. Muhammad preached kindness and consideration to women. Some practices like polygamy may seem strange to westerners, but in the context of 7th century war-torn Arabia, it allowed war widows to be taken into a family. And it may seem unfair to a western mind that a sister only inherits half the amount her brother does, but it still grants financial independence to a woman and is far fairer than primogeniture. Famously, the hijab is not compulsory in the Koran; neither is the ban on alcohol. Many of the rules we see as discriminatory were progressive for their time. And if some of the laws seem a little unbalanced for a modern society in which women work and earn, the Shia religion allows for modifications.

The difficulty is that Iranians live according to the laws of the Islamic Republic and the prescriptions of the prevailing social culture. In Iran, prohibitions on satellite dishes, parties, alcohol, books, independent journalism, foreign movies, American pop—on ideas and culture contrary to the revolution—are quite freely flouted by much of the urban middle class. But the constraints on the relationships between men and women are much less flouted and no one ever makes light of them. It turns out to be easier to ignore the law than to contravene sexual convention. The final irony for the westerner is that sexual attitudes are the result of a kind of collective will; in short, they are the most democratic feature of the country.

Flash fish

This is the age of aquariums: high spenders (usually young men) are paying a fortune to "aqua-scape" their indoor fish tanks—and parting with up to £250,000 for a single fish. Why?

Ed Docx

April 2011

We're waiting for the suicide fish. It is Monday night. We're in expensive territory—Notting Hill, west London—and we're staring at a huge aquarium roughly 14 feet long and three feet tall. There's water and there's rock in there. Not much else.

"When they due?"

"Pretty soon."

"What are they called?"

"I don't know, man."

The protein skimmers whirr and hum in the intervening silence. "You have to feel for them," I say, after a while. "I mean, if you're going to be a fish, then you don't want to be one of these suicide guys. You want to be... second wave."

"Yes. But we're trying to prevent wipeout here. That's what it's all about. If you don't use the suicide guys to test the water, and something goes wrong, you could have a very expensive mass extermination event on your hands. Could be carbon dioxide, could be pH balance, could be salt, could be temperature, could be anything—but you lose the whole tank." He draws slow and sober breath. "Wipeout."

I've known this guy almost 20 years. For the last 10 or so, we have trusted one another with the stuff of closest friendship. And yet this is the first time we've talked tank. I feel the need to have a reciprocal secret. (A tortoise hatchery?) I daren't ask him how much it's costing; my guess is easily £15,000 with upkeep north of £500 a month.

Welcome to the booming world of high-end aquariums. Latest figures show that sales have doubled in the past year at aquarium sellers from Lancashire to Southampton. There are rumours of oligarchs and Premier League footballers frantically trying to out-tank one another, with items such as a £3m aquarium made from solid gold and mammoth tusk. But it's not just the super-rich driving the new aquarium explosion. It's also the "glamour boys" on the "planted tank scene":

well-groomed middle-income professionals—stylish, savvy, suave—for whom the submarine flora are just as important as the fauna. Then there's the internet chatroom frenzy, the busy democracy of the forums, the YouTube channels: 623,000 hits on Dave Saxby's Reef Aquarium alone. From all corners of the land, men are talking fish tank again. Not since the underwater-chic begun by the Bond films of the 1960s and 1970s has there been such interest and demand. But where has this revival come from? And what does it mean?

"The whole fish thing used to be a bit naff or strange," admits Jeremy Gay at *Practical Fishkeeping* magazine in Peterborough. "But now it's not. Now, it's young men between 25 and 35 and it's suddenly become cool. A lot of these men have serious disposable incomes and they are ordering big."

"How big?"

"You can order fish worth up to £250,000—take the platinum arowana. We flew out to Singapore to see it. The irony is that arowana are prone to jumping out of the tank and dying. So you have to put a lid on, which makes them very vulnerable to a disease called dropeye. It's crazy. But you'd be surprised—some of these football players have a lot of money and they have to spend it on something. Talk to Roland."

Even if the platinum arowana stays deformity-free and is good for 10 years, that's £25,000 a year, which is a lot of money to spend on a pet that doesn't love you back. I call Roland: Roland Marcelin-Horne, creative director at Aquarium Architecture (London, Manchester, New York).

"I can't talk," he says. "I'm putting a tank in at the house of a Newcastle player. He's very high profile. Very. Wait a second." I listen to him walking outside (crunchy gravel, massed Bentleys circumnavigated). "Right, sorry, that's better. We did an Arsenal player before. And Stephen Ireland at Manchester City—before he moved clubs—it was way more than the £100,000 that was reported. Maintenance alone."

"He pays maintenance?"

"It's all about the maintenance. We did Belgravia Square at nearly half a million—sixth most expensive house in Britain. Later this year we're doing a really big one, for a Russian oligarch. Huge. You guessed it—him, I mean. No I can't say. Then we're back to Newcastle for another of their players. It's insane."

Practical Fishkeeping have also pointed me in the direction of the bespoke aquarium makers Aquavista ("we add life to art"); specifically, the Aquavista Dinosaur Gold, the monster £3m aquarium. The brochure tells me there are only going to be three in the world and they will each comprise: "a massive amount of pure solid 24ct gold, two extraordinary side veneers made from mammoth's tusk with a unique piece of dinosaur bone from the T-rex diagonally shaved into the tusk." My friend in Notting Hill will have to step it up. I note that the Aquavista Dinosaur Gold is not without practical attributes: it is "low maintenance—designed to simplify your life," and it is available at 5ft, 6ft, 7ft and even 10ft for those who want to "bring their walls to life."

What is going on? "Maybe it's *Finding Nemo*. Or *Blue Planet*," suggests Sue Church, director of Aquariums Ltd (Lancashire). "Or it could be the whole planted tank scene. All I can say is that we've doubled our turnover in the last year. Speak to the Takashi Amano men."

The Amano men are the new and growing cadre of Daniel Craigs on the "planted tank scene." They are aquascapers; they arrange plants, rocks, wood in their aquariums in an artistic form. Think *GQ*; think glamour; think art. To these people, the fish are secondary. Takashi Amano is their high priest, and his temple is the Nature Aquarium Gallery in Niigata, a city two hours north of Tokyo. On the scene, it's well known that Amano pioneered the whole *iwagumi* thing—an intersection of zen, feng-shui and bonsai—but taken to the tank. And so his school is usually more asymmetrical, minimalist. The rival Dutch school, meanwhile, is more about heavy planting—layers, colours, textures, terracing—and they tend to hold their own competitions through the likes of the Veni Vidi Vissie organisation. ("Vissie" is Dutch for fishes. Thus: "I came, I saw, I kept fish.")

The man to speak to in Britain about the planted tank scene is Dan Crawford, one of the founders of UKAPS: the United Kingdom Aquatic Plant Society. Crawford is an Amano disciple and the beating heart of British aquascaping. "We've got 6,500 members on our forum," he says. "The numbers speak for themselves."

I've been on the forums: UKAPS, *Practical Fishkeeping*, Tropical Fish, Tropical Fish Finder, Aqua-Fish. This is where men get together to discuss their problems—algae, parasites, how to go marine. It's busy and it's emotional. "I think it's because we do the aqueous art movement," Crawford continues. "Art incorporating aquascaping. We had a big exhibition in London. Packed out."

"But why are so many men into it?" I ask. A few conversations back, I've heard that more and more women like to get their toes nibbled by Garra rufa fish. Maybe it's something similar but non-contact. "Is it about calming?"

"No." He is emphatic. "No no no. It's stressful and hectic. Sure, what I do might be nice for you to look at. But, for me, it's stress, panic, high energy. If anything goes wrong, it goes crazy. There's so much to get right, look after, deal with. I have to keep everything in absolute balance. It's got to be perfect."

"We're talking competitions?"

"We can do. For example, we went over to Hanover and they gave us six hours to aquascape. We had to choose plants, choose landscapes: rocks and wood. So we do all that—fine—but it's not easy. It's pressure. It's tension. And then... well then we find that the Germans have grown most of their stuff beforehand. So they have a huge advantage. We had no idea pre-growing was allowed! We thought it was supposed to be a level playing field!"

I can hear the hurt in his voice. But for me this is just generating more questions. The most prestigious competition is in Japan. It's called the IAPLC: the International Aquatic Plants Layout Competition, and it's run by Amano's Nature Aquarium Gallery. They had nearly 2,000 entries from more than 50 countries last year. (You have until 31st May.) But how do they get their tanks there? It must be chaos at security: all that water slapping about; jet-lagged fish; airsick coral. Jeremy Gay at *Practical Fishkeeping* puts me straight: "They email photographs."

I'm shocked. "But what about...?" I can't say it. "Photoshop?" He sucks his teeth. "Photoshop is the fish keeper's friend."

He advises me to check the rules for the IAPLC. There's a whole section on how to take the pictures. But, then, in the "contest grading guidelines," I become further confused. They tell me that "since the planted aquarium hobby involves various forms of life, we don't just appreciate the beauty of a layout shown right after its completion; we pay careful attention to observe how long the layout has been kept in a healthy condition." How can they know?

I go back to my oligarchs man, Roland Marcelin-Horne. "Listen," he lowers his voice, "marine is where the top end is really at. That's what's driving it. The rich start it, then you get trickle down. Personally, I think the whole aquascaping thing is a storm in a teacup. I know those guys. I like them. But I haven't sold a single tank because someone wanted to grow underwater cabbage. That's not what it's about."

"What about women?"

"No. You can watch the rich wives losing interest the minute you explain it's hard work—with the feeding regimes and cleaning schedules and maintenance and keeping the balances level. Plus you can't take your aquarium out and about. Female customers are like hen's teeth. It's men who feel the need for fish."

"Right, so it's about men and fish and sublimated emotions?"

"Yeah. What I do is 70 per cent counselling men and 30 per cent fish welfare. It's like a marriage—these men get into it and they've spent all this money and they get scared."

"Of wipeout?" I suggest.

"Sure. So here I am: a shoulder to cry on. I'm the fish emergency service. I get calls day and night from men who are in a right state. They've spent a lot so they think they can ring me whenever the hell they want, and it's not like they can go anywhere else when things start to..."

"Tank." I say, helpfully.

"Exactly."

I've heard the men thing from everyone I have spoken to. Sure, some cite Disney's 2003 film *Finding Nemo* as the moment when aquariums started coming back. Some say it is Barbados and the rise of scuba diving. Others say it's the 1970s revival: chest hair, bad shirts, aquariums. Others again say that it's the Cheltenham & Gloucester pearl-diving commercial that was on television for so long. Some say it must be the Maldives. Some say it's to do with urban claustrophobia and the lack of outdoor gardening space. Others cite Brit art. Others say it's to do with the interior design extravaganza. Some say bling, some say gadgets, some say calm and some say creation. Others speculate that it's because aquariums have everything: art, science, nature. But be it aquascapers or oligarchs or footballers or hobbyists, tropical tanks, marine, planted or cold water, the forums or YouTube, everyone agrees: it is about men.

What are they getting back? Off the record, some shop owners point out that fish never know their keepers and that this is not the usual human-pet relationship. Others go deeper and say that it's about creating a parallel universe over which you have total control. Some outsiders go darker still and say that it's about keeping pretty things in total dependency in a see-through cage. But I've heard the opposite too: that men like to stare at fish for the same reason they become amateur astronomers, because it is a pastime which carries them into a world untroubled by gender politics. Make of this what you will. As for the suicide fish—the ones they send in first to test the water, to "stabilise" the tanks, to live or to die—well, it is oddly beautiful and tragic to report that they are called clownfish.

Lot 800: the Bainbridge vase

The story of an antique Chinese vase, found in a house clearance in Pinner and sold for £43m in a small auction room, was a suburban fairytale. Was it also too good to be true?

Sam Knight

May 2011

On a Thursday evening in late March, with the clock above his head showing 6.20pm, Peter Bainbridge climbed into the rostrum at his auction room in West Ruislip. A large man in his early sixties, with owlish eyebrows and thin grey hair that he combs back, Bainbridge was wearing a tweed jacket with a handkerchief in his top pocket. He folded himself into a wooden chair hidden by the rostrum and leaned forward.

Bainbridge was resuming an auction of antiques and general effects that had started at 11am. As yet, the murmurings in the saleroom—a beige warehouse crammed with dining tables, rocking horses and grandfather clocks from the 954 lots that day—had not died down. A freelance auctioneer had spent the afternoon selling off "the smalls": the clocks, books, records, china and bric-a-brac that clutter the homes of the nation. Bainbridge, as he always does at his monthly sales, was about to get rid of the furniture. He picked up his gavel and without waiting for the talking to stop, introduced lot 800, an uncertain family of pine furniture that included a coffee table, chairs, a "magazine rack-cum-television table" and two shelving units.

Bainbridge opened the bidding: "OK-twenty-pounds-to-go-going-to-start-at-twenty-pounds-anyone-for-twenty-pounds," he said in a voice that held no space for a pause. "Twenty-pounds-now-showing-ten-I-will-take-your-bid-now-ten-pounds-anybody-for-a-tenner-nobody-for-ten-pounds-OK." Finally he took a breath. "Remember if you don't buy now it will cost you double afterwards." There were no buyers, and 154 lots to go.

Next up was 801, which went without a fuss: a dining table and chairs for £20. Then Bainbridge was off: he sold a sewing machine, a mahogany bureau and an oak desk in quick succession. The saleroom, whose atmosphere was a cross between a National Trust tearoom and a bookmakers, began to wake up. "Let's sell these quickly before they find they're missing," joked Bainbridge, as he rattled up the bids on a set of old gates. Bidders, perched on chairs that were to be sold later that evening, either sat glazed, listening to the march of money—"thirty-thirty-five-forty-forty-five-fifty"—or else ticked through their catalogues, doing sums in their heads. When Bainbridge opened the bidding on something they wanted, they stiffened and nodded. A man in a black fleece delivered his winning bid of £240 on a set of garden furniture with a short punch to the air.

These, though, were the embers of the day's trade. By the time the auction entered its eighth and final hour, the room had thinned out and most of the lots were being sold to a group of a dozen regular buyers, men in jeans who milled at the back of the room. Some of the sales acquired an informal air: "Did I get that, Peter?" A teenage porter, wearing an apron with Bainbridge's logo (a rabbit leaping from right to left), leaned against the wall. Outside in the car park, hard up between West Ruislip Tyres and an old people's home, night had fallen. Buyers sorted through cardboard boxes of loot and an old red Volvo was trying to turn around, its engine screeching in the gloom.

Four months earlier, at another Thursday sale at Bainbridge's, lot 800 was a Chinese vase. "A Superb and Very Rare *yang cai* Reticulated Double-Walled Vase, six-character mark in underglaze blue of Qianlong and of the period," began its three-page description, printed on A4 paper for the occasion. It sold for £43m, around 40 times its estimate, and was by a factor of seven the most expensive thing that Peter Bainbridge had sold (he used to auction rare cars). In his own saleroom, which he has run since 1979, the record was £100,000, for a Ming alms bowl in 2008. This vase, at 430 times the price, was a leviathan. At £8.6m, the buyer's premium (an extra charge levied by the auctioneer to cover administration) was about the same as the total turnover for the auction house for the past decade.

The sale made the television news that night. In a country short on money and fond of its knick-knacks, the story was a November tonic. Cash in the attic. On acid. Details that crept out—the vase had recently been valued at £800; it was from a house clearance in Pinner; the owners had to step outside "for a bit of air" when the hammer came down—were gifts to headline writers. A "wobbly bookcase" it was kept on and an "adventurer uncle" who brought it back from his travels (both tabloid inventions) only added to the fun. But it needed no embellishment. The vase is the most expensive work of Chinese art ever auctioned and, by £20m or so, the world's most valuable porcelain.

It was shaking the international art market before it even got into the newspapers. Most of the people at the saleroom that evening were dealers, specialists, agents and collectors in London that week for the annual autumn sales of Asian art. They had come to West Ruislip from a day-long sale of fine Chinese art at Bonhams, and got into taxis heading back into town calling and emailing their colleagues in Beijing and Hong Kong as they went. "When I first heard the result, I had to chat with my customers and calm them down," an agent in Shanghai told me. Months on, that community, which travels the world dealing in the heightened and opaque world of Chinese art, is still wondering what to make of what happened that night.

That is because the future of the vase is nothing like resolved. Within days of the sale, there was speculation on the internet that the bidding had been rigged by Chinese agents, seeking to bump up prices ahead of the big sales in Beijing two weeks later. Then, in December, a respected American dealer expressed doubts about the vase's authenticity. Since February, there has been a drip-drip of stories in the British press, mostly unsourced, questioning whether the anonymous buyer—a mysterious "businessman in Beijing"—is going to pay, or pondering the possibility of a conspiracy involving the Chinese state.

Whatever the reason, the most expensive vase in history is in limbo, in a high-security vault at an undisclosed location, not yet paid for. When Peter Bainbridge finally agreed to speak to me, he insisted, as confidently as he could, that the sale would go through. "If this whole transaction is two feet deep, you have covered a foot of it," he said. "And the other foot is very interesting." The next day he flew to Beijing, to get to the bottom of it himself. As the weeks have gone by, the sight of a tiny auction house at the end of the Central Line wrestling with the whims of China's macho, multi-billion pound art market has gone from agonising to comic and back again. It is also, according to those who make their living in this world, a warning to others. "The whole market," one dealer told me, "is not for the ill-informed."

The vase turned up at Bainbridge's last September. Along with some mahogany furniture, it was from the house of Patricia Newman, an elderly woman who had died in Pinner, about three miles up the road. Newman's sister Gene, and her nephew Tony Johnson, a solicitor who lives on the Isle of Wight, had come across a leaflet for Bainbridge's when they were going through the dead woman's possessions. After the sale of the Ming bowl in 2008, Bainbridge invested the proceeds in a mailshot across northwest London, aiming to increase the number of probate instructions and house clearances that provide most of his stock. On the evening of 22nd September, when he and Luan Grocholski, a consultant valuer, were going through the monthly haul, a porter lifted the vase onto one of the shelves reserved for ceramics.

Grocholski was cataloguing something else at the time. But the vase—16 inches tall, with bright yellow shoulders and a pale green base, enswirled everywhere with decoration, and with four panels showing cavorting fish—distracted him. It was, he said, "a sort of light source," and he couldn't help going over to it. "My natural reaction was to think, 'It can't be real,'" he told me, "I just thought, 'What an amazing copy, what an amazing fake.' Amazing, wonderful, superb... but." Picking it up, he saw on its base the reign mark of Qianlong, the 18th-century emperor who was the last great imperial ruler of China. He told the room that a genuine vase of this kind could fetch up to £1.5m. "They all went, 'Oh really,' and opened their eyes wide," he said. "Then I put it down and we went off to supper."

Over dinner at a nearby pub, the vase flickered in Grocholski's mind. When he went back to finish cataloguing he took it and sat alone in the office, turning it over in his lap. His mind began to turn as well. "The more I looked at it, the more everything started going the other way, the seesaw from being fake to real," he said.

"You're looking at the enamelling, and the quality of it, and the gilding, and this and that, and the mark, and the way it's done and the overall feeling of it... Suddenly you think actually there is no reason for me to think it is a fake. Why isn't it real?" Grocholski asked Bainbridge to remove the vase from the next sale and let him take it home to research it. That night he drove to his terraced Victorian house in Highbury, north London, with the vase packed in a Waitrose box.

Grocholski is a tall, sloping man with a persistent cough. The son of Polish aristocratic émigrés, he has passed his working days in discovery of old things in British houses. The way he speaks, invoking "one" ("one would have liked...", "there is an awful lot one doesn't know..."), is marked by gentility and the deprecating jargon—the kit and nice things—of a life lived in the antiques trade. When I went to meet him one afternoon at his house, Grocholski answered the door accompanied by a writhing King Charles spaniel. "This is Hettie," he said. "One false move and she'll lick you to death."

Not academic, but interested in the arts, Grocholski left school in the 1960s and took a year-long course at the Victoria and Albert museum. At the time, ceramics struck him as the most arcane and terrifying of fields, with its unknowable subtleties of paste and glaze. Yet it became the mainstay of both his first job, as a porter and cataloguer at Phillips auction house (now part of Bonhams), and at his second, as a valuer at Sotheby's in the mid-1970s. At Phillips, Grocholski worked under a ceramics expert called Gordon Lang, who went on to become a celebrated teacher at the Sotheby's Institute of Art. At Sotheby's he had occasional contact with Julian Thompson, one of the foremost porcelain connoisseurs of the 20th century.

It was an invigorating time, and Grocholski, who was in his twenties, was drawn to the fragile china—British, European and Asian—that passed through his hands. "It can be a sensuous material," he told me. "A sort of almost edible material." He had a feel for it. While at Sotheby's, he challenged a decision by Thompson, then head of the ceramics department, to reject an 18th-century vase that Grocholski had spotted in a client's house, converted into a table lamp. Thompson, who at first believed the vase was a copy, was persuaded otherwise and the cleaned-up piece sold for £15,000, a considerable price then.

But as of last September, Grocholski hadn't worked at a leading auction house for more than 30 years. In the late 1970s, he left Sotheby's to work as a roving valuer, instructed by solicitors and auction houses operating in the national churn of probate sales and house clearances. It was in this world that he met Peter Bainbridge, a young estate agent turned auctioneer, who was about to open his own saleroom. At first Grocholski worked occasionally for Bainbridge, but in the last 10 years the two had become close, and now he was involved in almost every sale.

Grocholski put the vase on his desk next to his computer and set about investigating it. He photographed it, searched the internet and walked the galleries of the British Museum and the V&A, which house Britain's finest porcelain collections, amassed across four centuries of trade, diplomatic exchange and war with China. All the visual and sensory signals from the vase told Grocholski that it had been fired, glazed and enamelled at Jingdezhen, the site of China's most sophisticated kilns, during the reign of the Emperor Qianlong (1736-95), a period of prodigious porcelain-making for the imperial court. He could see that the vase was highly unusual. Not only was the top half enamelled in yellows and pinks—a palette borrowed from European art and known in Chinese as *yang cai* (foreign colours)—but it was also double-walled, or reticulated, and so of extraordinarily complex construction, and would have needed to have been fired in the kiln several times.

"The loneliness of the outside expert," is how Grocholski described his research. "I'd never handled a thing like this." He had scarcely any solid information: the Johnsons only recalled that the vase had been in the family since the 1960s, and no relative was known to have been to China. For a time, Grocholski focused on finding a matching vase anywhere in the world, and came tantalisingly close in the collection of the National Palace Museum in Taipei, which has a Qianlong piece of the same construction, but red and with panels of painted landscapes rather than carved fish. Then Grocholski wondered whether a matching vase might make his more rather than less likely to be a copy. "The weight of responsibility was considerable," he said.

Still, Grocholski did not seek outside help. He did not approach Sotheby's or Christies, or any of the 30-odd prominent Asian art dealers in London, for fear of complicating the sale. When I asked him why he didn't consult with an academic authority, he said: "There was no one that I know well enough." Instead, he sat with the vase. "One lived with it." The more he read and probed, the more his confidence grew. Finally, in late September, with his mind all but made up, Grocholski turned to his old colleague Gordon Lang, who was then dying of cancer. Grocholski drove the vase to the Trinity Hospice in Clapham, and showed it to Lang. "He was already very ill," said Grocholski, "but he did see it and he thought it was all right." Lang died on 8th October. Around the same time, Grocholski called Bainbridge to tell him he believed the vase was genuine.

Bainbridge did not question his friend. Instead, he took out a full-page ad in the *Antiques Trade Gazette*. "Peter went for it," said Grocholski, "in a big way." Asian Art in London was about to start—a seven-day series of exhibitions and sales that sees around £20m change hands each year—and they decided to schedule Bainbridge's November auction, featuring the vase, for the same week. Grocholski estimated its value between £800,000 and £1.2m. On Monday 8th November, the beginning of Asian Art, the vase was put on display for the afternoon in a company boardroom, borrowed from one of Bainbridge's friends, above an Eat sandwich shop on Dover Street in Mayfair.

The biggest creatures in the Chinese art world came to see it. Removed from its box and placed on a grey blanket, the vase was inspected by a procession of the curious and the expert from noon until 6.30pm. For Grocholski, it was an enormous validation. The leading US dealer in Chinese antiques, James Lally, came, as did Giuseppe Eskenazi, London's finest. Jules Speelman, whose family has dealt in Asian ceramics since the late 19th century, ran his finger round the base, complimenting the wear. The great Julian Thompson, by then frail with illness, came and smiled his approval. No one seemed to doubt it.

For Grocholski and Bainbridge, though, the revelation was in the reaction of the Chinese who came into the boardroom. Dozens of dealers, agents and collectors—

many in London just for the week, clutching their catalogues from Bonhams and Christie's—stopped by and admired the vase. "It was like, I don't know, it was like a hot water bottle radiating happiness," said Grocholski. For Bainbridge, who is prone to flights of oratory, seeing the vase reintroduced to people who instinctively understood it made a powerful impression. "My whole viewpoint changed," he said. Bainbridge found himself imagining the labour of porcelain-making in 18th-century China. "There would have been no light," he told me, "just the light of the kilns... You know, sweating bodies racing around, dealing with their various duties. There would have been huge mess everywhere, I imagine, clays all over the floor, lots of these high-pitched instructions going on. Or would there have been silence?"

Either way, the day in Mayfair could not have gone better. When Grocholski left that night, his only fear was that his estimate was too low. "It was like a taxi meter," he said. In his mind, "the figures were click, click, clicking upwards."

It was the perfect week to sell the vase. Many of those who saw it in Mayfair went to a nearby reception the same night at Eskenazi's, the five-floor headquarters of Giuseppe Eskenazi and his son Daniel, London's most glamorous dealers of Asian art. In 2005, Eskenazi senior paid $27.7m for a 14th-century blue-and-white jar at auction at Christie's in New York, a record price for Chinese porcelain that stood for five years. That evening, he was celebrating 50 years of business with an exhibition of "Twelve Chinese Masterworks." The centrepiece, a dragon vase painted in the studio of Emperor Yongzheng (Qianlong's father), had already sold for $25m. Five clients, all from mainland China, were rumoured to have been willing to meet the asking price.

In another year, the purchase of the Eskenazi vase would have been breathtaking, but 2010 was an annus mirabilis for the Chinese art market. In April and June, records were set for works by a living Chinese artist and for calligraphy, with a painting and a scroll selling in Beijing for $14.8m and $64m respectively. In October, shortly after Grocholski had decided on his estimate for the Bainbridge vase, Sotheby's sold a similar Qianlong piece to Alice Cheng, one of Hong Kong's leading collectors, for $32.6m, eclipsing the record set five years earlier by Eskenazi. Using auction results as a guide, the Chinese art market grew by 150 per cent last year, with sales in China, Hong Kong and Taiwan worth more than $8.3bn. In March, an annual study by the European Fine Art Foundation reported that in 2010, China overtook Europe to become the world's number two art market after the US, with 23 per cent of the world's sales. A week later, Artprice, a respected compiler of auction data in Beijing, announced that China was number one.

It is not easy to grapple with these kinds of forces. One afternoon in March I went to see Giuseppe Eskenazi at his offices off Bond Street. Drilling was taking place outside and in the window a 1,200-year-old earthenware horse had its head cast down, looking pained. Eskenazi drew me a graph of the prices in the market in which he has dealt for the last half-century. After the lull of Japan's recession in the 1990s, the line crossed into the 2000s and began to climb astonishingly quickly as new clients from mainland China—"big punters," according to Eskenazi—arrived on the scene. "Up to a point," he said, "we can't find enough objects to satisfy a market like that."

There are various explanations why China's art market is growing so fast. On the one hand, there is brute economics. According to the Hurun report (China's rich list), there are now 189 US-dollar billionaires in China, around six times the number in Britain. They have few places to put their wealth. Currency controls prevent them moving their funds offshore, while in mainland China, there is inflation, a flat stock market and a property bubble—the outlet for spare cash during the last 10 years of growth—that the government is now trying to prick. Almost by default, expensive, collectible things have become an asset class worth piling into. "How are they going to spend their money?" Colin Sheaf, the head of Asian art at Bonhams, asked me before answering his own question: "Whack it on a piece of Chinese art and keep your fingers crossed."

But antiques also have a special allure. Pearl Lam, the daughter of Hong Kong billionaire and a leading gallerist of contemporary Chinese art, explained to me that "cultural enhancement"—the acquisition of knowledge and artefacts from China's pre-communist past—is an important vocation for many of the country's first-generation rich. Most grew up under Mao's abhorrence of the "four olds": old ideas, old culture, old customs and old habits. "If you don't have it and you've never had it, then you want to have it," said Lam. With money no object, you expect to get it too. But at the apex of China's antiques market, where the best pieces of porcelain and calligraphy carry the seals and inscriptions of the imperial court, there is a permanent shortage of supply. Competition, as a result, is heady, and nowhere more so than in public auctions, which remain the most reliable way to guard against buying fakes. In the phrase of Nicolas Chow, deputy chairman of Sotheby's Asia, who runs the company's Hong Kong sales: "We see some very, very gutsy collecting styles."

No one pretends the world of Chinese art is an easy place to operate, however. One major, and contrary, player is the Chinese government. With one hand, it plays sponsor: in 2002, it set up the state-funded Lost Cultural Relics Recovery Programme to buy back artefacts that were sold or looted from China; Poly Auctions, meanwhile, one of Beijing's most profitable auction houses, is state-owned. With the other hand, though, China plays wrecker. In 2009, two bronze heads, taken by French soldiers during the sacking of the Summer Palace in Beijing in 1860, were auctioned at a sale of Yves Saint Laurent's estate in Paris. A dealer, widely believed to be working for the Chinese state, sabotaged the sale by winning the auction but then refusing to pay.

Then there are the big punters. Beyond its attractiveness as an investment, and as a source of prestige and knowledge, Chinese art is also a currency for scoundrels. As long ago as the 16th century, China's porcelain, jade and calligraphy markets have been associated with the twin sins of fakery and bribery, across spectrums that run from dutiful historical replicas and honest gift-giving to sophisticated counterfeits and organised crime. Antiques frequently turn up in the prosecutions of corrupt Chinese officials. "Art has always been a suitable thank you for services rendered," the agent in Shanghai told me. In 2010, Wen Qiang, a former senior justice official in Chongqing province, was executed after being found guilty of rape and taking over £1m in bribes, including 36 art objects and 69 paintings. A year earlier, an official in charge of construction projects in Zhejiang earned the nickname

"Bureau chief: antique collection" for the trove of porcelains that police found buried under his house.

When you stop to consider its hectic entirety, the world of Chinese art is a fraught place to do business. On a rainy day in Mayfair, I met Elton Chau, a dealer who has been trading Chinese art in London since the 1980s. Before we even sat down to talk, Chau, a small man carrying a silver-coloured umbrella, started shaking his head. "The market has gone crazy," he said. "Some of the prices people pay now, they are frightening." Chau no longer takes clients whom he has not met face to face.

Like most of the people who wanted to buy the Bainbridge vase, Chau saw it first in the *Antiques Trade Gazette*. "That is amazing," he thought. He made an appointment to see the vase alone in West Ruislip where he could inspect it closely and without interruption. Then he called a client in Beijing and told him to fly to London and see it for himself. The client, whom Chau did not name, came and instructed him to bid up to £15m. From discussions with fellow dealers and agents, Chau was convinced that what he called the fish vase (many Chinese people struggle with the name Bainbridge) would fetch twice that.

Just before 6pm on the evening of 11th November, Chau was in the crowd at Bainbridge's to see Grocholski, wearing a grey suit, red tie and an armistice poppy, emerge from the office carrying the porcelain. Bainbridge was in his place at the rostrum. By chance, it was lot 800, an auspicious number for Chinese buyers. "The vase. Let's welcome it," said Bainbridge, leading a round of applause. "It's a very, very solid item."

The bidding opened at £800,000. At first it fell down to £500,000 before a series of telephone bids—handled by Bainbridge's wife Jane, among others—pushed the price over £1m. Then the bids moved in £200,000 increments. Grocholski stood behind the vase, watching his estimate fall away, his hands folded in front of him, as the auction took on an abstract quality. "Of course it was a lot of money," he said, "but as it goes up, it's only figures. It becomes less and less, it's... It's a game really."

There were seven bidders at £20m. At £30m—a record for Chinese porcelain—Bainbridge flicked his hands to the rest of the room and said: "Now the rest of you can join in." By the time the two final bidders, one a young Chinese agent in the front row, wearing a black V-neck sweater, closed in on £40m, Bainbridge's gestures were solemn. When the price settled at £43m, he began his peroration: "Ladies and gentlemen, we are coming to a conclusion now this evening. We have the most wonderful, wonderful sum of money." Then he began to count down, lingering over the number, repeating it three times, raising his left, then his right, and then finally both hands, a conductor guiding his orchestra to their last magnificent note. "Sold!" Bainbridge shouted. "Sold!" On his second swing, Bainbridge broke his auctioneer's hammer and the room erupted with noise. Grocholski stooped and carried the vase out.

There was a month of celebration—of interviews and plans—before the sale suffered its first serious knock. In a conversation with a journalist from CNBC, James Lally, the leading American dealer who came to see the vase, said he was "very sceptical" of its authenticity. "There are a number of people who do not find that piece convincing," he said. "And I think people who were bidding on it, some of them on the telephone, were taking an enormous risk."

Lally's comments surfaced in the British press five days before Christmas, and all the dealers and experts that I talked to were surprised that he made them. Dealers and auction houses do not disparage each other's stock. Most disagreed with his analysis too, albeit off the record. When I asked a ceramics expert at a major London auction house, he said the vase was "absolutely right." Jules Speelman said the vase "struck me as real." But the verdict is not unanimous. "Frankly my first impression when I saw the pictures was that there was no way that was Qianlong," a prominent academic who has not handled the vase told me. "Other people have that opinion too." In an email, the expert said there were three aspects to the vase—its carved relief fish panels; its green latticework, which was not used on imperial wares; and the unusual motifs displayed on its neck—that made it unlikely, in his view, to have been created in the 18th century. There is no way to settle the question definitively. Thermo-luminescence testing—in which a small hole is drilled in the vase and its porcelain is dated in a laboratory—is not considered accurate for objects less than 300 years old.

The comments from the sidelines infuriate Bainbridge's. "Because it's so much money," Grocholski told me, "you find all the sharks and piranhas swimming towards you." When he bumped into James Lally at a memorial service for Julian Thompson, who died in January, Grocholski confronted him about his remarks. Lally was civil but he did not retract them. Peter Bainbridge is sure that such comments—as well as media speculation that his buyer does not have the money to pay—have damaged negotiations to conclude the sale.

The persisting anonymity of the buyer has fuelled the rumours as well. At first, even Bainbridge's did not know his identity, only his agent's; now they guard it zealously. Research by *Prospect* in Beijing, which included an interview with the chairman of an auction house who claimed to know the buyer, could ascertain only that he was a businessman with interests in real estate and the steel industry. Knowing his name might not help in any case. As Elton Chau told me, there is little incentive for him to identify himself now. "Even if he has bought it, he will say, 'You got the wrong guy,'" Chau said, adding: "It is mainland Chinese. It is a mystery. End of story." Buying a major antique abroad can subject Chinese collectors to uncomfortable questions about their wealth. "The Chinese government doesn't like people to be high profile," one such buyer told me. "As soon as you are high profile, the IRS [tax authorities] will follow you."

In the terms and conditions published on the back of every Bainbridge's catalogue, it says that the saleroom receives a 20 per cent buyer's premium and a 17.5 per cent seller's commission on every lot. Applied to the vase, that should come to £16m. But after months of delay, Bainbridge acknowledges that he is now unlikely to receive that. "Standing here, right now I don't know the figure. The reality is that it will not be that figure," he said. "But nevertheless it is over £1m."

We were speaking on the phone just before 9am, and another day was beginning at the saleroom. Bainbridge occasionally had to break off to tell someone what to do, or answer another phone. But in a quiet moment, he allowed his mind to wander. “Yes,” he said. “It is deeply embarrassing to the trade. But at the end of the day, you know what? It’s just trade. It’s just money. The bottom line is money. All this. Everything that is going on is money.” Bainbridge was invited to Sotheby’s Christmas party after selling the vase, and he was struck by the champagne that was being served. “Two hundred pounds a bottle! What does that say to you?” he said. “Huge huge monies. The turnover of these places. They are just scary aren’t they?”

Families

The legacy of the sixties

Peter Hitchens, repentant reactionary, and his brother Christopher Hitchens, unrepentant radical, disagree about the late 1960s. Was it the start of a slide into moral and political nihilism or a flawed but authentic progressive convulsion?

Christopher Hitchens and Peter Hitchens

March 1998

2nd February 1998
Dear Christopher,

If there is anything worse than a young conservative, it is an old revolutionary. Young Tories are now practically extinct, but the western world is infested with paunchy radicals. My own path—a silly flirtation with revolution in my teens and 20s followed by a comfortable return to Tory certainties in middle age—used to be a cliche. Now I am an exception—asked, in wondering tones, how I come to be a reactionary. The disturbing thing about the late 1960s is that they are still going on; and we have not had to grow up.

The 1960s were not the emotional spasm they appeared to be, but a genuine upheaval with permanent effects. The year 1968 was not the beginning of this, but it was the moment when all its strands—political, moral, sexual and artistic—were woven most closely together. This was a cultural revolution far more destructive and iconoclastic than the Reformation—and lacking any true liberation. It reduced beloved institutions to rubble, while elevating musical, artistic and literary garbage. It introduced dope into western daily life. Its corrosive effects on language, manners, true human kindness, the education and upbringing of children, have been a disaster to anyone who has the slightest tenderness for the next generation. I regret that I was involved in it at all, and squirm with embarrassment when I recall most of what I said and did. I recognise my responsibility for the loss of things which I should have been cherishing and defending, while I was helping to knock them down.

You ought to agree with me. You went deeper into this than I ever did and understood it better than I. You cannot be pleased by the nurseries of ignorance we call schools and universities. You cannot be glad that heroin is sold openly in pit villages such as Grimethorpe. You cannot be happy that rock music is the nearest most people now get to poetry, or that faith, class and deference have been replaced—not, as you might have hoped, by rational self-confidence, but by the syrupy celebrity worship epitomised in the recent festival of the Goddess Diana.

Nor can you be delighted by the achievements of the political causes, foreign and domestic, that we espoused. Vietnam holds public executions of "economic saboteurs." Africa is an economic and political slum, from Cape Town to Cairo. The Clintons, that perfect counter-culture couple rooted more deeply in the movement than they now care to admit, turn out to be as inspiring in office as Warren Harding, liberated only in the president's unconventional sexual tastes.

The favourite social causes of our generation—unrestricted abortion, easy divorce, radical education, sexual equality, homosexual law reform, the end of censorship and the abolition of capital punishment—have all been victorious. In every single case, the warnings of the crustiest and stupidest conservatives now turn out to have been sober and accurate prophecies. The family is disappearing. Life, born and unborn, is cheaper than it has been for almost two centuries. Millions of women, willingly or not, abandon their children to the care of paid strangers. Sexual tolerance led not to civilised contentment but to demands for legal and moral equality between homosexual partners and married couples. Morality has been replaced by a cold hedonism which promotes sterility rather than fertility.

An ethical person is no longer one who behaves well, but one who publicly conforms to orthodox opinions. As for the liquid manure which gurgles out of Hollywood and television studios, who can now say that Mary Whitehouse did not have a case when she predicted this and warned of its effects? And who can now read the evidence of clerics and literary persons, who declared that *Lady Chatterley's Lover* was a puritan and moral book, without a snigger?

We have not merely changed the rules of politics and morality. With our complacent acceptance of narcotics and our worship of talentless rock music—both of which provide exaltation without effort—we have broken the link between pleasure and reward as well as that between crime and punishment. By mocking the ideal of the gentleman we have elevated ambition and greed, unrestrained by concern for others. Surely this is not what we wanted? We have cut down the forest of custom and law which protected us. Yet to oppose or criticise these changes is to become a lonely dissident.

It is fashionable in Britain at the moment to blame our social decay on Margaret Thatcher and the "cuts" which she failed to make in social spending. As it happens, I accept that both the Thatcher and the Reagan administrations lacked a moral centre, and I believe that this is why they failed to achieve anything lasting. However, the truly serious diseases of our society are the work of our own spoiled generation: we wanted everything designed for our convenience and gratification, chose causes because they made us feel superior to our parents rather than because we were truly concerned about them, and then called our selfish wails a revolution.

Yours fraternally,
Peter

3rd February 1998

Dear Peter,

I think we might start as we mean to go on, and leave my circumference out of it. (After all, in your eyes, I was worse when I was leaner.)

In the autumn of 1996, I was interviewing Václav Havel in Prague. He spoke very warmly of Bill Clinton and declared himself—rather indiscreetly, I thought—in favour of his re-election. "I feel a bond with Mr Clinton," he said. "Like me, he is a man of the 1960s." A definite gloom descended upon me. As a relatively unrepentant *soixante-huitard*, I felt that I could trace some of the filiations connecting 1968 to 1989. Sixty-eighters I had known, or came to know, had become valiant eighty-niners. I mention Adam Michnik, Jan Kavan, Miklos Haraszti, Hans-Magnus Enzensberger, Peter Schneider and the late Rudolf Bahro—not in order to drop illustrious names but to show "where I'm coming from." In the old debate between EP Thompson and Leszek Kolakowski, for example, I always thought that Thompson had the right of it because he believed that some of the 1960s spirit, however unintended, had begun in 1956.

Bill Clinton, on the other hand, has always seemed to me a gruesome combination of baby-boomer narcissism and political correctness. All decades are arbitrary, of course (and I suspect that you would rather periodise history by reigns), but the 1960s did have a definite shape and definition. By its close, in a phrase that I detested at the time, "the personal had become political." Much of what you do not like in the modern world can indeed be blamed on the ethos concealed in that slogan. But it was the exhausted and demoralised *terminus* of the time, rather than its most authentic expression.

I am writing this from my current roost at the University of California at Berkeley. What was the position as viewed from here in the spring of, say, 1967? The college and state authorities claimed the right to invigilate and suppress most forms of political expression. Volunteers from the campus took their lives in their hands if they journeyed—as many did—south of the Mason-Dixon line, where millions of Americans were denied the essentials of citizenship. Meanwhile the university served as a think tank and laboratory for an unjust war of aggression in Indochina. And much of the state of California was a proving ground for thermonuclear experiments which calmly envisaged the extinction of the human species for the sake of a dishonest superpower quarrel. Thanks in part to a cultural and political rebellion with which the name Berkeley is identified, the extension of civil rights became unstoppable, while a lousy war was actually stopped—in large part by a movement of citizens.

My chief regret, looking back on that period, is that I didn't play a more active part. Two of the great initiatives which also featured locally—the struggle for decent treatment for the Spanish-speaking underclass and the movement for nuclear disarmament—still await their dénouement. I was, I might add, relatively unmoved by the poetry of Allen Ginsberg and totally unmoved by the music of Frank Zappa. But Václav Havel says that these voices came to him as liberators. It's not much of a test of one's broadmindedness to see what he must be driving at.

Take the same moment in Europe and elsewhere and you find that military fascists in Greece have just joined the sub-Nato club comprised of Spain and Portugal;

that a British Labour government is capitulating to a racist settler revolt in Southern Rhodesia; that Northern Ireland is a sectarian political protectorate of a cynical "Conservative and Unionist" party and that Israel has taken the leap from tiny David to the role of occupying Goliath. Nelson Mandela has two decades of confinement still ahead of him. At Oxford University, the PPE course ends before the study of Keynes—and official permission must be sought for everything from apparel to the distribution of leaflets, to say nothing of equal overnight rights for heterosexuals in college (male guests had always been allowed). I probably did more to alter the conditions in the last category than in any other, but I did at least witness and applaud and argue for some of the later triumphs in the other areas too, all of which were substantially *soixante-huitard* in origin, and some of which still need more attention of the same kind. I would not take back a word or deed of it.

Nor would I—do you invite me to do so?—restore the ban on DH Lawrence. Furthermore, Zimbabwe and South Africa are much less "slummy" than they would have been under the old dispensation; and Vietnam, if our lot had had any say in the matter, would have become independent in 1945. Grimethorpe was fairly rugged when I saw it last during the miners' strike of 1974, but the prevalence of illegal hard stuff is the work of serious cartels with occasionally frightening friends in high places; hardly the outcome of a flower-child ethic. I am in favour of decriminalisation of all narcotics and also the unfettered availability of all forms of contraception. But I don't get your drift about fertility. Apart from your status as a Jeremiah who sees little hope for our species, do you want the human sexual urge to lead to the production of more *bambini*? (I realise that, like all Christians and monotheists, you are stuck with the belief that we are (a) created sick and (b) commanded to be well.)

Looking back, I am most of all struck by how little the theories of the ownership of the means of production had to do with the outcome of anything. I wouldn't have believed that at the time. There is also the matter of unintended consequences. (Endless grudge suits about harassment, say, instead of any talk about workplace democracy.) You could reply that I am picking the good bits and leaving the bad bits out. But in order to say that you would have to be a different kind of critic, one who is not merely issuing an undifferentiated Whitehousean lament.

Fraternally,
Christopher

4th February 1998

Dear Christopher,

As a person of girth, I can assure you that it is the politics, not the podge, that I object to.

You have found my weak point with your mention of Václav Havel and his comrades, but I think I can explain their forgivable error. They were engaged in a genuine, dangerous liberation struggle rather than the vainglorious play-acting on our side of the curtain. There was no nonsense about repressive tolerance from Comrades Gierek and Honecker. It is true that some eastern and central Europeans may have taken inspiration from our silliness, and mistaken the self-pitying whine of rock music for the sound of revolt. However, I suspect this was only because they thought we were more serious than we were. Being so serious themselves, they could not conceive that we were so trivial. They may also have felt that the banal contentment of the Nato countries lacked nobility as a goal, even if it was what millions desired.

Do you perhaps overstate the horrors of pre-revolutionary life? In your Oxford, the PPE course may have ended before Keynes. In today's Oxford, undergraduates are enrolled who have never heard of Keynes—and could not spell his name even if they had, although they are of course free to engage in any kind of sex, while eminent college principals publicly excuse illegal drug-taking. Could these things be connected? You say the Berkeley and California authorities "claimed the right to suppress most forms of political expression." What sort of language remains to describe real dictatorships?

Narcotic cartels thrive because we removed the moral barriers against drugs. DH Lawrence was never banned, just subtly restricted so that true pornography *could* be prohibited. Break the link between the sexual urge and procreation, and you get—well, what we have got. And I knew you wouldn't like it, but as a monotheist I have to point out that of course the dismantling of faith is to blame for the Spencer cult and many other pagan manifestations that you rightly despise.

Yours fraternally,
Peter

5th February 1998

Dear Peter,

Do not think for a *moment* that a more generous and expansive tone is going to save you. As head of the family it is my job—nay, it is my *duty*—to inculcate some lessons that you will not soon forget.

My old college was good enough to award me a scholarship to visit the US, and by way of return I still offer myself on the hospitality list for those who benefit from the same programme. As the years have passed, the main change is that about half the recipients are young women. (That's up from a whopping 0 per cent in 1970, when there were no female members of the college at all.) It would be condescending to say that they seem bright and well read, because I am aware that admiration for youth is a trap set for middle age. What I can say for sure is that they are no worse than my contemporaries were.

As late as Harold Wilson's "victory" in 1966, it was illegal to be grown up and "queer" in Britain. Felons were executed by hanging, and the debased concept of "deterrence" made some people argue that it didn't matter if the odd innocent went through the trapdoor as well. There was book and theatre censorship, the latter imposed by someone styling himself "The Lord Chamberlain." These were indeed the days of traditional standards.

You may think that you have caught me in a slothful phrasing about "political expression," but if I had been writing about a totalitarian system I would have elided the word "most," and substituted "forbid" or "compel" for "suppress." I would also have omitted the word "claim." Casuists and neo-conservatives may have fooled about with the genuine distinction between "authoritarian" and "totalitarian," but

I give them credit for being deadly serious about the authoritarian option. They preferred it to democracy, as well as to absolutism—at home, as well as abroad.

A considerable part of the grandeur of Martin Luther King, Jr was that, with a pretty full plate in front of him—including daily threats to his life—he insisted on going the extra mile and denouncing the Vietnam War and nuclear blackmail. The entire black and white establishment united in saying that this proved his "extremism." You might want to reconsider your choice of the term "self-interested."

Once you are done with murder and theft and the other human universals, there is no serious behavioural problem to which prohibition is the solution. And there is no way of "breaking the link" between the sexual urge and procreation. A bit of distance between those two things has, however, been found helpful by many people who are ethically superior to both of us. It is also the profound aspiration of many in those poor countries which you loftily wrote off as "slums."

Faith in the supernatural and the paranormal is not my responsibility. But did not the same Church of England, a state church, which sanctified a royal wedding while knowing it to be a sham, play hypocritical host to the obsequies in an ancient abbey? And was this paganism? The struggle against cretinism must be waged every day and in every decade, and is not much forwarded by those who grizzle that it's been all downhill ever since whatever year it was when their own memories began to go a bit dim.

Yours fraternally,
Christopher

6th February 1998

Dear Christopher,

In the Dallas Museum of Art there is, or used to be, a rather frightening painting of the prodigal son returning, years too late, to a ruined and deserted homestead. I am afraid that our generation, the most indulged in human history, has wasted its substance on riotous living, shrugged, and charged it to our credit cards. If we ever realise that it is time to turn for home, we too will probably have left it too late. I am frustrated by the Panglossian refusal of the left even to consider the possibility that the past 30 years have been a dreadful mistake. Your side has just as much to fear as mine from the approaching breakdown of social peace and the dark age of ignorance which will accompany it. If my tone is generous, it is because this subject matters too much to be lost in *ad hominem* bickering.

So let me teach *you* one or two lessons. I suspect that you were exceptional when you were chosen for your scholarship. I think it likely that your young visitors are also outstanding and may have given you a false impression. Friends of mine in the universities no longer bother to dispute that there has been a serious fall in standards, particularly in the body of knowledge expected at entrance. Interestingly, it is only governments (of both parties) which still seek to lie about this. I would have thought that might at least make you suspicious.

I am sure you don't mean to give the impression (although you very nearly do) that pre-1966 Britain punished buggery with the noose. However, this would accord with the dark picture you paint, of iron censorship and cruel intolerance. This is where we have to remember which question we are trying to answer. Mine is not: "Were things bad then?" It is: "Are they worse now? If so, why?" My monotheist view warns me that human society is not perfectible, and my reactionary position warns me that motion is not necessarily progress (ideas which ought not to be as eccentric as they are).

It seems to me that there is, or ought to be, some tolerant midpoint between the dreary excesses of Old Compton Street and illegal homosexual scuffles in the Hyde Park gentlemen's convenience. I would also prefer not to have to defend any censorship at all, even the gentle restraining hand of the Lord Chamberlain. However, the torrent of coarseness and pornography which now overwhelms television, the cinema and the stage suggests to me that we may not have the proper moral equipment needed to handle liberty. And this is my reply to your assertion that there is no serious behavioural problem to which prohibition is the solution. I partly agree with this, but I think you will have to admit that the law can be a useful support for the true remedy, which is a universally accepted moral code, enforced by convention, disapproval and shame rather than by courts, prisons and gallows. It is this invisible web of protection which the enthusiasts of 1968 (and of 1789 and 1917) sought to tear to pieces. They also hoped to break down the pillars which held it up—love of country, loyalty, a shared acceptance of what is good and beautiful, religion, tradition, deference and respect for family and authority, and perhaps above all the great virtue of self-control.

They succeeded rather well. It is astonishing how short a time it has taken to smash up the family, to popularise abortion (the most violent, but not the only way of breaking the link between the sexual urge and procreation), to abolish history and literature, strip the altars, burn the flags, spit on the crown, give dope and contraceptives to children but deny them poetry or parents. Every wretched slogan shouted on the streets in 1968 has come to pass in the real lives of the millions. How can you still be pleased?

Yours fraternally,
Peter

7th February 1998

Dear Peter,

I suppose that you keep a high horse conveniently tethered nearby, and leap aboard to flog it round the paddock, whatever the topic may be. Well, I have a patient old donkey on my Animal Farm, and what he says is that history goes on for a very long time. As I think *I* conceded (taking my turn at the concessionary tone), there were "1960s" slogans that mutated into either silliness or nastiness or both. To the one I cited I could add: "Take your desire for reality"—a popular Parisian poster of the time. Taken literally, these helped to raise the curtain on the "me decade" and the "New Age." But, as I have also tried to remind you, they originated as notes of desperation or defeat when it became obvious that the short term was not to be millennial. Against that, I recently read an interview with Mikhail Gorbachev, in which he defined himself as one of the *shestidesyatniki*—"people of the 1960s"—who were changed forever and for the better by the events and debates of that period.

Glasnost and *perestroika* are grand words and always will be. They eclipse, for me, the downsides of sex and drugs and rock and roll (which do have their upsides as well).

You—if you will forgive me for saying so—sound a bit like one of today's Russian blimps, growling about how everything has gone to hell on a sled since the firm hand was withdrawn. I appreciate that you identify more with those who would restore the Orthodox dispensation but, having seen the Serbian cousins of this movement at work, I'll pass on that too.

An interesting question arises: which of us is the nostalgic one? I admit to finding political life in the 1960s more vivid and authentic and worthwhile than I have ever found it since. The current age of populism—and the manipulation of that populism by elite devices and techniques—has no charms for me. But this is a result of the 1960s only in the sense that the "gilded age" of corruption was the outcome of the American civil war. That is to say, it is true, but not the truth. And the standards and experiences of the abolitionists (who had not sought the war but did not shirk it) were mobilised for new battles under different flags. What could not be restored was the *ante bellum* "ideal" of an organic society in which each knew his or her place in some ineffable contract. Your yearning for something like this is utopian, but only in the most arid sense.

My students at Berkeley freely confess that they arrive with some large holes where their education should have been. But they were educated for a consumer society and not by my comrades; we will, nevertheless, contrive to keep the Dark Ages at bay. It is true that the television and cinema screens are full of crap (most of it rather sexless) but there are several excellent and flourishing bookstores within strolling distance to which I can direct them; and on the shelves are works by old literary and political allies of mine which for moral seriousness will bear comparison with any throne, altar or crown on offer.

After 30 years, I quite understand that there's no going back. But there are ways forward, even through the inevitable thicket of unintended consequences. You deny this to yourself by adopting an ethos of "deference" exploded long before the first baby ever boomed.

Fraternally,
Christopher

Worst of England

The anti-modernist Kingsley Amis and the post-modernist Martin Amis have spawned half a century of snarl and sneer in British fiction. They are both big enough to represent the successes and failures of their respective generations, but cannot (or in Martin's case, cannot yet) compete with the best American novels

Andrew Marr

July 2000

The survival of the novel—that is, a work of fiction written to do more than while away a few hours of boredom—is rather surprising. As a developing form the novel was pretty much exhausted a lifetime ago—by, say, 1922, the year in which *Ulysses* was published and Kingsley Amis was born. As with figurative painting, the "modern" novel would twist and struggle to find a way forward and then more or less give up. But whereas the visual arts turned to *new* forms—pop images, video and installations, the stuff of Tate Modern—the novel settled back into its early-modern or classical form and kept on going. Philip Roth's last three novels, for instance, *American Pastoral, I Married a Communist* and *The Human Stain*, are rich, high works of a completely traditional kind (silver age if not golden age); they would be completely comprehensible in terms of form, if not history, to a contemporary reader of, say, Émile Zola or Henry James. The experimental novels produced with such excitement by modernists—Celine, Wyndham Lewis, William Burroughs, the French new wave, Woolf, and so on—have gone nowhere.

Why is this? "Because they were all bloody unreadable," would presumably be Kingsley Amis's answer. That is not true and, in any case, the triumph of the conventional novel form is a standing refutation of the cultural pessimism that informed Kingsley Amis's curmudgeonly opinion. More likely, it is to do with the different markets. A Damien Hirst can become successful with the patronage of a single Saatchi, but a novelist needs to find hundreds of thousands of individual patrons in order to live well.

The truth is, the novel remains the handiest tool for millions of us to use when thinking about our lives and their shape—the novels of childhood, of early sex and sentimental education, of family and divorce, the novels of bereavement, old age and loss. Film rarely does this job. It does spectacle and horror, escapism and jokes, but not life. The novel's nearest rival is the television soap opera; it has bigger audiences but a vacant glossiness and a necessary absence of catharsis. No, the chances are that if you are averagely intelligent and educated you will think about your generation, and what is happening to it, through the eyes of serious novelists—John Updike, Ian McEwan, PD James, Alasdair Gray, Iris Murdoch—very much as the Victorians did. Because of this the novel is required to update its information; the surrounding furniture of music, sexual ritual, social atmosphere, political worry and fashion, everything from emails to Aids, has to be right for new readers to turn a page with a whoop and think, "yesss… that's how it is now, for me, for us." The great novelists of the canon are essential for an educated mind, but we need the contemporary tellers, too. And the achievements of the latter—the reports they send back to the rest of us about how we're all getting on—shape our imaginations and choices too.

This is a long way of saying that novelists matter, more than journalists or film-makers, and is a prelude to the subject of this essay: the Amises. It was going to be an essay on failure, but it has turned out rather differently. Its origin was a semi-flip remark I made to the editor of *Prospect* a few months ago, to the effect that for me the two Amises were "the worst of England" and their half-century of snarl and sneer was the most interesting thing in recent literary life.

Some of this, at any rate, I still stand by. To attack Martin Amis's novels, as distinct from his dentistry, hauteur, alleged greed and so on, is to invite the wrath of a large protective shield of Martists in newspapers, literature and publishing. It's not done. But surely I am not the only person who has been sent by newspaper reviews to the latest great, wise, hilarious, life-enhancing Martin Amis novel, only to find myself consumed by nausea and boredom after a few chapters. Not all his novels, admittedly: *London Fields*, his best by far, and *Time's Arrow*, a single good idea sustained right through with manic intellectual energy, will stay on the bookshelf. But *Money*, *Success*, *Night Train*? Utterly brilliant phrases, sentences of pure verbal genius, fine paragraphs, so-so pages and, taking them all in all, sloughs of despond, every one of them. As for *The Information*… a stinker, no?

Kingsley was a different matter. Nobody with any ear for the English language could resist *Lucky Jim* or *The Old Devils*. But the succession of women-baiting, self-consciously bufferish performances (the very worst were *Stanley and the Women* and *Russian Hide and Seek*) which came garlanded with squeaks of delight from the puff-merchants of the press, plus his apparently serious loathings of great contemporaries, foreigners, Jews and so on, put him beyond the pale.

What slightly spoils this diatribe, however, is that to prepare for it I went back to Kingsley Amis's novels and enjoyed myself more than was convenient for my purposes. *Jake's Thing*, for instance, famously rancid with misogyny, turns out, on re-reading, to be surprisingly tender in parts, and intensely moving on the humiliations of impotence. *The Old Devils* will last as long as novels do; but it is not the only brilliant treatment of old age—*Ending Up* is one of the most delicately tragic funny books I have ever read. And so on.

Then came Martin's memoir *Experience*, certainly the oddest but also one of the best books he has written. It has terrible flaws and jarring notes, but it is utterly compulsive too. Early on, he throws a pre-emptive punch at any mere critic. There is a good, structural reason, he writes, "why novelists should excite corrosiveness in the press... When you write about a composer, you do not reach for your violin... But when you write about a novelist, an exponent of prose narrative, then you write a prose narrative. And what was the extent of your hopes for *your* prose—bookchat, interviews, gossip? Valued reader, it is not for me to say this is envy. It is for you to say this is envy. And envy never comes to the ball dressed as Envy. It comes dressed as something else: Asceticism, High Standards, Common Sense..."

This is, of course, mere bullying. The case of Martin Amis would not matter a tinker's cuss if he was not one of the finest prose performers alive. There are plenty of examples in *Experience*. His account of his father falling over on a traffic island in the Edgware Road (pages 338 to 339 in the hardback) is a masterpiece of funny-sad writing; if I'd been able to write like that just once I would consider mine a life well lived. So yes: envy. No one who relishes a sinewy sentence and a compacted block of thought, compressed and kneaded into surprising freshness, could resist the tribute of envy. The force is with him.

But that makes what he does with that force even more important. Yes: he has had a lot of rubbish written about him, not least about his avarice. (When you think of the money that company-destroying corporate lawyers, dim crooners and oafish money-traders manage to get their fat hands on, advance payments to serious novelists should be a matter of general relief, not abuse.) But to imply that Martin Amis's talent should put him beyond criticism is nonsense on stilts, with a scowling mask and an ostrich-feathered hat.

In fact it is a little worse than that. You live your professional life in and around a public family. You have your media and literary friends—polemicists as powerful as Christopher Hitchens and James Fenton, many literary editors, about 5,000 admiring younger writers, your father's circles of poets and critics. As you say, you've been name-dropping ever since you first said "dad." You would not have grown and thrived without your great gift but, hey, none of the rest has exactly stalled the career, has it?

You have played your image alongside your novels: the tough-kid 1970s literary hooligan, the snooker lout, the charmed circle of brilliant mates, the private slang leaking into the books, the film star friends, the famous women. There has been a violently-coloured penumbra around the actual books which has been, let's face it, part of the deal. Martin Amis is no Salinger, not a man to lock himself away in the forest. And now, in the memoir, we have further material thrust upon us: the Fred West connection, the lost-and-found daughter, the divorce and remarriage, the struggle and then loss of the remarkable father. And it is all recounted in prose which, while thinned down with white spirit, is still close enough to the clotted writing of his novels for an idle reader to confuse fact and fiction. To turn around now, with injured innocence, and complain about media intrusion into your private life, about "how often my free will has been compromised by fame"—well, it's rather late in the day, that's all. Whatever Martin Amis's problem has been, too much publicity it ain't.

What, then? The problem is evasion, a cold obliqueness to life which is accomplished in the novels through bravura writing at the expense of closure, genuine catharsis or structure. The energy is intense but febrile, like an opera crammed with thrilling arias but without a plot, heroine or jot of real emotion. This would not matter much, perhaps—after all, nobody is obliged to read the books—except for the suspicion that the problem of Martin Amis is the problem of British men of his generation—many of us, anyway. Like his dad, he is good enough to represent more than himself; he is the message as well as the messenger.

Here is a crude proposition. Kingsley Amis was the worse man but the better writer. That, of course, is a generational judgment made by a 40-year-old. Kingsley Amis had the characteristic virtues and vices of British males of his time; he was still driven, even tormented, by the old British Protestant work-ethic, but he was, as his son notes, a baby all his life. The self-pity, the mixture of spite against women and utter reliance on them, the morose hostility to outsiders, the blub-blub pessimism about his country, the conservative timidity in cultural matters, the booze-bottle as teat... none of this is attractive, and it is ruthlessly self-exposed in his letters.

Kingsley Amis may have been a living caricature: the club-man who had little time for "abroad," the vigorous fucker and drinker who managed to feel oppressed by "the permissive society," the poet and prose-master who made much of his enthusiasm for dirty limericks and Dick Francis. But he was also somehow emblematic. His post-1945 England was indeed a country that had lost its way and its confidence, a nation of anti-modernists, of mildly resentful, hard-working, women-hating, culturally conservative men redeemed—some of the time—by their quiet, stoical courage and humour. Larkin, bleaker and more courageous than most, was their poet, and Kingsley Amis, funnier than most, was their novelist, and both men were confident about who they were. They were not, in the French phrase, comfortable in their skins—that was part of the point—but they were self-assuredly uncomfortable. This confidence gave Larkin's poetry its deadly compression, those killer closures; and it gave Amis's novels their comic structure, their resonant conclusions. These were books which knew where they were going.

Where did this leave Martin Amis? One clear clue is provided in *Experience* which contains, interleaved through its disjointed narrative, a series of letters he wrote as a teenager to his father and step-mother, Elizabeth Jane Howard. Though he cringes from them now, they are precociously fluent for a schoolboy: "Thanks awfully for your letter. So we all appear to be working like fucking fools. I seem to be flitting manically from brash self-confidence to whimpering depression; the English is all very fine, but the Latin I find difficult, tedious and elaborately unrewarding... In my last few days in London I read *Middlemarch* (in three days), *The Trial* (Kafka is a fucking fool—in one day)... Much as I'd love to see you both, it does seem that I'll be doing too much fire-ironing and pie-fingering (I'm sure Jane could adapt that to one of her swirling mixed metaphors), to be able to get away..." The fluency, of course, is borrowed. Young Martin's breezy rhythm is remarkably close to his father's.

He arrives, therefore, as a young writer, with the gift of astonishing loquacity but also the son of a certain kind of Englishman who was, for post-1960s youth, utterly redundant. Kingsley Amis, however, seems to have been a hard man to rebel against—too funny, too tolerant and too lacking in fatherly discipline in the first place. So Martin develops that encrusted rococo English he's famous for, sentences that preen and double up and go nowhere—a perfect cover for the inherited fluency. His novels don't have the self-confident structure of his father's. He creates low-life grotesques and Hogarthian caricatures to replace the plausible, shrewd, just-caricatures of the Kingsley Amis books. He is less naked than his father, less fully confronting life's trouble.

Some things don't change: Kingsley Amis's most compelling novelistic gift was his ear, his talent for mimicry which resurfaces, untouched, in his son's work. Both are masters of reported inarticulacy. Also, the son, like the father, abandons his family and is tormented by the choice. The son drinks and screws and surrounds himself with a reliable band of male friends to share in-jokes; it's a snooker club, not the Garrick, but the principle is the same. Julian Barnes seems to perform a similar role for Martin to the one Philip Larkin played for Kingsley, until the rift over Martin dropping Barnes's wife as his agent. The Kingsley-Larkin friendship also cooled, although less dramatically, and then triumphantly revived later in the two men's lives. In Martin Amis's account of that "delightful" rejuvenation, with the return of old endearments and verbal energy, there is perhaps a wistful message for Barnes.

So the son is like the father in much, but he has the liberal politics, the more generous attitude to women (although I still think he's a poor writer of female character), and the more confused attitude to his own identity which all go with his generation. Again, there is a wider message. Millions of men of roughly his age, say from their mid-thirties to their mid-fifties, broke out of the shell of British post-war maleness, its puritanism and pessimism, its misogyny and insularity, only to find themselves adrift and confused, freed from their fathers but not free, lacking a robust sense of self or purpose. Like Martin Amis, they are not very good at stability, and seem younger at 50 than their parents were at 30. Like him, but unlike their Americo-sceptic fathers, many of them are fixated by US culture. They—we—reject the big picture and struggle to make sense of anything much.

This revolt against structure and therefore meaning is exemplified in *Experience*, which dodges awkwardly through space and time. There is, after all, an almost too-perfect Shakespearean plot buried in the book: the daughter lost and found; the good cousin lost to unspeakable evil, and not redeemed; the father lost and the other father found; the wife and children abandoned and the wife and children found. The hero errs, is human, is tested (by a dentist) and is reborn. There is even the comic underplot, featuring a comic villain, Eric Jacobs, the biographer. It adds up to a richer stew of plot-lines than *The Winter's Tale*. Imagine what Tom Stoppard, say, or Michael Frayn, could do with that on a London stage.

Instead, this-being-here-this-being-now, it has been cut up, disgorged in pieces in newspaper interviews and profiles and presented in a deliberately disjointed book. *Experience* sets hares running and fails to follow them. It ends on a jarringly discordant and weak account of a trip to death camps in Poland and evades questions any reasonable reader wants to know about. There is a picture of a baby which "cannot be named for structural reasons"—yet dammit, there are no pictures of the main tragic protagonist, Martin Amis's teeth. He concludes: "My life, it seems to me, is ridiculously shapeless. I know what makes a good narrative, and lives don't have much of that—pattern and balance, form, completion, commensurateness."

But nor, characteristically, do Amis's novels; structure and meaning are joined at the hip, but Martin Amis has always had a structure problem. His novels start, continue and finish; they rarely travel or conclude; they lack completion. Why is this? *Experience* is a book haunted by at least two other books: Kingsley Amis's own *Memoirs* (and, less so, his *Letters*); and Saul Bellow's *Ravelstein*. Bellow is a surrogate father to Amis; that friendship, Bellow's recent illness and quotes from drafts of *Ravelstein* recur constantly in *Experience*. And *Ravelstein* is also a book made on the disputed ground between memoir and fiction, a novel bearing an uncanny closeness to a portrait of Bellow's friend Allan Bloom, author of *The Closing of the American Mind*, who died of Aids.

Ravelstein, however, is a book of tremendous confidence: poised and beautifully formed, a model, in Amis's words, of pattern and balance, form completion, commensurateness. It is spare; but full of sinewy wisdom, a judgment flying high above the ground and missing nothing. The same could be said for late Roth, DeLillo, Ford, and some Updike. Somehow, the male American novelist has an openness to history, to the wider culture and a sense of men's condition that the British male novelist does not—certainly including Amis, who is probably the most conscious of the American issue. Is it because of the grandeur and glamour of "the American century" or the easily-mocked but triumphant cultural earnestness of part of the US elite? At any rate, our story seems smaller by comparison, our male imagination (for this does not apply to female novelists or less so) inward, pinched, shrivelled, unconfident. And perhaps it is just that Amis is too good a novelist not to reflect those cultural failures—a man whose stylishness is doomed to fail because of his time and place. The dodginess and brokenness of *Experience* is the brokenness of the experience of many of us.

I am not saying that the Americans are optimistic in a simple way, just big in every way. Philip Roth, whom Amis (rightly) attacked for his post-modern, writing-about-writing novels of the Zuckerman era, has since managed to give triumphant shape to lives lived, to have the boldness and courage to spread his empathy, to make judgments on good people struggling with fate, and to achieve closure. This doesn't mean a neat, happy, invigorating or simple conclusion. But for some reason, Roth and other male Americans have an openness and a breadth of historical understanding which allows them to make old-fashioned, well-built novels about the genuine catastrophe—the one which happens to all of us—while British male novelists have been twisting away into genre and grotesquerie. Not true, I know, of people disdained by the literary set, such as Nick Hornby or Tony Parsons. But it is true of the most talented, Martin Amis above all.

His father is dead. His father's letters, the last great slew of his writing, are published. The shadow of post-war man, with all its virtue and failure, is lifting from the country. The worst of England, and some of the best. Now Martin has started to write a little straighter—to look his life if not in the eye, at least in the face. Is it possible that he, like Roth, will move beyond a mediocre middle age into a triumphant late flowering? He has the gift and the intelligence, but has he the generosity to get beyond the old evasions, the coldness, the camouflage of that deadly, fish-eyed stylishness? If he does, a generation will be the richer for it.

L'invisible

A second child often gets much less attention than the first.
Can a father make it different for his newborn son?

Sam Leith

June 2011

When I had my first child—a daughter, Marlene, now nearly two years old—I hit on what seemed to me an effective metaphor for what was going on. I was moving from a Ptolemaic universe into a Copernican one. Before you have a child, you are the centre of your own universe: everything revolves around you. Parenthood gives you the proper—the Copernican—sense of your marginality. This new thing takes its place, and you are in orbit around it.

I went on to realise—a much more important realisation—that the nature of new parenthood is that you think you're the first person it's ever happened to, and there is nothing you can think about it that hasn't been thought already. A friend to whom I was expounding my theory, said: "Yes, yes, I know someone who calls it 'a Copernican revolution of the self.'"

Well. The image stands. The first child is a cataclysm: a great reversal. The cliché is that "nothing prepares you for it," but actually everything prepares you for it, or tries to. When the editors of Sunday supplements seek parenthood columnists they look to new dads or first-time mums. When people tell you their boring stories (which you put up with because there's a quid pro quo: you get to bore them with yours) they come under the rubric of "becoming a father" or "becoming a mother."

It's the second child, actually, that nothing prepares you for. It's regarded as less of a deal, a repetition, albeit a happy one: more of the same. And yet it isn't. It's new in a more profound and less discussed way.

To go back to my initial image, you're adding another heavenly body to the astrolabe. This is a less dramatic but—it stands to reason—a much more complex transformation. The bonds of love and rivalry, care and dependence that are, in this little universe, the forces of gravity, are now acting on mother and father and two children and in complex ways between each and all four of them. You're not dealing with three relationships: you're dealing with six.

We do recognise that, but only at a more or less subliminal level. One thing I felt strongly before the arrival of the second, for instance, was a change in the way I conceived of us as a unit. We had been, hitherto, a couple with a child. With two kids, I felt, we'd earn the name of "a family."

But in terms of front-of-the-mind thinking, the arrival of a second child is taken somewhat for granted in our culture. What makes it unique—and trickier than the first in terms of what you expect, and how you feel, and how you manage—gets occluded; as second children themselves can do.

Even the advice you get tends to be about managing its effect on the first child: don't let your first one see you fussing over the new arrival; shower her with extra attention and love; keep an eye out for first child/second child/sharp object interactions. (Surely every family has a version of the tale told in mine, of my infant uncle being intercepted having not only found but loaded his dad's shotgun and explaining: "I'm going to kill the baby.")

We hear much about the psychologies of the oldest child, the youngest child, the only child. What, though, of the second child? My younger brother Alex—there's two and a half years between us—has always had the family nickname *l'invisible*. His catchphrases are "HeelllOOO!" or, as we talk about him as if he's not in the room: "I'm... RIGHT... HERE." At his wedding, I made much of his invisibility as a running joke in my best man's speech. I was being an older brother: celebrating, colluding, stealing laughs, showing off at my younger brother's expense.

That's what we do, we first children. We hog the limelight. The lives of our siblings, in childhood, are cycles of worshipful emulation and serial rejection. Naturally, the second child tries to give himself shape with reference to the elder sibling, and is resented for it. "Stop COPYING ME!" is the infuriated shriek with which he is asked to efface the self he's trying to construct, by the very model around which he's trying to construct it. "I'm Nobody! Who are you?"

A second child is shaped by a predecessor not only in him or herself, I suspect, but as far as his or her parents go. Is what you expect from a second child, what you want or fear, ineluctably shaped by the first? Is a second child necessarily secondary?

My locus standi, here, is not calm reflection after years of experience, but being in tiger-gripping, nappy-wrangling, posset-wiping, bum-cream-smearing medias res. At the time of writing my son Max is three weeks old. So I'm at the beginning of the process that ends with my knowing it all.

I think there's some value in writing it down now—at just the point at which the abstract idea of the second child is becoming concrete. For I will forget that point: I will forget what it's like to be here. Because one of the things about parenting is that you forget, constantly.

What did we do, you ask yourself, when she was little—when she slept 16 hours a day? How come it felt like we were so busy? You remember incidents but not when they happened—and not the day-to-day texture of life. You have forgotten the washing and cooking and washing and cooking, the scrambled egg nappies and the vomit, the walking up and down the stairs again and again with the high, tremulous, unceasing, not-quite-human sound of a newborn's cry at your shoulder. Friends with younger children ask: "What did she do at four months?" or "When she was six months, did she behave like that?" You have no idea.

That forgetfulness goes all through the process. Each situation that arises cancels other possibilities out. When one child is asleep on your chest and the other playing sweetly in the sunshine in the park, you can't imagine anything but bliss; when both are throwing shit-fits and you haven't slept properly for weeks, you can't remember ever not having been in despair.

As with the parent, so with the child. Parenthood is, in a way, a long process of mourning. "It goes so fast," people say, and they sound sad. The child in the photograph, six months ago, is not the child patiently spooning yoghurt into its ear at the table beside you. The child six months ago was a different child from the one you lifted for the first time into a plastic hospital bassinet. Versions of your daughter quietly unselve and disappear, week in week out, and are replaced by new ones that you love as much, and in whose features you can trace the likeness of the ones you lost.

Marlene now says "gogaly" and "cooloo" and "pingo" and "peacarry" for "gone" and "squirrel" and "kaleidoscope" and "pick me up." In a few weeks, she will not. Perhaps we'll try to capture the odd usage on tape, but most likely we won't get round to it, and they will vanish for good. We will remember them, probably—or try to. She will not. As an adult, my daughter will remember nothing at all of the life we share now. So, one fear: are you looking to the second child, in some subliminal way, to be an aide-memoire, a ghost of the first, an attempt to recapture the experience?

You spend the first few months of your first child's life panicking. You agonise: "Is that a purple rash? Or a red one?" You debate whether crying is a good reason for a visit to A&E. You think, basically, that a stiff breeze has a better-than-even chance of killing your offspring. And a whole industry exists to assuage and exploit these fears. It says: what if your child died? Wouldn't you feel bad if you hadn't taken this precaution? It's unlikely—yes. But what if? What if you didn't buy our product and your child died? Think how you'd feel.

It sells you cat nets (two sizes; Moses basket and cot). It sells you sterilisers. It sells you monitors that scream if your child stops breathing. It sells you reins and ropes and reinforcements, stairgates and socket-locks. It sells you hypoallergenic fabrics and eggs that glow arctic blue if the nursery is a degree colder than the optimal temperature for the preservation of newborn life.

So you think, second time round, that you'll see these merchants coming. You will be a bit more relaxed. One of the benefits of that—it's an impulse, at least, that I can identify in myself—is the hope that going over the process a second time, when you know slightly better what you're doing, will give you the chance to pay closer attention. If you're not terrified of crashing the car, you'll be better able to enjoy looking out of the window. The ratio of pleasure to fear will be higher; you'll live more in the moment; notice more of the detail.

Rather than a reboot of the experience of the first, perhaps it's more kindly thought of as an opportunity to live the experience of parenthood—at once entirely generic and entirely particular—differently: to relearn what you forgot. As you heft a baby onto your left forearm, you think: "Yes. I remember this." But even as you remember, the quality of light outside the window has changed.

One of the things you worry about in advance is: "How could I ever love a second child as much as the first?" People will warn you about this, and will promise: "Amazingly, you just do." You don't quite believe them, for while the child is in utero—an abstract proposition, an idea of a child—you can't feel about it as you feel about a living human with a name and a chin. You think of it as secondary. It is, for the moment, invisible.

But then it becomes a person, and: "Amazingly, you just do."

The truth seekers

Derek Parfit and Janet Radcliffe-Richards believe that philosophy should guide behaviour. Their marriage shows that it can

David Edmonds

August 2014

In the 1980s there was a seminar held regularly in the wood-panelled Old Library at All Souls College in Oxford. It was known informally as "Star Wars." Four giants of moral and political philosophy would take turns to lead the discussion and spend the best part of two hours sparring with each other at one end of the room, which would be packed mostly with eager, awestruck postgraduate students. I was one of them and attended for a term.

The four philosophers were Derek Parfit, Amartya Sen, Ronald Dworkin and GA "Jerry" Cohen, all of them in their scholarly prime. In 1982, Janet Radcliffe-Richards, who had just moved to Oxford, decided to go along to see for herself what everyone agreed was the best show in town—dazzling, preening intellectual pyrotechnics. She was then in her late thirties, and a lecturer in philosophy at the Open University. She had recently published a book entitled *The Sceptical Feminist*.

Sen, who would go on to win a Nobel Prize in economics, already knew Radcliffe-Richards and after the seminar went over to greet her. "Who was that?" Parfit asked him. After extracting her name and being told that she had recently separated from a partner, Parfit wrote her a letter, which she says she will publish one day. "The most remarkable chat up letter in history," Radcliffe-Richards calls it. He'd bought *The Sceptical Feminist* as, according to her, "a sort of audition" and proceeded to pursue her assiduously, oblivious to the fact that he was in competition with four other men.

Today, Parfit is considered by many of his peers to be the world's most important living moral philosopher. His first book, *Reasons and Persons*, published in 1984, is routinely described as a work of genius. He is now married to Radcliffe-Richards, herself the author of three widely admired books characterised by unflinching logic and a willingness to tolerate uncomfortable conclusions. Not only are Parfit and Radcliffe-Richards arguably the world's most cerebral romantic partnership, they are a fascinating study in the extent to which a philosopher's professional convictions, particularly in the sphere of moral philosophy or ethics, shape his or her personal conduct—as Parfit thinks they should. I recently visited them in their north London home.

Janet says she was initially "utterly baffled" by Derek. He lacks certain common traits and doesn't pick up on many normal social messages. He has no envy or malice (though he is no stranger to pride). During the "courting" process there were none of the usual wooing signals—no flowers or chocolates—but he did once thrust into her arms the complete keyboard scores of Bach. He also lent her an old desktop computer sold to him by Ronald Dworkin. It kept crashing. "It was an indication of the strangeness of what was going on that when Derek suggested he come round at midnight to deal with the computer, I thought he meant it." He didn't.

In 2011, the night before they were due to get married in a register office, Derek and Janet were walking down Little Clarendon Street in Oxford on the way to a low-key celebration at an Indian restaurant. They had been together for 29 years, and had taken the decision to marry largely on pragmatic grounds. They felt they were getting old, and formalising their relationship made it easier to settle issues such as inheritance and next-of-kin. There were to be only four witnesses at the ceremony: Janet's sister and brother-in-law, her niece and her niece's partner.

As they approached the restaurant they passed a wedding shop. In the window was one of those meringue bridal dresses, all petticoats, hoops and trains. "That," said Janet, jokingly, "is what I shall be wearing tomorrow." "Do you mean that exact one," replied Derek, in all seriousness, "or one just like it?"

It was the kind of literal-mindedness that Janet has become accustomed to, though it still tickles her. It had taken her some time, after first meeting Derek, to figure him out. "You shouldn't take up with Derek if you want a normal domestic relationship," she says. "But I knew by then that I didn't."

Janet and Derek are both now Distinguished Research Fellows at Oxford's Uehiro Centre for Practical Ethics, where I am a research associate. I was supervised by both of them as a postgraduate. Derek supervised my BPhil dissertation and Janet was the supervisor for my doctorate. My PhD was on the philosophy of discrimination, a subject on which Janet has written a great deal, though Oxford University Press is still waiting for the book she promised them.

My BPhil dissertation was on "future generations" (or population ethics), a topic that falls within the broad category of moral philosophy. It deals with questions such as what obligations and duties we have to people as yet unborn and whether we make the world a better place by bringing in more happy lives. Parfit didn't so much shape this sub-discipline as create it. Most of the writing on the subject takes issues he has raised as its starting point.

One conundrum that has exercised him is the so-called "non-identity problem." Imagine that a woman knows that if she conceives a child now it will be born with a disability, but if she waits a couple of months she will have a "normal" child. Now, most people would probably say that she should wait, and not just because of the effect that a disabled child might have on the family and wider society. The stronger intuition is that it is better for the child.

But a moment's thought allows us to see that this idea is misguided. If the woman delays conception she will not make the life of the disabled child better; she will have a different child. Provided that the disability is not too severe, the woman who does not delay getting pregnant is not making things worse for the handicapped child—if she puts off her pregnancy this handicapped child would not exist at all.

It took Parfit's brilliance to recognise that this moral dilemma had far-reaching implications. Decisions over climate change or other forms of environmental degradation, for example, have a similar structure. Suppose we have to choose between two policies. Policy A will conserve our resources, while policy B will deplete them. If we choose A, then the quality of life will be lower for a period than if we choose B. But after 300 years, say, it will be much higher, and will remain so indefinitely thereafter.

Different people will be born depending on which policy we opt for. After three centuries there might be nobody alive who would have been born whichever policy we choose. In *Reasons and Persons*, Parfit suggests we will grasp this complex point more clearly if we ask ourselves, "If railways and motor cars had not been invented, would I still exist?"

Normally, when we think that something is bad, we think that it is bad because it is bad for one or more individuals. But in these non-identity cases there is nobody for whom the decision is bad. Parfit claims that this makes no difference. If in either of two outcomes the same number of people would live, he argues, it would be bad if those who live have a lower quality of life than those who would have lived.

The reasoning seems watertight. But more perplexing difficulties arise when we are faced with decisions that will create different numbers of people. Parfit draws us down a path that leads inexorably to what he calls the "Repugnant Conclusion." This has to do with the very real practical issue of what would be the ideal population size. The Repugnant Conclusion holds that "For any possible population of at least 10 billion people, all with a very high quality of life, there must be some much larger imaginable population whose existence, if other things are equal, would be better even though its members have lives that are barely worth living." Parfit's label for this conclusion makes it clear that he regards it as unpalatable, but he and other philosophers have found the logic that got him there hard to refute.

As well as future generations, *Reasons and Persons* makes seminal contributions in other areas of philosophy, including time (and our puzzling bias in favour of the future over the past) and personal identity (what kind of changes can we survive and which changes involve our ceasing to exist). The book overflows with rich and intricate arguments, which are often advanced through the use of wonderfully strange and creative thought experiments.

Two years ago, having hit the mandatory retirement age, Parfit had to vacate his rooms in All Souls for a small house he had bought in the centre of Oxford. The change in circumstance would have been a shock for him if Janet had not returned to Oxford at that point. Derek had lived almost his entire life in institutions—he was a scholarship boy at Eton, then went to Oxford as an undergraduate, to study history, and after winning a Prize Fellowship at All Souls aged 25 he never left. All Souls is a unique Oxford institution in having no undergraduates, only academic researchers.

"Derek has no idea what it is for a building to exist without a manciple and domestic bursar," says Janet.

"Are you implying that I require looking after?"

"Not at all. That's what's so interesting. You don't demand looking after at all."

Nonetheless, had Janet not been around, his habitat would have rapidly turned feral. One of Derek's friends is the Harvard professor Frances Kamm. Derek regards himself as semi-American, and has spent many semesters at Harvard, New York University and Rutgers. When he stayed in Kamm's apartment he noticed that the plughole in the kitchen sink was blocked. She hadn't known, because she had never used the sink. "Kamm is the person who is most like me," says Derek.

He does not know how to operate his oven, though his dietary regimen is scrupulously maintained. Ludwig Wittgenstein once stayed for an extended period with friends in Ithaca and told them that he didn't mind what they cooked for him so long as it was always the same. Derek does mind. He eats the same staples every day. For breakfast there's muesli, yoghurt, juice and an enormous cup of instant coffee, industrial strength and often made with hot water from the tap because boiling it would require putting on the kettle. In the evening he has raw carrots, cheese, romaine lettuce and celery dipped in peanut butter. Food has to fulfil two basic criteria: it must be healthy and involve the minimum of preparation. Like Janet, he is vegetarian.

"Isn't this rather a boring topic of conversation?" asks Derek. This is not auspicious. Derek once wrote that he can't remember ever being bored. Janet and I retire to the living room upstairs, leaving Derek to his muesli and instant coffee.

Published in 1980, *The Sceptical Feminist* was a book that seemed calculated to annoy everybody, though Janet denies any mischievous intentions. The "sceptical" bit, which infuriated some feminists, was the assertion that many standard feminist arguments were shoddy or incoherent. The "feminist" bit was a brilliant deconstruction of the illogical justifications used by men to validate their position of privilege over women.

Consider a rule like "Women should be barred from driving buses" (examples such as this felt much more urgent in the unreconstructed 1970s). What's wrong with it? It can't be merely the different treatment for men and women that it implies. After all, someone who fails to get a job is treated differently from the person who gets it. In a labour market distinctions are inevitable. Alcoholics are not allowed to become pilots, but we don't conclude that alcoholics are thereby discriminated against.

What is wrong, Janet argues, is that the rule cannot be justified even in terms of the general standards set by those who propose the policy. Most of these people profess to believe in a meritocracy, but this moral standard is not consistent with the arbitrary disadvantaging of one group.

Janet likes to quote John Stuart Mill. Often those proposing a rule such as the one prohibiting female bus drivers will insist that women aren't good enough drivers to be permitted behind the wheel. But as Mill pointed out, "what women by nature cannot do, it is quite superfluous to forbid them from doing." In a genuine meritocracy, in other words, if all women were really hopeless at driving buses, they wouldn't be employed—it would be unnecessary to have an additional rule excluding them.

This argument reflects a trademark Radcliffe-Richards manoeuvre—she grants an opponent their premise or premises and shows that their conclusions nonetheless don't follow. The abortion laws, she argues, don't make any logical sense. If the foetus really is a human being, why should we draw a distinction between a woman carrying a deformed child, a woman who has been raped and a woman who simply got pregnant by mistake?

"The nearest we can get to a coherent account of [current] law," she says, "is that it is to punish women who have sex when they didn't intend to have children. The idea is that if you were raped it's not your fault, you haven't gone in for sex as an end in itself. If you have a deformed foetus you were properly intending to have children, but were just unlucky and that wasn't your fault. But you couldn't just have an abortion because you didn't want a child after having sex."

When Janet takes up a subject she does so from scratch, working from first principles and eschewing established templates and frameworks. This is the source of her originality. In her second book, *Human Nature After Darwin* (published in 2001), she examined aspects of philosophical reasoning through the study of Darwinism. She was particularly interested in claims about innate differences between men and women, which had been left open in *The Sceptical Feminist.*

Assume, for the sake of argument, that men are more disposed to take up random sexual opportunities than women. Would this imply that society should try to thwart or otherwise re-direct male urges? Or should we just accept that men and women are likely to behave differently and will make different choices? Janet is convinced that there are sexual differences—that men are more competitive and status-driven, for example—but this is not what really concerns her. She cares about the "so what?" She wants to show that feminists have nothing to fear from natural or genetic sexual variations.

In conversation, Janet is more nimble than Derek. She is also an in-demand interviewee and public performer (she lectures fluently without notes). For a couple of series, she was a regular panellist on the BBC Radio 4 radio discussion programme, *Moral Maze*, although she wasn't rude enough really to excel in that format and she had what must have been the exasperating habit of telling the presenter and her fellow panellists that they were posing the wrong question.

Unlike Derek, who is proudly a philosopher's philosopher, Janet's writings have shaped debate on practical matters—on feminism, naturally, but also on bioethics. More recently, she's gained attention for her work on the ethics of organ transplants. Most people have an instinctive aversion to the idea of a market in kidneys or hearts, especially as those most likely to be willing to sell their organs would tend to be the poorest in society. But, Janet argues, it is far worse to prohibit such a market. "Of course it's dreadful if people have to sell their organs. But how does a ban on them selling their organs improve things?"

She cites the case of a poor Turkish peasant desperate to raise the funds to pay for his daughter's leukaemia treatment. "And we rapidly passed legislation, and sent him back, presumably to watch his daughter die. Then we patted ourselves on the back. Well, really!" As for the campaigners against the trade: "There are these sanctimonious rich American surgeons with second homes on Cape Cod travelling the world, presenting themselves as heroes for saving poor people from exploitation. And of course what they do is force the desperate—for money or kidneys—into a black market where there's no protection." Her voice drips with contempt as she says this.

Later, as I'm exchanging domestic trivia with Janet, Derek walks back into the room. The conversation undergoes a handbrake turn. We stop gossiping. The talk is all philosophy. And it is Derek who does most of the talking.

His current preoccupation, and the main focus of his second book, is the question of whether there are objective ethical or moral truths. That book, *On What Matters*, appeared in 2011 in two gigantic volumes, totalling nearly 1,500 pages. It received the ultimate imprimatur of cultural significance—a lengthy article in the *New Yorker*—and was also the subject of a substantial review in the *New York Review of Books*.

While Janet won't duck controversy when she believes an argument is either bad or dangerous, or both, Derek says he finds conflict over ideas and values uncomfortable. "I'm unusual among philosophers in the extent to which I'm worried by disagreement." It unsettles him that many leading philosophers, dead and alive, believe that there are no objective reasons for action. Take the example, discussed by the late Bernard Williams, of a man who treats his wife terribly and doesn't care. Williams claims that although there are several things we can say about the husband—that he is nasty, sexist and brutish—he has no reason to improve his behaviour. We cannot insist that he has a reason to be nicer if he cannot be motivated to change. But Derek's book is a prolonged defence of the claim that whatever the man's actual desires or motivations, he does have a reason to behave well.

Questions such as whether morality is objective and what constitutes subjectivity and objectivity are fundamental questions in the area of moral philosophy known as "meta-ethics." But do they matter outside the seminar room? Parfit thinks they do and argues that people who have doubts about the objectivity of ethics are less likely to behave well. He struggles to remember a passage from a poem by Yeats, and turns to Janet for help identifying the lines: "The best lack all conviction, while the worst/Are full of passionate intensity."

I suggest to Derek that it is unlikely that a person's meta-ethical views will sway their actual conduct one way or the other. Over the past few years there has been some fascinating empirical research into the links between the opinions and the behaviour of professors of ethics, much of it conducted by Eric Schwitzgebel, a philosophy professor at UC Riverside in the United States. It suggests, for example, that although ethicists believe that people should give more of their income to charity than do non-ethicists, in practice they are no more generous. Parfit retreats a little. He concedes that it is an empirical matter whether subjectivism—the view that there are no objective moral truths—corrodes our ethical responses, but "it would be surprising if it didn't weaken at least some people's moral convictions." And he frets that his arguments about future generations might undermine the belief that something must be done about climate change.

I suspect that the source of this anxiety is his extrapolation from the case of one individual—himself. I am quite willing to believe that if he were persuaded that subjectivism is true it would change his behaviour. When I ask what his and Janet's philosophy have in common, he answers that they both accept that there are "normative" or ethical truths out there waiting to be discovered. The thrust of his moral thinking has tended in an impersonal direction. It's consistent with this that both he and Janet have signed up to the Giving What We Can campaign, which requires people to make a public pledge to donate at least 10 per cent of their income to charities that work to relieve poverty.

There are no offspring to whom they could bequeath assets. Given that one half of the couple is a specialist on Darwin and evolutionary psychology, and the other on future people, their decision to remain childless is striking. Janet long ago came to the conclusion that there were already too many people in need in the world, and felt no urge to create any more. Derek was indifferent to the prospect of kids. Janet has never regretted not becoming a mother: "In fact, the more I see about ageing parents the more I'm glad that I have no one to feel resentful about if they don't look after me."

Derek is now 71, but he remains the Alexei Stakhanov of the philosophy world. He rises late, but then works with only a few short breaks until 11 o'clock at night, seven days a week. This has been his habit for half a century. It is not an entirely reclusive existence, however, since he's in constant email contact with philosophers around the world. The acknowledgements page in Shelly Kagan's book *The Limits of Morality* is typical. After thanking a number of people, Kagan writes: "[The book] got still longer thanks to the extraordinary and painstaking attention showered on it by Derek Parfit. Derek commented on the whole, not once, but three times, and I have incorporated his suggestions in well over a hundred passages."

A former student of Parfit's, Jeff McMahan, who will soon become the White's Professor of Moral Philosophy at Oxford, recalls arriving for a supervision with him and leaving 14 hours later. On another occasion, McMahan showed up not long after getting off a transatlantic flight. The philosophy began immediately. It didn't occur to Derek that his guest might need a glass of water or to go for a pee.

The deluge of draft papers and manuscripts into Parfit's inbox continues, and his extensive notes are returned quickly. "The only thing I pride myself on is the speed with which I can send people comments," he says. He reads when he's eating, when he's on his exercise bike, when he's putting on his socks and when he's brushing his teeth. Each year he goes through dozens of toothbrushes, which he purchases in bulk. He has been known to read 80 page articles during a single brushing session. One of the reasons he dresses in the same outfit every day—black trousers, white shirt—is so he doesn't waste time selecting clothes. His friend Ingmar Persson, the Swedish philosopher, calls him the "most erudite of living philosophers" and says his hard graft has "contributed to make his work tower high above everyone else's." His modus operandi is to write multiple drafts and then to re-draft (he quickly wears down letters on his keyboards). He is not secretive about how his work is progressing. Numerous pre-publication versions of *On What Matters* had long been circulating in the academic world, each of them varying slightly from one another. The acknowledgements section in the book runs to over 250 names.

When his world is not filtered through books, it is mediated by the lens. Or rather, it used to be. For decades his main "hobby" was photographing St Petersburg and Venice, returning numerous times and taking countless shots of the buildings in different light: in St Petersburg each photograph captures the snow under grey skies. "I may be somewhat unusual," he told the *New Yorker*, "in the fact that I never get tired or sated with what I love most, so that I don't need or want variety." His admiration of certain architectural styles has led him into trouble. Many years ago he insisted that he and Janet buy a house together in rural Wiltshire after falling for its charming Georgian façade. It was miles from Oxford and outlandishly overpriced. In the eight years they owned it, Derek took precisely two walks in the countryside, both reluctantly. The top floor study had breathtaking views, but the curtains were kept closed.

The photographic holidays are no more. After three years of snowless Februaries in St Petersburg, Derek regards that project as complete. A reformed duomaniac, he's now a mere monomaniac: from now on, it's all and only philosophy. He's busy on another book, *Does Anything Really Matter?*, in which he'll respond to critical responses to *On What Matters*.

His reputation, though, is already secure. He has just been awarded the prestigious Schock Prize and two generations of philosophers in their forties, fifties and early sixties revere him. Roger Crisp, a professor of philosophy at Oxford, says Parfit is the most impressive philosophical interlocutor he's ever met. "In his work on personal identity, Parfit has taken the Humean tradition much further than any previous thinker," Crisp says. "He has done the same with the rationalist tradition which stretches back to Plato via Immanuel Kant. And he has transformed the utilitarian tradition."

McMahan, with whom Parfit used to stay when visiting Rutgers, and who called his basement, the "Parfit Suite," says that his writings, especially on population ethics, have "forced a rethink on almost everything in ethics, including the value of life itself." What makes Parfit so special, he says, "is that, like a good chess player, he sees many moves ahead—he can see the implications of claims that no one else can see."

Reasons and Persons is an archetype of a particular approach to philosophy in general and moral philosophy in particular. It proceeds carefully, and methodically, constructing arguments and testing intuitions with thought experiments, from which it generates principles that can be transposed, or so it is claimed, onto the real world.

Many moral philosophers practise their discipline in this way, though none with Parfit's depth or sheer inventiveness. It would be wrong, however, to give the impression that he is universally venerated. For many philosophers, Parfit's approach is wholly misguided. Among the objections made to it, perhaps the most powerful is that ethics does not lend itself to a sort of algorithmic analysis. As Roger Scruton puts it in a caustic forthcoming review of *On What Matters*, "One way of being a bad person is to think that [moral dilemmas] can be resolved by moral arithmetic." Another notable critic is Simon Blackburn who, in his review of the book, asked whether it was really, as Peter Singer suggested in the *Times Literary Supplement*, the "most important publication in moral philosophy" since Henry Sidgwick's *The Methods of Ethics* in 1874. Or was it, Blackburn wondered, instead "a long voyage down a stagnant backwater?" He left the reader in no doubt as to his own verdict.

In the 1940s a Viennese paediatrician Hans Asperger carried out pioneering work on a group of troubled children. But it was only in the 1980s that Asperger's syndrome became recognised as a medical disorder. There are a number of symptoms. They include literal-mindedness, the failure to read social signs and narrow, obsessional preoccupations. Because Asperger's is relatively new to the psychological literature, few people older than 40 have been diagnosed with it.

Several of Derek's friends mention "Asperger's" when I ask them about him. What does he himself think? Might it explain the quality of some of his social interactions and his unusual lifestyle? "There may be something in this suggestion," he says, though he also attributes it to a boarding school education. The same friends also comment that his remarkable nature has required a huge amount of adjustment on Janet's part. She agrees. "But the adjustment was relatively straightforward once I had figured him out and stopped looking for what was not there. His way of life gives me enormous independence."

Although Janet returned to Oxford to teach in 2008, there is still a great deal of shuttling back and forth between there and London, sometimes together, but often separately. Not surprisingly, she says, "many people don't realise that [Derek and I] are connected." But the couple have always communicated constantly. Whenever I went to Janet's house in London to discuss my doctoral thesis, the sessions would invariably be punctuated by calls from Derek. Janet was then teaching at University College London and spent most of her life in the capital. Derek was in Oxford. They spoke many times every day. Here was obviously an extremely close and affectionate relationship between two people who were intellectually, morally and aesthetically compatible. Yet, at some level, Derek seemed strangely unaware that Janet was 60 miles away. "It matters to him that I exist," she says, "but it matters much less that I'm around."

Derek Parfit died in 2017

Acknowledgements

The editorial team of 2020 would like to thank everyone who has worked on the magazine over the past quarter of a century. The original idea for this book was 25 of our finest essays from the past 25 years. But when we began delving into the archive, re-reading every issue, our shortlist kept growing longer. We owe a debt of gratitude to every commissioning editor who has ever worked at *Prospect*. You made this job much tougher—and more enjoyable.

Huge thanks to everyone who currently works at *Prospect*, in particular Sameer Rahim, Stephanie Boland, Alex Dean and Rebecca Liu, who helped to draw up the shortlist, as well as Mike Turner and Chris Tilbury, who are responsible for the design. We'd also like to thank Louise Banbury for copy-editing and Susha Ireland for proof-reading.

We'd like to thank the authors of each essay for allowing us to republish their work, as well as the families of those contributors no longer with us.

Thank you to everyone—and the list is long—who has helped to fund *Prospect* over the years. That includes you, of course, dear reader. Many of you have been with us from the start, but whether you have subscribed since Issue 1 or have picked up a copy for the first time today, we appreciate your continued support.

Finally, we'd like to thank David Goodhart and the late Derek Coombs. Without them, *Prospect* would never have existed.

Tom Clark and Steve Bloomfield, London, March 2020

"Prospect is not only a good read, but a necessary one for anyone with a serious interest in politics"

Ian Buruma, former editor of the New York Review of Books

"I only take two publications on my travels, Prospect and the Herald Tribune"

Michael Palin CBE, actor, writer and television presenter

"Political writing for grown-ups, well beyond the party political playpen... Europe's outstanding political and cultural monthly"

Andrew Marr, BBC presenter and political commentator

"Prospect has the knack of addressing the crucial subjects just before they explode into general consciousness. Never predictable, its depth, breadth and energy are admirable"

Polly Toynbee, the Guardian

"Prospect has become the focal point for informed debate in the UK"

Martin Wolf, chief economics commentator of the Financial Times

"Erudite, enjoyable and thought provoking, Prospect is journalism at its best"

David Cameron, former prime minister

"Prospect is simply the best of its kind: provocative yet detached; thoughtful, and elegantly written. An important read without being self-important"

Jonathan Dimbleby, broadcast journalist

"The best journalistic and intellectual monthly in fifty years. Simply it has become indispensable and essential reading"

Will Hutton, British political economist and former editor-in-chief of The Observer

"The louder and more hysterical public discourse becomes, the more I find myself drawn to the calm intelligence of Prospect magazine"

Evan Davis, journalist and presenter

"I always enjoy Prospect because it's a source of new ideas and enlightenment that don't come pushed through any particular ideological filter. And it's beautifully produced too"

Steven Pinker, cognitive psychologist

"In an era where politics swiftly descends into chaos, Prospect restores order through the power of argument and analysis"

Cathy Newman, Channel 4 News presenter

"Prospect has a knack of identifying key issues before they hit the mainstream"

Jonathan Evans, former DG, MI5

"Prospect has a breadth, intelligence, and proudly liberal outlook, which is needed now more than ever in our national conversation"

Tristram Hunt, director of the Victoria and Albert Museum

"More than ever we need the serious in-depth analysis that Prospect supplies about the major issues of the day"

Margaret MacMillan, historian and author